A CHANCE FOR THE TOP

CAROL DIX
A
CHANCE
FOR THE
TOP

BANTAM PRESS

LONDON · NEW YORK · TORONTO · SYDNEY · AUCKLAND

TRANSWORLD PUBLISHERS LTD
61-63 UXBRIDGE ROAD, LONDON W5 5SA

TRANSWORLD PUBLISHERS (AUSTRALIA) PTY LTD
15-23 Helles Avenue, Moorebank, NSW 2170

TRANSWORLD PUBLISHERS (NZ) LTD
Cnr Moselle and Waipareira Aves,
Henderson, Auckland

Published 1990 by Bantam Press
a division of Transworld Publishers Ltd
Copyright © Carol Dix 1990

British Library Cataloguing in Publication Data
Dix, Carol, *1946-*
    A chance for the top.
    1. United States. Companies. Women managers. Sex
    discrimination by companies
    I. Title
    658.40082

    ISBN 0-593-01762-5
    ISBN 0-593-02032-4 pbk

Printed in Great Britain
by Guernsey Press Co Ltd, Guernsey, Channel Islands

To my daughters Alice and Yasmin

Contents

A CHANCE FOR THE TOP

PART

I

INTRODUCTION

Who Are the Women MBAs?

Just what does it take to make a woman push herself to the top in those traditional male spheres of business, management, potentially high earnings and visible outward success?

Behind this book, and the interviews with women business graduates who form the basis of my investigation, lies that one fundamental question. The women whom I sought out for interview may not yet be wildly successful, but they all share determination and an ability to show guts in taking such a risk with their lives. No one expects or encourages a woman, even today, to put herself through several years of hard work and study, in her late twenties or early thirties. No one tells a woman, even today (unlike her male colleagues), that she has to be a success to achieve peace of mind.

The women in *A Chance for the Top* share one other basic criterion for my study: they have all taken a Masters degree in Business Administration (MBA) – the high-flying postgraduate degree that has been made famous by America's Harvard Business School and that currently is an obsession with a growing number of major corporations and companies in the western world.

Any professional woman or one carrying with her an under-graduate degree might shrug her shoulders at the emphasis on words such as 'determination' and 'risk'. Isn't hard work merely hard work, that falls within the realm of many? But, for all its hype, the MBA does have to be seen to be different: this degree is one undertaken by adults who have progressed from student life usually into some form of professional work. Before undertaking the course, potential graduates need to consider specific factors: such as the possibility that they are returning to academic study

3

after several years spent working; or that they have the strength to change career direction at a midpoint in their life.

The MBA route is not an easy path to follow. Hurdles are placed at the runners' every step: hurdles that will test not only his or her academic and practical ability, but also their motivation, stamina and determination. For prospective women MBA students, in particular, for those from an Arts background, the likelihood is that they are about to enter an academic regime, based heavily on mathematics, the like of which they have never previously entertained. But something, somehow, has captured their imagination.

Did they believe that this degree would help boost them from their own current routine into a new challenging environment? Could they explain that dream and the motivation behind it?

These and many more questions were unleashed for me as soon as the initial challenge had been posed. The rest just flowed, as though relentlessly. When I decided to embark on this journey of investigation into the lives of this particular group of women, I also launched myself into a voyage of self-discovery.

Like many women reading this book, I have been actively or passively involved in all the major changes to the woman's role, and the ideas affecting or influencing that change, over the previous decades. I have devoured books or articles that purport to explain why women fear success, refuse to give up entirely on their dependency culture, have allowed themselves (willingly or unwillingly) to be subordinated, have surrendered their own personal goals and ambitions to support the achievements of the man in their life, or their children, or both.

I came to research this book at a particularly poignant moment in my own life: in my early forties, newly separated from my husband of ten years' standing, a single mother with two nearing-adolescent daughters to support, plus a professional life to nurture and develop, I suddenly found myself fascinated by women who were outwardly doing far more than myself to follow an ambitious path of personal success.

The idea of interviewing women MBA graduates, to assess just how the degree had changed their lives, was devised by myself and my Bantam Press editor, Ursula Mackenzie. Both of us were aware of an American book published several years ago that was written along similar lines, *Women Like Us*: What is Happening to the Women of the Harvard Business School, Class of '75, the women who had the first chance to make it to the top, by Liz Roman Gallese (New York, Morrow, 1985). I had read the book while still living in New York (my husband is American) and had been struck initially by the rather sad note of quiet despair the author depicted for these women, who came across as solitary in their struggle to encroach on male territory. I remember thinking that such an attitude wasn't necessarily essential.

I had recently returned from New York, and was living in London, wondering how best to make a change in my own working life, when Ursula and I discussed the notion of writing such a book about British women MBA graduates (or at least those women who had taken the degree and live on this side of the Atlantic). Slightly bewildered as I had been out of England for so long, my main fear was that there would be simply six such women out there, 'and they'd all be Americans'. But a few initial phone calls to some of our major business schools changed my mind. Women MBAs may not be forcing out the walls of the male bastions of corporate culture in their droves, but over the last twenty years (since the MBA was introduced here as a degree), considerable numbers of women have been pitting their wits and skills against the MBA examiners and post-MBA employers.

The MBA is conceived to be as daunting, as difficult, as demanding a course of study and self-improvement as one is likely to find. Notoriously male in concept, it is often thought to attract the grab-it-all-type of young man (who has long been a cartoon figure of fun in his Porsche or Golf GTI, mobile phone to one ear and cigarette dangling near the other) as he careers a steady, but selfish, curve through our contemporary world. In reality the strenuously academic course is generally taken by men or women who are in their late twenties to mid-thirties, and some who are younger or older. It is not for recent undergraduates as some years of work or life experience are seen as essential.

By definition, the MBA attracts someone who is very self-confident, with a strong personality and sense of direction. The hope is that once graduated, he or she will be capable of earning one of the highest available salaries, and should expect to be respected and revered by his or her colleagues. For some, it is

5

seen as the stepping stone to high-flyer promotion at a young age; guaranteeing to double or triple their current income level. There are tricks within the small print of the guarantee, however, as the MBA also necessitates a heavy investment of time and money at a stage when the student would normally be earning well, in line for rises and promotions. Doubling your salary after a two-year break may not in reality be the type of quantum leap that MBA graduates like to brag about.

The other major reason for taking an MBA is to effect a brilliant career change. And this, as I mentioned earlier, is very often the reason women opt for such a course of action. Notoriously directed when young into 'soft' or typically 'female' type of undergraduate degrees or first jobs – particularly teaching, social work or even the media – a woman may reach the point when she realizes that this is not sufficiently challenging to sustain her interest for the rest of her life. For her, the MBA may be a passport for a major change: promoting her from a passive, dependent role to a fully-fledged managerial, and well-paid, professional commitment.

The MBA is no longer new to Britain, but it is not a three-lettered word that trips easily off the average tongue. Many jokes fly around as to its meaning: master of building, and makes better acetates, are just a couple of acronyms I have come across. The first of these degrees was offered in 1965 in Britain, and even fifteen years ago you would have found no more than an handful of women MBA graduates throughout the country. In the past ten years, however, there has been a rapid increase in the proportion of women taking management studies, at both postgraduate or undergraduate levels. Today, women account for 40 per cent of the undergraduates in many British business studies departments, and for 10 to 30 per cent of the MBA graduate student population.

The Impact of Women
on Business, and of
Business on Women

There are said to be some seventy different MBA courses on offer in Britain today, which vary from the prestigious two-year full-time course (three year part-time) at the London Business School, to those at the Manchester Business School, the University of Warwick, Sheffield Business School, Imperial College Management School, London's City University Business School; and those at Cranfield and Ashridge Management Schools, Kingston Business School, the Open University, various American colleges based in London, as well as in-house courses offered by some major corporations. Would-be graduates from the UK can apply to influential colleges in other countries, whether INSEAD, in France, or Harvard, Stanford, Chicago or Columbia Universities in America.

In October 1990, the Cambridge Institute of Management Studies will be admitting its first students, thereby offering the University's seal of approval to business studies. Budding entrepreneurs and managers, once derided by our intelligentsia as mere 'tradesmen', will soon be joining their ranks.

Dr Charles Handy, who lectures at the London Business School, and is the author of the much quoted *Age of Unreason*, developed the sandwich-structure model on which the Cambridge Institute's studies will be based. It is now widely mooted that Britain will require another 10,000 MBAs throughout the competitive 1990s and that, unlike our major rivals, we lack a system of quality management education. But, while the number of MBA graduates from British universities has risen from 18,500 to almost 28,000 between 1978 and 1988, many still remain sceptically unconvinced that business is a worthy subject of study.

If MBAs in total are a relatively new phenomenon to hit British business, then women MBAs are certainly a strange and, although important sector within management ranks, little documented group. No intensive studies have yet emerged on the influence that their presence is having on the business community, let alone any investigation analysing the implications of such resultant change on both men's and women's lifestyles in the future. In a recent article Bruce Lloyd, the past chairman of the Business Graduates Association, looked into some of these issues.

'As women move towards greater, possibly even complete, economic independence, the world is likely to become a very different place for both sexes. We are only at the beginning of a revolution in attitudes and lifestyle that could well dominate the way we all live in the next century. But have we begun to understand the implications of these radical changes?'

MBA women represent a select group in the vanguard of the changes taking place within industry and society in general. In the 1960s, there were very few women on the MBA courses in the US or the UK, but during the 1970s there was a rapid increase in the corporation of women pursuing management studies at both undergraduate and graduate level. The increasing number of women, he argues, could be a significant indicator of some of the social and economic trends to be anticipated for a much wider section of society in the twenty-first century. Therefore, concludes Bruce Lloyd, there must be much we can learn from their progress, attitudes and stresses.

Why indeed do we continue to ignore the impact on society of women's economic independence; the effect on companies of women's successful adaptation to business and management practices; and the influence their own demands will have on the hitherto male-dominated work world?

Before we look into any great alterations that may or may not occur, we should spare a moment to consider how women are in fact changing the average life of the *male* business person. In their books *Reluctant Managers* and *Women in Charge*: The Experience of Female Entrepreneurs authors Dr Robert Goffee and Professor Richard Scase, who respectively teach at the London Business School and at the University of Kent in Canterbury, point out, 'Male managers can now less easily assume that their partners will be prepared to make sacrifices in order to help them in their careers . . . Married women won't move for their husbands if it affects their own career, interests or their children's lives.' In fact the days of the 'corporate wife' are probably long gone. They point out that rising divorce rates also mean that marriage can no longer be assumed to be permanent, and therefore no longer a secure asset for the male manager. Men are now being advised, by doctors and employers, to strengthen their emotional commitment towards their marriage and family, even if it jeopardizes their jobs, because personal happiness and greater marital stability is seen as a boon to a successful working life.

So, although we can argue that women bring with them a greater burden into business life, in that their emotional commitment to marriage and family tends to remain strong despite pressures from work, men are slowly having to join them in sharing that burden. The concept of 'life priorities', taking equal place with commitment to work, is now being seen as an acceptable part of the portfolio of a good manager. He or she is allowed to be only partially committed to the job.

The winds of change — blowing in women's direction?

Dr Charles Handy was speaking recently at a major conference that I attended on women and education. He implied that as women are now entering the business world in far greater numbers, and in far higher positions than ever before, they will force companies to change — as the companies adapt more to women's needs — because the harsh facts of economics will blow the wind in women's favour.

He claims that the workforce of the future will require 70 per cent brain power over muscle power, and some 60 per cent of new jobs are going to be in the management/professional area rather than manual worker fields. This is going to lead to a *massive* skills shortage, he believes, especially when we consider the much-talked about shortage of school-leavers as we move into the 1990s.

The forgotten 51 per cent of the population is ready and willing to take up their positions as equals in the workforce. However, any company thinking about opening its welcoming arms to the forgotten half of the population, must bear in mind that women also produce the necessary 2.2 children for the continuation of that same population. Consequently, we cannot expect women with brains and professional expertise to be exactly the same, in the workplace, as their male counterparts. Organizations, desperate for the talents of well-educated women will have to woo them hard. This will change the status quo dramatically.

In the past, organizations' attitudes to workers, both male and female, ran along the following lines: adapt to our ways or leave. Dr Handy believes that now women in particular can afford to argue certain implicit alterations to that adaptation rule. For example, women with children need to have control of their time. They cannot afford to sell a company their time from 8 a.m. − 8 p.m. every day, when that would be taking too much time out of domestic or a family's needs. Women can argue that there is no time in their busy lives to travel long distances to work: therefore part-time, or some home-based, working hours should be viewed with respect and treated as being of equal status. What we need is a greater emphasis on *what* we produce within our working lives, not so much on *how* it has been produced. As is often mentioned, women favour less hierarchical structures of management, they prefer to operate at work on a set of people-centred ethics rather than totally business-centred concerns.

He also points out that the notion, long-held and determinedly adhered to, that education should finish by the age of eighteen or twenty-two is ridiculous. Rather than women 'retraining' to fit themselves back into the work-force, we should be looking to individual life patterns that will necessitate several spells of 'educational break' points. We should be moving to a concept of a 'flexilife'. Dr Handy ended his talk with two quick phrases that could move mountains if they became locked into the common jargon of our time:

1) Let's not turn the clock back and make women into men of yesteryears.

2) If we treated men like women, rather than women like men, life would be far more interesting.

Why are there so few women MBAs?

One big reason, that can easily be cited, is that the timing of the course affects women far more obviously than it does men. If the full-time MBA students tend to average twenty-seven years old, and the part-time students (who are fitting in the degree around full-time jobs or other commitments) are in their mid-twenties to early forties, then these mid-adult years come at a crucial time for women. By her late twenties, the average woman, even if she is intent on developing a good career, will likely be turning her thoughts towards marriage and starting a family.

At the back of every woman's mind, as she approaches thirty, is the salient factor that usually she will have to have been with a company or employer for two years before she will become eligible for maternity leave. Giving up one career path, therefore, to change direction in one's late twenties will mean delaying the question of motherhood for at least four years. This is a sum every woman can calculate: not all will be prepared to make the sacrifice.

The level of risk and the type of commitment involved are also rare among the female sub-culture. Still feeling like the first-generation immigrants we are, daring to tread upon sacrosanct territory of the hitherto male work-force, simply getting our feet upon the career ladder in one area may feel like a major achievement. To throw it all in, on the whim that the mythical MBA will bring about greater security, prestige, money, and/or all of the above, could appear madness.

Ageism is rampant and rife in most companies and, where a man may genuinely fear the possibilities of re-employment if he is made redundant or tries for a different job once he is in advance of his forty-fifth year, then a woman who deliberately leaves a job, or is trying to return after several years out of the work-force, will have doubly strong fears.

But first we should look down the list of reasons why a woman may not even have thought of doing an MBA. The comments I made previously about female choice of career and subjects for further education are pertinent. As for the others, I think they deserve a quick re-airing, because they are, or have been until very recently, the driving force of western women's lives:

· Real women don't like maths (even if secretly they're rather good). Not only do they hate maths, but they indulge in that collective excuse-me dance of, 'Oh, I could never do maths at school, I'm just so dumb' (where, for dumb, we are supposed to read attractive to men).

· Real women know they are smart, clever, able to control and organize their own lives, men's, and most other people's, but they won't be seen admitting to it.

· Women who want to attract a man (or men) in their lives – hopefully as a permanent fixture – feel they have to leave something unfinished about themselves. Hence, one cannot be earning as much as or more than the average male at one's peer level and still expect to be fancied.

· Women who hope to be married and/or have a family are unlikely to get themselves locked into a fast-track career path in case they cannot find the key to unlock themselves. They may need to be able to move and follow *him* wherever. And even if aged twenty-three they are firmly set on a fast-track career path, it is more than likely by the time they are approaching thirty, they will be looking for the key that unlocks this perceived 'trap'.

· Real women are not powerful. Power is a male attribute that comes in the package with the penis. Women don't want to be powerful (until they go beyond middle-age, at which point like Margaret Thatcher they seem to realize they've been missing out on much in life).

· Real women like money that comes by other people's efforts: they love goodies, and gifts (preferably from men), shopping, nice houses, holidays and clothes. But even if they know they can earn all that money themselves, they will engineer to do something so it looks as though there are gaps in that ability. If a woman can buy herself *everything*, what is there left for a man to do?

12

Let me move on to consider just who are the women, having eschewed such frivolous concepts, who have really taken modern life at face value – the ones who have declared to themselves (if to no one else), 'OK, I'm going to have the male world, and the female world, I'm going to prove it can be done.'

Are women who go into business life different from men?

People who work with female MBA students point out that on the whole these women come from different backgrounds from the average male graduate students: that is, the majority of women come from arts or social sciences backgrounds. As you will read in the following chapters, this arts or 'soft' type of background does eventually bring many women to a point where they want to change. They may want to adapt to the male work world, to fit more easily into it or to live and conduct their work life like a man's. They want a 'chance for the top'. And why not? They see the way to proceed is by learning the game the men play: adapting the well-worn jargon, adopting their rules and coming in at full speed, playing them at their own game.

When researchers are looking at the future prospects of women MBAs they have to focus their gaze more deeply into the fact that women from an arts background may still be regarded basically as 'soft'; that their previous raising and training may leave them ill-equipped to keep up the fight; and, particularly in an all-male terrain, they may have greater difficulty in finding jobs.

However, within the business schools, there is an awareness that these same so-called 'feminine' traits can actually fit women better for management. As one lecturer quipped, when it comes to teaching 'operations management', a subject that should be best understood by the average male engineer, it is in fact better grasped by the average female historian. The statement is an exaggeration, he admitted, yet it rings with truth as a generalization.

The registrar for admissions from one of the business schools also commented that the women MBA students tend to be on average of far higher quality and calibre than the men because they have already undergone a strenuous hidden process of self-selection to bring them to the point of application. These women have had to overcome fears of failure, rejection and of an assumed inability, but by making the decision, they alone have what it takes to succeed. A greater proportion of women than men who apply are therefore selected to take the course. But, still, the number of women students compared to that of men is at most 25 per cent in any one year.

Women MBAs will bring with them to their graduate studies certain other in-built factors:

> They will be of the prime age for childbirth and settling down, which can lead to conflicts between their desire to improve their career and to begin a family.

> They may have husbands or partners who, far from being supportive of the course, will be downright destructive.

> Marriage and relationships when put to such a test often break up. Which way will the woman's loyalties lie?

> If she already has children then there will be extra domestic tasks and time that has to be found out of the day for the children's nurture and spiritual welfare.

> Women worry about other people in their lives and are more than likely determined to continue devoting a certain proportion of their daily time to those people. The average man might, by comparison, decide that now is the time to devote 100 per cent of his time to career and future. And he will do so regardless of other people in his life.

The interviewees and their responses

I make no pretensions about having written a sociological thesis, or one that bears any statistical relevance for future theoreticians. This a slice-of-life book; fuelled by the enormous energy and interest that I discovered in the women I interviewed. My MBA

14

graduates were tracked down partly through contacts with several business schools; and partly through women's networks in the City and beyond, whom I found to be unceasingly generous in lending time and thought to my project.

The main emphasis I must underline is that I was not setting out to write a book about how to take an MBA, nor how to make the most money on graduation. *A Chance for the Top* is aimed at women in general, who I felt would be fascinated by the themes surrounding women's struggle in today's business world.

I met every one of the women in a variety of situations. We talked either at her workplace, squeezed into a quiet corner of the office, or over lunch, or with a sandwich in the park. Sometimes, if there was the opportunity during the day, evenings or weekends, we met at their homes. Each interview was meant to be an open-ended exploration: I had no axe to grind, no evidence to bolster, and no argument that I was determined to prove. Rather, I wanted to delve into these women's lives to gauge their feelings and experiences.

Knowing little about what I might expect to learn from the average female MBA graduate, now turned businesswoman, I will confess to a sense of nervousness and hesitation when I embarked upon the project. Were they going to be imposing, overwhelming, frightening? Would they be M. Thatcher-type clones, severe in suit and thought? Would they belittle me as some irrelevant waste of their time? Would they freeze me out with disdain? Worse, would they imply I had no right to ask such questions, when really there was no difference in being a female businesswoman than a male?

I am delighted to report back that without exception these women were just the opposite of this composite ogre I had created for myself. They were charming, generous-hearted, interesting, eager to talk, quick to fit my demands into their busy schedules, and above all, open with their thoughts and desperately inquisitive about how other women were handling their lives. They ranged in age from late twenties to late forties, and were poised at various steps on the ladder to whatever they individually perceived as success. By and large they were attractive, well-dressed, well-read, flexible women – certainly not the type of person whom one would consider locked into a rigid frame of thinking.

We were able to laugh together about some of the rigours involved for women entering the hitherto male domain; such as the 'dress-for-success' pressure and whether one could dress to please the feminine consciousness and still fit the male world. They were also all prepared to discuss the difficult problem of men in their lives: whether these were men encountered on a daily work basis or more romantic partners (real or imagined) in their domestic lives.

And, without a fault, they broached the topic of children and how best to juggle the conflicting demands of a fascinating work life with the very real needs that have to be met of a family (depending on their place in the spectrum of where such a family fit with their present-day lives).

Bear in mind that these women are not visible to the outside world. They hold down positions that, until a few years ago, would have been considered exclusively 'male'. And, in that sense, they probably continue to be the type of jobs most teenage girls would frown upon. Who would want to work in industry, or be a management consultant, or sweat it out in the City?

Just what was it about these women I found so appealing? I asked myself that question as I started to write, for I genuinely had found the interviewing an uplifting and stimulating experience. They were to some degree high-achievers, but by no means were they all very successful at the time we met. There were, however, some common traits among the women that struck me personally from the vantage point of my own comparatively confused stance in life:

· They were reaching out for a level of success that was not within the norms of 'traditional' female success, which made them by default risk-takers, women able to take on a challenge, in command of a sense of adventure.

· They gave out a sense of being in charge of their own lives and of others' lives – which enabled them to be very caring.

· They exuded an air of self-confidence and of justified self-esteem.

· They shared a level of economic independence which, whether married, partnered, or not, gave them an emotional independence.

· They definitely shared a high degree of intellectual energy, curiosity, and inquisitiveness – which made our conversations often quite exhausting as ideas flew back and forth.

16

· They tended to have a good sense of humour.

· They were high-energy women, with a feeling that new challenges would be taken on throughout their lives.

· They actually seemed happy people, with no time for moaning or complaining – something which has long been seen as a typical female trait and one more than likely induced by being denied power and control in our lives.

The points for discussion: some issues I felt the book should explore

· How ambitious and aggressive are women today prepared to be?

· Why did you decide to pursue an MBA, at a stage in life when other women might be preparing to slow down, or opt out to have a family?

· How easy has it been pursuing a career in a traditionally male field?

· Have you experienced any prejudice – or major problems – at work or at home since becoming an MBA?

· How do you see your long-term career goals?

· Has any woman, or man, acted as mentor or served as a good role model?

· How do you feel about yourself as a woman, fitting in your personal life with a demanding career?

· Where does 'femininity' fit with business suits?

· Is the pursuit of a fast-track career, and very high salary, ever something that makes you feel guilty?

· Do male colleagues or romantic partners feel threatened by your success and/or greater earning power?

· Are you surprised at your success in life, or was this part of a plan from childhood?

· How drastic was the difference in salary, once you had the MBA letters after your name?

· What advice would you give to other women?

What can you expect from the interviews?

Firstly, I want to make plain that while writing the book, I decided that each story merited its own unedited play. I felt that because I had met these women, and each one somehow managed to convey her very individual story, it would be more interesting and, in the long run, more productive for the reader to get the same feel for the person, her conflicts, joys, and problems. There are, obviously, many common themes running throughout the twenty interviews which I would like to delineate:

· The pursuit of money is less enticing for women MBAs than the pursuit of new challenges and a constantly intellectually demanding way of life.

· Determination is a strong factor in these women's lives, often originating from childhood – even if they did not pursue a straight-line career or have a strong sense of what to do with their lives when they were young.

· Self-confidence seems to be the one big selling point of the MBA. As some have pointed out, whatever actual information, techniques or new skills one might aquire, the single most tangible asset (maybe more so for women than for men) is an enormously elevated level of self-confidence: the feeling that you can tackle anything, anywhere.

· Quality of life is a most important consideration to most women, and MBAs are not different. They discuss the basic conflict, quite openly, of finding themselves in the male workplace where length of hours and 100 per cent loyalty to the job are seen as prerequisites of the large salary and high-powered status. Many women, while going along with the heavy commitment in time, question inwardly whether they will be able to keep it up in the long run. If they have families or even a partner, how can this be a healthy way of living?

· If the men they meet are truly threatened by women being as or more powerful, earning as much or more financially, then women question whether they need such men in their lives. Should this be the woman's worry or the man's?

· Even with the lure of a high salary, these women would move to another job for more responsibility, autonomy, sense of achievement, peer-respect and above all, *power* – rather than for mere cash.

· Women earning high salaries do not feel rich. They still seem anxious about money. Indeed, as the truism states, the more one earns, the more one spends. A higher salary means a bigger house, bigger mortgage, and, in one case, better-quality but excruciatingly expensive curtains! Working mothers on high salaries point out that losing half of the couple's income, during maternity leave, can come as a bigger blow than if one was on a lower salary. Consequently, they are more likely to return to the high-paying job. They will then spend more on nannies and other household help.

· These working mothers recognize that they have to buy their way out of the traditional female, housewifely chores. They pay not only for a nanny, but for regular housecleaning, gardening and sometimes cooking. As one woman put it, 'I had to get to grips with myself to ask the cleaner to polish all our shoes every week. I don't have the time, and that's what we're spending our money for.'

· High-powered, high-earning women, when they find a partner, tend to mate with a nurturing type of man, who likes to cook and is happy to take his share of duties with the children. Interestingly, even if they marry a man who earns as much or more, they seem to find men who do not feel threatened or act competitively towards them. Needless to say the greater proportion, even of my small sample, is not married. (Is this because there are not many such men around?)

· Many women find they have chosen a 'soft' educational degree course and profession and then, later on in life, have wished to make a direct change in career path.

· Equally many women do not follow a strong career path early in life, opting for the 'free flow' form: which may include moving cities or countries with, or in pursuit of, a man. They will have experienced a variety of jobs, maybe part-time, not always at their technical or educational level.

· Some, but not all women, feel they fail at the 'office politics' or 'games-as-men-play-them' type of tactics found in the male-dominated work-force.

· Certain women feel they can master the game, once they have learned the rules, jargon and techniques (which is largely what is seen to be taught on the MBA course). Others feel perpetually perplexed as though living in a fog.

· Some women are more obviously going to succeed or continue succeeding than others. Do we ultimately feel they show more of the traditional male characteristics, or is the ability, or disability, to continue with success a uni-sex conundrum?

· Will women MBAs go on to climb to the top of the ladder? Some women do seem to reach a level where they feel they have achieved enough, by anyone's standards, and are prepared to give up the struggle.

· Are female qualities recognized in the male work world – and can they as easily lead to success? For example, if women prefer a more people-oriented style of management to the male more object-oriented style, which is most likely to dominate the workplace of the future?

· Many point out ways in which women don't help themselves and for example, fall by the wayside: they seem unable to fight for promotions, and fear exaggerating their abilities or applying for positions that pay too much!

· Is the MBA really the much-vaunted stepping stone to success or a passport to newer and better opportunities? Most women take a stance of some kind on this line: as one woman cynically observed, 'Some people take an MBA because they are losers to begin with, and it doesn't prevent them from continuing to be losers. There are the twenty-five-year-old high-flyers on the course, the career-changers and then there are those hoping to find that mythical boost to their lives. But they'll never find it.'

Women, money and power

There was a newspaper article lying on my desk assessing psychoanalysis and how it affects women these days. Its title read 'What do women really want today?' and without thinking, in a moment of annoyance, I scribbled 'Money!' next to the question. Do women want money, and lots of it? If we are growing braver in admitting to our open, naked ambition, are we not mostly still rather weak in admitting to a desire for money?

I asked many of the women interviewees about their attitude towards money, as I had just been reading a fascinating American book called *Unbalanced Accounts*: How women can overcome their fear of money. The book had led me to question whether women treat money as seriously as men. If you were earning a very high salary, would you play around with investments, indulge in the stock market? The answer tended to be no. Even the high earners among my sample smiled cutely on being asked the question and confessed that they let their money pile up in the bank or they made sure it was all spent. Money is the basic image of our independence, of our freedom from needing men, and ultimately perhaps we see in it our recipe for loneliness. Without money, there is always the last hope that still we have a need for protection, that someone somewhere will ride in, on white charger or red Porsche, to sort out the rest of our lives.

You are also less likely to hear a woman confess that what she really wants out of life is 'a Rolls-Royce, or Maserati'. Although many women do enjoy driving round in top-of-the-range sports cars, indulging in fashions, furs and jewels, fine houses, and exotic holidays, they are far more likely to talk in terms of their priorities involving personal happiness, husbands, babies and good health.

Power, however, seems to pose less of a problem. On the surface, qualified and self-confident women can move successfully into powerful positions, without totally souring their 'feminine' identity.

But how can women assume a powerful role with ease? Furthermore, do they really want the responsibility which comes with power.

How to handle new-found power

In *Paths to Power*: a woman's guide from first job to top executive, Natasha Josefowitz, a professor of management at the College of Business Administration at San Diego State University in California, asks her readers to ponder the basic 'I wants' in life, to discover how badly they want to be in charge. She suggests they should ask themselves some of the following questions to ascertain their attitudes:

· Am I willing to let the important relationships in my life suffer because I will have to stay late, work at weekends, travel?

· Will I be terribly upset if I am talked about or even hated by some people?

· How will I handle being unfairly accused, misquoted, and misinterpreted?

Other questions include those involving levels of responsibility, the ability to fire people, and whether they are willing to be married to the job as well as to a partner? These, she concludes, are the prices men have paid for top positions. Can women expect to perform as effective leaders and not pay the same price? Or, more pertinently, do women want to make these sacrifices?

Ageism and the working woman

Many of the interviewees brought up this topic: that what may hold good for newly-graduated, (and it is assumed) attractive young women in the workplace can be completely different once they are seen to be 'old'. When do you become classified as old (and therefore not so attractive)? Once you have married, or had children, or given up wearing four-inch heels to the office? Your style of dress, and amount of money spent on more discreet fashions, will also place you in a certain category. If you are a career-changer, or a return-to-work after several years out with the children woman, then there will also be huge obstacles to overcome, both seen and unseen.

At the conference on women, education and the workplace, that I referred to earlier, the mostly female audience listened intently to the male personnel director of a major corporation who was supporting Dr Handy's view that companies and industries will have to adapt themselves to accommodate women's needs and demands as equal workers. Feeling somewhat confused and bewildered by the nice female-oriented comments, I raised the question that, despite all these protestations, in my experience and that of so many others, any woman over thirty-five trying to force her way back into a job, will find her age an insurmountable hurdle. Jobs tend to be advertised for twenty-five to twenty-eight year olds. Companies make it obvious that they consider hiring a young woman exciting and no threat, whereas the older woman, who by comparison has no plans to leave on behalf of pregnancy, is treated as a no-hoper in the race.

Dr Josefowitz's book includes valuable sections on how you should psychologically prepare yourself to handle job interviews and the stereotyped views you will confront: whether this is your first time out as a young woman or later in the game of life as a mature returner. She lists the current prejudices that, all too likely, are swimming around not too far from the surface of your interviewer's mind. As other women have pointed out, it is advisable to raise some of these common prejudices yourself at the interview, to make the situation clear for all. *If it is not mentioned, that does not mean it has not been thought.*

STEREOTYPES

ENTRY: THE RECENT GRADUATE	RE-ENTRY OR LATE ENTRY: THE HOMEMAKER
Enthusiasm of youth	Wisdom of maturity
No life experience but knows latest development in the field	Rich life experience but is not aware of latest development in field
Has credentials: can brandish a diploma, a list of courses taken, and summer job experiences	Has competencies but does not know their value; does not know how to brandish a list of volunteer experiences
Seen as flexible, able to learn	Seen as rigid, set in her ways
Seen as a risk: may marry, have children, get transferred with husband	Seen as stable and reliable
May be ambitious; will demand equal pay	Will be grateful; will accept lower pay
Because of affirmative action, may have good opportunities	Because of age, may be discriminated against
May be discounted because of youth	May be discounted because of age
May job-hop; sees herself as having options	Will not move; does not see other options

24

High self-esteem; optimistic; expects to be promoted fast	Low self-esteem; pessimistic; does not expect promotions
Wants to travel	Wants to stay put
Willing to work late; has higher energy level	Willing but unable to work late; gets tired quickly
Has no family commitments	Family commitments may interfere with work schedule (unless family is grown)
Will be seen as daughter or sex object	Will be seen as mother
Vertical orientation: socializes with bosses	Horizontal orientation: socializes with co-workers

The glass ceiling

A common phrase in American women's business jargon is the 'glass ceiling' which refers to the invisible obstacles placed in the way of women's attempts to reach the top. You can't see it, but the ceiling is definitely there: allowing you to look through at all those men in their grey suits on the board of directors. The discussions can be long and heated between women on who engineered the construction of that piece of glass. Did it come from the women themselves who deep down won't let themselves push right to the top? Or does it come from the men above them who are not willing to allow women access to that final last mile, their secret domain?

One primary cause, or effect, of the glass ceiling seems to be the desire or resolution felt by so many women to set up in business on their own. Again, you come across the chicken and egg argument: Do women set up their own businesses because they don't fit in to male companies? Is this the only way they perceive furthering their careers? Does the impetus come because they honestly prefer to be independent and don't want to make themselves part of the male corporations or organizations? Or does the responsibility of family life mean corporate hours are out of the question?

In my interviews I discovered several women stating that their ultimate intent was to set up in business. In spite of their current prestigious position, running one's own business seemed to be the final goal. Only one or two had actually taken the plunge, and they were at the point of suffering the fears and inner doubts of any new business venture.

At this point, therefore, I leave you with these basic questions before turning to the women themselves to provide the rest of the story:

· Are women at heart natural entrepreneurs, gifted with an individualism that drives them away from the rigidly structured work-force to go off on their own?

· Are women forced into this desire because they just cannot fit their working hours and domestic lives into the strictures imposed by an outside work-regime? Working for themselves, or running their own companies, affords them instant flexibility even if it can lack the outside recognition and status.

· But, by going it alone, are women giving up the fight to make the male work-place adapt to their needs rather than for the opposite to slowly take place?

· Is working for yourself more 'feminine' and working for a corporation more a 'masculine' ideal or tradition?

PART
2

UNUSUAL CAREER
CHANGES

The MBA course, by definition, is one that can help both men and women in a mid-life career change, so most of the women profiled in this book could fall under this category of unusual career changes. However, I have attempted to divide up the stories into sections that best reflect the underlying themes behind a book of this kind. These following four women illustrate the type of career breaks, hurdles and leaps, that can be made by women interrupting their careers to take an MBA. Their original careers were in traditionally female areas: one made the break from a career in advertising; another was an editor in publishing; the third had been an art teacher; and the fourth was a social worker.

Those who take on the biggest challenges in life are not necessarily the bravest people. That is my own philosophy culled from months of interviewing so many different and varied women. When I say brave, I am referring to the fact that the women I describe may not necessarily come across as bold, daring, assertive or even aggressive; not even necessarily imbued with a natural self-confidence or easy flair. Yet they are women who have deliberately gone out of their way to bring about a massive change in their lives.

They had set out as young women on a traditional path that was carpeted with female stereotypes. Suddenly, their lives seemed not to be following the safe orderly route as expected, and they spotted an opportunity which has enabled them to break out of their conventional mould. Long gone are the days when a woman could convince herself, for example, that when the right man came along, she could give up the effort and rest in easy security for the rest of her life. These women have faced the often lonely decision that no one but themselves would be easing their path into the future decades.

Harriet S.

'What am I going to do with the rest of my life?'

Why are women not more ambitious from the very outset? Why is it still rare for a woman to take her career so seriously that she will embark on a mid-life change, and prepare to send herself off into mid-life orbit? This type of question was raised many times during my interviews with the women for this book. Sometimes, we would find ourselves comparing women in Britain with those in America, many of whom have made much greater advances out into the realm of outspoken ambition and unequivocal success than has been witnessed on this side of the Atlantic. At other times, the question came from within the conversation itself as we pondered some of the decisions women make for themselves over the years.

Harriet is just such a woman. Now forty-two and single, she is successfully running her own business in the field of executive search (more commonly she would be known as a 'head-hunter'). She talks easily of the ambivalence she experiences between this type of success and the more traditional view of what success should mean for a woman: the kind achieved through marriage and family.

The same age as Harriet, I was able to empathize with her views as we spoke. Our generation, post-war baby-boomers, the first-wave of neo-feminists, grew up through the Sixties and, by the standards of today's young people, tended to start late on the serious-about-career path. The generation of women now around the age of forty often stands on fairly shaky foundations with feet splayed in two very different and separate camps.

All those questions I referred to in the opening chapter, about seeing ourselves in terms of our attractiveness as partners to men or about our perceived position in the world, very often bring up questions and offer no ultimate answers. Harriet is a very intelligent and perceptive woman: she expresses the complexities of her social group – the single, working, post-forty woman – with passion and a wary sense that somewhere along the line she has been betrayed.

I should explain here that an unfortunate but inevitable split began to manifest itself between the interviewees who are married (and happily so), and those who are unmarried (even if happily so). Although I would ask all the women about their relationships with men, and whether their being ambitious and obviously striving for success left men around them feeling threatened, the responses were markedly different. The married women quite naturally steered the conversation around men with whom they dealt at work. The unmarried, just as naturally, would talk about men in their personal lives. I say this to explain why it could seem that someone like Harriet appears to concentrate more on the 'man' issue than others reported here, and I send her my apologies. Harriet is by no means obsessed with the issue; it was simply that her feelings and ideas were more deeply-perceived, well-presented, openly discussed and, I felt, would ultimately be of great interest to other women.

Harriet took up seriously the challenge thrown down to her: that it was time for her to take care of her own life. Although she had a reasonable (by most people's standards) career in advertising, she decided to stop waiting around 'until' marriage or the right man came along. At thirty-five, she faced up to the reality that it was more than likely no man would come along to rescue her: now was the time to do something about her future.

Women who are turning thirty tend to focus on marriage and motherhood as the most important factors in their immediate future (or career if they've achieved the former and not the latter). Women coming up to forty suddenly look around at people in their late middle-age and panic: 'If I'm going to hope for a decent, interesting, well-financed next two (or three) decades then I'd better set the wheels turning in that direction.' Where once they may have lacked direction, allowing a certain flexibility in life to propel them, suddenly the road ahead can appear appallingly narrow and straight.

Why an MBA?

'I'd read an article in a magazine about "until women". It dealt with the problem I had not consciously thought about until then, how women do things with the idea it will be until we marry, until we have children. I was just coming up to my thirty-fifth birthday, working in advertising and becoming increasingly aware that this was not a career for women in their fifties, when I found myself thinking, "Hold on, Harriet, you've always said you'll continue working until you get married, but what if you never marry and have children?"

'It had become pretty obvious to me by then that, contrary to my earlier view, I no doubt would continue working even if I were to marry. And I just had to find a new career, one that would see me into my later years. Advertising is highly competitive. Women do not tend to move through to senior, or executive, positions. I knew of friends who had taken MBAs. I also knew that you could do the degree in one year at certain centres often outside London. I just set my mind to it, took the entry exam, went for the interview and, within six weeks, found myself giving up my job, arranging the loan to finance myself for the year's full-time course, letting my flat in London, and moving to rented accommodation in the bleakest countryside!'

I was curious, however, about Harriet's swift dismissal of advertising as an unsuitable career for her future development. To most women the fact she was doing reasonably well at thirty-five, with a company car, a secretary and her own flat in London, would be enough. Surely the job carried prestige and glamour? Why give it all up to return to the student life?

Harriet is an extremely lively woman: talkative, funny, very generous to friends and colleagues. She is the type of person who cannot help but get herself involved. Through her earlier student years, she was active in undergraduate politics. As a graduate student she became equally involved. As a working woman she sits on a lot of committees and networks, absorbed by them all. We met over lunch in a crowded cheerful wine bar where the waiters all knew her.

Pale, pretty and smartly dressed, she carries herself with assurance and self-confidence. A meal other than that appearing on the menu was ordered, her own favourite wine and table were requested. She was extremely helpful and encouraging to me with my project; happy to give me other names to follow up, articles to read, and any information she could possibly find to hand. Even as we talked, the thought hit me – and obviously I was not the first person to be so affected – that Harriet should try for a political career. When I posed the question, she grimaced. 'But that brings me back to all the old problems about ambivalence. A real political career entails 100 per cent commitment. I just don't think I'm capable of that right now.'

Ambivalence

'Even if I look back to my school days, I can see that I have been a funny mixture of the ambitious or competitive on one hand and, on the other, the traditional me which hangs on to the view that "real" happiness will only come through marriage and bringing up a family. There have been various points in my life where the decisions I have made reflect this ambivalence. I'm forty-two now and have never been married. Yet, I still keep one foot in the camp that says to myself that I won't have really achieved until I'm married.

'I was ten, and not from a wealthy family, when another girl in my class decided to try for a scholarship to a small girls' public school nearby. I simply felt I was as clever as her and so decided I'd also have a go. In fact we won two of the three county places. So I was educated at a very good girls' public school. But when I reached seventeen, that's when the tussle began. I was convinced that I did not want to go to university. In that school, it was assumed either you'd go on to a prestigious university or that you'd become a nurse (until you married). But I felt at the time it would be rather wonderful to become a bilingual secretary.

'I applied for a place at Keele to study International Relations (not that I really knew what it entailed) but, although I was offered a place, I turned it down that year. A man I was interested in was going to London University, and I much preferred the notion of secretarial college and moving to be near him in London! During that year between school and university, I learned speedwriting and also did some supply teaching at a girls' secondary modern school: which in itself was a real lesson for me. To put it mildly, talking to those girls taught me more about sex than I ever knew. However, after my first stint of working in an office as a secretary, I couldn't wait to get out and by that stage was ready to begin a university life. I was lucky because in the end I was offered a place studying International Relations in London. It was part of the Economics degree course which, fortunately for me, veered away from any formal economics.

'But instead of turning into the hard-working good student really trying for a top degree, I became heavily involved in student politics during the time of the sit-ins at the LSE. It was a great time, and I had a lot of fun. But I came away with only a lower second-class degree. Once graduated, I'd applied to Belgium to the College of Europe, to study for a special diploma. But my mother seems to have stepped in at this point in my life, and she engineered for me to be interviewed for a job. I'm sure she felt that by continuing in further education, I'd be distancing myself too far from ever meeting a man and achieving a happy family life.

'The job was as a personal assistant in an advertising agency, but it turned out to be far too secretarial a role for me. After I had been there a year or so, I asked if I could move into an account manager's position, but was smartly informed that they did not employ women in those positions. However, by default, that original job had set me on the advertising track, and to move on, all I had to do was change agencies. Then I began doing rather well, even though at that time advertising agencies were not comfortable with women employees, certainly not those obviously strong and ambitious women wanting to work on an equal footing with men.

'The next stage came when I was made redundant. It came as an enormous blow, a real knock to my self-confidence. The truth was they had only one promotional slot available and I was pushing to move into it. But their choice was between a man with a sick wife and two children, and young, single, pushy Harriet. They promoted him and got rid of me. I found another job within a week, but still I was shaken.

'By this point I had become involved with a man from Canada, with whom I thought I was in love. He was returning to live in Montreal and I emigrated out there to join him. We lived together for a time and I settled easily, finding a good job in advertising, at double my former salary. At first, this felt like a very good move. But later, when the relationship broke up, and I began building a life for myself in Montreal, it dawned on me that this experience in Canada would hold no water if I wanted to return to London. Three years later, after I'd had a very bad skiing accident, I knew it was time to come back. This was in the mid-seventies, during the height of the depression in the advertising industry in London. Yet, within four weeks, I had secured myself a job, with a small agency, where by now all my varied experience finally paid off and I was seen as an asset to the company.'

Life as a thirty-five-year-old student

And yet it was at that very same point that Harriet began looking closely at her life, wondering what was going to happen to her as she grew older. Somewhere at the back of her mind was the feeling she could do more; that she could achieve something more stable for herself. Maybe she would even go into business on her own? And suddenly, she found herself signed on as a full-time student, living in the depths of the countryside in a rented house that had no central heating, sharing with two male students, working night and day at her studies and living cheaply off bangers and mash or meals at the local pub.

'My London friends thought I was mad! I'd given up the easy life back here – the good life – restaurants, cinemas, tennis, sailing, skiing holidays, all for the gamble that by taking an MBA I could do more for myself in the future. Any woman who pursues such a course has really made a huge commitment to her career and, as you can imagine, with my own level of ambivalence I was secretly terrified.

'The MBA is only a passport not a guarantee to finding another and hopefully better job. That year of being a student was very tough for me, as it was for several others on the course. I'd failed my economics exams as an undergraduate at university and now

I was struggling to understand statistics and accountancy. But in itself, the fact that the year was so very different, meant it had to be good for me too. There were people around me with whom I'd never normally have associated. Yet, because we were all thrown into this strange situation, were all struggling under the same pressures, we were bound very closely together.

'In our first week, I remember one of the lecturers giving us the hint by saying, "You're all equals now. Any prestige you've been used to has gone. No one has a job title, secretary or company car to give them status. Life here is a great leveller." For me it also meant that I gave up my London friends. I couldn't possibly go down to London to see them where I'd have to listen to their problems and conversations, all of which now seemed so completely irrelevant to me.

'I went off to take the MBA to help me change career and, as I achieved that goal, I have no complaints. The salary increase in my case has not been so dramatic, as I was already quite highly paid. But I would never have made the move into executive search without the MBA qualification. In my new business, I am in the position where I can quite comfortably interview a finance director or a product manager, from a variety of fields. I must be capable of talking to them at their level about the staff they wish to employ. And that might mean switching from one type of company or industry to another in the same day.

'The MBA lends you an insight into how businesses are run and teaches you to analyse the situation. As an MBA student, you become used to being put on the spot and being made to defend your case in front of fellow students and teachers. You have been introduced to the latest management thinking. Ultimately, I found that I gained the confidence that made me believe I could achieve anything.'

The move from advertising to head-hunter

The phrase 'career change at thirty-five' may bring to mind the image of a woman who knows she wants to move into a specific profession or field; of a woman who knows what she wants out of life. But Harriet had gone along to her MBA course merely seeking an indefinable 'something else', with no idea at the time what that would be.

'We had a careers' weekend during my time at business school. As it was only a year's course, by the second term many of my colleagues were already beginning to apply for jobs. Various employers attended the weekend and we students underwent a variety of psychological exercises aiming to teach us more about ourselves and what we might want out of life and work.

'It had become clear to me that people would be a very important element in any job I pursued. My own opinion, that had been slowly forming, was that I should move into academia as a lecturer. Well, when I made that statement in the group session, it was greeted with howls of derision. They all agreed academia was far too political and mean-minded for an open-hearted spirit like myself. But, during that session someone mentioned executive search. Ironically, later that day I was interviewed by one such company and they offered me a job, even before I'd taken finals. I started work a week after leaving business school and the very next week was off to Chicago on my first business trip. Things certainly felt very good at the time.

'A year or so later I moved to another executive search company where I was made a partner. From there, I eventually resigned to set up my own company.'

Why do so many women dream of starting up their own businesses?

Harriet is firm in her belief that women do *not* always fit into the corporate culture. She raised several questions herself in search of the answer: Is it that men do not regard women in the same light? Or is it the lack of opportunities for convivial networking, that are available for men in the gents or out on the golf course? Or does it come down to the fact that women just don't necessarily want to play the game (rather than that they cannot)? Harriet also developed the discussion of women's greater honesty which can make them appear ingenuous and apolitical.

'I do think women are more prepared to speak their minds at

work, and that having done so, they end up being classed either as agitators or simply awkward people who don't fit. Women are just not so good at being political animals. Other situations that I have also noticed include the fact that women are not so likely to make a fuss if promises of promotion, or higher salaries, are not adhered to; women are more prepared to accept a role that is lower than their qualifications should allow; and that women often are unprepared to blow their own trumpets either for promotions, promises or even pay.

'I had reached a point myself in my last company where, despite being a partner, I felt uncomfortable with the environment and just knew the time was right to try and go it alone. I've been very lucky since setting up my own company in that already I'm doing well. I rent office space alongside one of my old advertising companies. There's just myself and a secretary, but we have the companionship of the advertising crowd. If I continue to be successful, I'll have to decide whether to encourage the business to grow or let it remain small and contained.'

Ambition and ambivalence

Whether she will one day find a man who will become her life-partner, not business-partner, is a worry still very much on Harriet's mind. The notion of whether a super-charged, super-businesswoman could still be attractive to a man brings a smile to her face. 'I haven't been married and I'm not ready to say it's all over for me yet. But, the big question is: If I commit myself to a very big work schedule, if I build up my business to become a huge success, won't I in effect be saying that I don't really want or need to be married? I have to admit I haven't yet reached that stage of determination.

'If I grow the company I know that to the outside world I'll be seen as an aggressive businesswoman. If I leave the company as it is, then I'll be seen as a small businesswoman, doing quite well, maintaining her position. And, let's face reality, to men that would mean I am still approachable. It's all too easy to see that men could be threatened by someone like me. I suppose there is always the chance that, if I were to meet a man who was equally confident in his world, then it would not be a problem. But, as a huge generalization, I do think men see successful women as daunting and certainly we're far more threatening than the average younger, and prettier woman.

'It's a very difficult situation for me right now. I'm not going out with anyone and yet I would like to be in a relationship. I've read a lot of the research on female executives that is currently emerging from America, and it all indicates that these successful women may have been married in the past, but that if they are holding down a high-powered position then they tend to be single and know that they have sacrificed a home life, in allowing their job to become all important. That's just what men do: they work all hours of day and night, and their wives are meant to be happy to see them home at nine or ten o'clock at night. When I look at an average week, I only go home to sleep and to get ready for work the next morning. And I own a four-bedroomed house. But in my type of work I'm often out in the evenings, it means leading quite a work-related social life in order to keep up the contacts. Plus, I'm involved in a lot of associations and organizations – mostly women's networks.'

Is finding a man still important?

Echoing the cry voiced so often by today's post-forty single women, Harriet expresses her resentment that she really tries to be out there meeting men. But her efforts are all to no avail. There just are not any divorced or single men, ready and available, to be met.

'I know a lot of single women and within the same circle there are no single men. I have a lot of really wonderful women friends and no similar men friends. I do everything possible. I'm a member of two tennis clubs, I organize singles' sailing weekends which are a lot of fun, but already I know everyone who comes along. I go skiing. There does come the point when you say to yourself, "What else?" The only other way would be to experiment with one of those expensive executive marriage bureaux – but I'm not sure if it's worth two thousand pounds.

'Besides, my realistic self says that I'm only likely to meet a man through friends or through my work. These things happen accidentally, not through forced arrangements. But, yes, I will confess it is a major concern of mine. I'm anxious that if I become too successful, it would finally put off any potential male partner.

'It's one of the trickiest topics for women to confess to, because it exposes a vulnerability, a weakness that otherwise we don't feel in our lives. I know a lot of women friends who are now seeing counsellors, not because they have a serious mental problem, but because they have to come to grips with what they really want out of life.

'Sometimes, I think that my problem goes back to that ambivalence, that a part of me is clinging to the idea inherited from my mother that I must want to be married. But then I ask, "Why do I go around making myself miserable over nothing?" I've carved out a really good life for myself. Just because I was brought up to believe in marriage as the be all and end all, do I really want marriage in my life? I have very strong expectations of what such a relationship should bring to both partners, which in itself would make settling with a partner difficult.

'But, even with all that knowledge behind me, when you grew up assuming you would be married by now and bringing up children, that you would obviously be living as part of a family, it's bloody hard to give up on that notion just because you're forty-two and tell yourself it's not that necessary. What do you fill the blank with, once you banish that fantasy from your mind?'

Karen D.

Coping with Challenge

Karen is the managing director of a small book packaging company. She arrived in this position from a background of editorial work for several of London's major publishing houses. Now forty-two, she gave up her first career in publishing ten years ago, to take a full-time MBA course. Although that might not sound, at first, as though she has made a direct career-change, making the move from editor to managing director – with a variety of experiences along the way – has been one mammoth leap for Karen.

Karen is courteous and meticulous by nature: I knew that because having arranged our meeting, she sent me directions by post of how to find the office building and where to locate a car park. As we shook hands and made our introductions, I could detect a slight North American accent.

Karen herself brought into our conversation the topic of how she does not conform to the classic MBA image. She has, and is first to admit it, a very quiet speaking voice. 'I tend to mumble and swallow my words,' was how she phrased it. How does someone with such a quiet voice compete in the competitive environment of an MBA class? How did she battle her way up the career ladder, through high-ranking jobs with major video and record companies, to this position?

The lesson learned from Karen is that to exploit your talent and even to be assertive, a woman does not necessarily have to raise her voice. She can hang on to her previous identity and face up to the challenge by learning new tactics. But, as Karen describes, that process for someone like herself can be halting and fraught with problems.

40

'It is still quite novel for someone from a soft, artsy background like publishing, to opt for an MBA. But I know exactly why I went. I was reading an article in *Cosmopolitan* one day (not even a magazine I usually read) about business schools. I think at the time it focused on INSEAD in Paris, which was then trying to encourage more women to enrol. It was as though a penny had dropped. Suddenly I could see what it was I wanted in life.

'I had reached a point with my career in publishing when I just felt stalled. And I had no idea how to push it any further. I knew nothing about finance, accountancy and management. To my mind, I thought that publishing was pretty badly run as a business, but I would not have been able to offer suggestions or help improve the situation. And, further, after seven years in the industry working for three different companies, I found myself working as an able and competent Number Two to someone else. I realized that I was a very good Number Two, and felt that that would always be my forte. But then, on reading the article, I knew I was going to have to break away.

'My American background was conventional and middle class. I attended university, but it was an all-girls' college in New England, one of the Seven Sisters, and I was pretty miserable in those years. I'd decided I wanted to go into publishing, but I knew that I would never even get a position as an assistant editor in the States, so I came first on an exchange programme to visit England and wound up staying here with a job at the BBC. At the time, I imagined I'd stay two years. That was twenty years ago.

'After the spell at the BBC, I found a job in publishing as an editorial assistant. Originally my decision to stay on in England was because of a man, but even after he and I had long parted, I knew I could not return to America because then I'd have to start all over again in publishing. I only had to picture myself as a little junior editor, stuck in the corner of a large building in New York, putting semi-colons on manuscripts, and it filled me with horror and determination to stay.

'By comparison, in London, because my jobs had tended to be with smaller companies, I'd learned about publishing through all its stages: production, editing, even up to taking the authors out to lunch. I kept saying to myself, "I'll stay another year". But you know what it's like: you get a credit card, buy a flat, and one day it's too late to turn back. Besides, I must have subconsciously decided to stay here, because when I decided to try for business school it was London or nothing. I didn't even get the brochures for the American schools, even though the British ones have rather a low profile back in the States.'

But Karen's words had sparked my imagination. As such a non-assertive person, how did and does she survive in the business world? Surely, I asked her, you had enough self-confidence to take yourself and your career very seriously, to say that you believed in yourself sufficiently to take the risk of trying for an MBA?

Self-confidence and the MBA

Immediately Karen picked up the gauntlet. She was determined to talk about the issue of self-confidence, and the lack thereof, experienced by so many women at work. 'I suffer from that lack acutely. I can come across as cool, calm, collected and competent. Occasionally I appear arrogant, I fear, because of my natural reserve. But what the outsider does not see is that every day I have to sit here and wind myself up even to make a phone call if I think it will be difficult.

'Basically I am now running my own business: I have a 25 per cent stake of the company. It is up to me to make this business work. It is rather like coming into the office every day, sitting down and looking at myself in the mirror. The business only has the life that I breathe into it. If I don't pick up the phone, make calls, make things happen, the business will go down the tubes. I'm timid, not a natural salesperson, and all the time I'm having to overcome these things. Maybe it's part of the attraction that lured me into this type of work — it's good for me! Psychologically, it feels like a real grown-up position for me to be in: this is part of making me grow up.

'The only reason, I now know, that I have problems is ultimately because of me. And that may be largely because I'm female. I was brought up to marry and have children, to support my husband through his career. I never consciously challenged that prescription for my life. I just didn't follow that course. If I had been brought up knowing that I would be my own breadwinner, that I would have

42

to work all my life, it might have made a change to my degree of self-confidence. Let's face it, as a girl, I would never have seen myself as the managing director of a company or living abroad.

'My first career fitted in with that picture. Publishing is "nice". It's a career that involves nurturing and caring for others, and socially it conforms with the female self-image in the world. In the seventies, I used to think that I loved working with books. But I'm just no longer wedded to that sort of naïve attitude. Before I used to work on very classy books. But here it might be joke books or just anything between covers. My work now is commercial and I'm proud of that. The product for me is the business; making the business work is all-important. That's a one hundred and eighty degree change in my thinking.

'Still, I remain basically shy and certainly, professionally, very shy. Which is why going to business school was so good for me. As an MBA student, as nowhere else, you're challenged; you have to think on your feet; you have to get up and give presentations. I did what was necessary, but even there I ducked a lot. Looking back, I know I should have volunteered more in class. It offers a wonderful opportunity for women especially to overcome that diffidence.

'You see, it's not only a lack of self-confidence I'm talking about, but also a fear of speaking out in public, of airing our views. Women don't want to be thought stupid, they're terrified of being rejected. But we have to learn to speak up. If, over time, you don't speak up and give your opinion, the situation begins to change and soon no one will even ask for your opinion. They'll begin to take you on board as someone who is not a participator.

'It's a lesson I keep having to re-teach myself: that whatever task I'm afraid of tackling is not going to be any less difficult if I procrastinate. In fact, it is likely to be harder. Business life in that way is just like business school. If you don't force yourself to overcome your fears, there in a protected environment, which is not even the real world, then you may never overcome those problems in the outside world.'

Where did the MBA take her?

I asked Karen to describe the tortuous route, following her MBA, that led to her present position as managing director of a business she now partly owns. The self-effacing woman, afraid to handle some of the trickier and more terrifying aspects of the business world, thrust herself out into the jungle in no uncertain terms. And, maybe to her own surprise, she has quietly succeeded.

'One thing I've learned about myself is that what I can do, and do best, is get on well with people. This probably holds true for a lot of women: I can manipulate situations in a non-aggressive way. When I look back at myself in publishing, I can see that I was not good at spotting bestsellers. But I was good at making things happen, organizing people, seeing things through, and at meeting deadlines and budgets. However, to have risen to higher ranks within that type of publishing, I would have had to have been one of the bright-star commissioning editors. Consequently I felt stalled and stuck. Originally, when I set out on the MBA course, I intended to take my new-found information back into mainstream publishing and, as it were, rescue them!

'The MBA course was probably the best two years of my life. Because I hadn't enjoyed my first degree when I was younger, I made the most of the opportunity, at the age of thirty-two to have an adult student life. I was helped with funding the course by my parents, who had supported my brothers through graduate school, and by a government grant which was still then available for business school. I had not been earning a high salary in publishing and I was content to live cheaply as a student. Besides, I worked very hard there, five nights out of seven, so there was not much to spend money on. And, although I had no maths background whatsoever, I did not find the work terribly hard: it was just the volume of work that was daunting.

'Towards the end of the course, once we began job hunting in earnest, I started looking around for a position with the then newly-emerging cable television industry. I wanted to stay loosely within the media, and this was in the early days of video. I had a long-term strategy in mind which was to go in, learn as much as possible about video, and then take that back as wonderful electronic information to the publishing industry. Anyway, I landed a very good position with a major company, but the job I was hired for was shelved the day I started. So that rather put an end to my long-term strategic planning. I found myself stuck with a job in the record-industry side of the company, with a group of men who seemed just like classic record-industry spivs. I hated it, but stuck it out for a year.

'The job involved me in co-ordinating buying for our markets all round the world. Later, I moved into long-term planning, writing policy documents, and assessing budgets. Then I moved on again into research and planning, and wrote the business plan for a whole new arm of the company. It was fascinating work, although eventually our section was sold off and we were all made redundant. I was then out of work for three months, before I landed another job within the music business, where I found myself running a major record manufacturing outlet.

'In this position, I was working almost exclusively with men, compared to my publishing jobs that had been almost exclusively with women. But the music industry, on its manufacturing side, is a very male world. It took me some time to realize quite how odd the situation was. I'd been going to meetings, for example, for weeks with a group of ten to fourteen others before it dawned on me that I was the only woman. Actually it was a lot of fun, although given the choice I do prefer to work in an environment that reflects the world as it is. The colleagues reporting to me were all men, including several who were considerably older. But I survived. Even one man of fifty-four, who seemed outwardly to resent me, finally came round. It felt very good to be on top of such a situation.'

Men, career and the single woman

Being a thoughtful woman, in her early forties, it would be impossible for Karen to have an intimate conversation about life and her hopes for the future, without raising the question of the dread post-forty single-woman lack-of-men crisis. Karen has already referred to the fact that she was raised the conventional way: her upbringing and even education geared her towards the life of the married woman, supporting her husband through his career and doing her best for their 2.2 children.

'I'm not married and have no children. I've never consciously made a decision to concentrate on my career to the exclusion of marriage.

45

What I think happens is that, without the other commitments, one day you wake up to realize work has taken precedence. Throughout these recent years, I have been coming into work at around eight and not leaving until seven most nights. Work takes over, it expands to fill the time available. And if no one is pressing you to be home, or ready to go out at a certain time, then you have time available. I'm trying now to do something to redress the balance. I've begun by letting my hours slip a little: now it's more like eight thirty a.m. to around six p.m. Large corporations have a life of their own and executives tend to stay late. But, with my own company, I can fit the hours around my life.

'My decision to go to business school was probably motivated somewhere along the line by the fact I was then thirty-two and still single. I was beginning to think that maybe I would not marry and have children, so that meant I was not going to be able to drop out of the career-game conveniently at some point. There would be no excuses for not having made it. If I wanted to keep up the sort of lifestyle I enjoyed, then I was going to need to earn a lot more money than I was in publishing as a young assistant editor. At that time in life, I was really at the low end of the pay scale.

'And, in the long run, I've been proved right. When I was working in the music industry, I was earning very good money with a company car and all. Now, on a profit-sharing basis, if I make the business a success, the sky is the limit. At present though, I don't pay myself a vast amount and I have decided against taking a company car. Money is not that important to me. I like to earn so I don't have to worry, so that I can afford interesting holidays and feel secure that I'll have provided for myself in old age. But I don't need to earn eighty thousand pounds a year for that. I own a nice three-bedroomed house, in which I've just invested a huge amount for improvements. And I find I can pretty much buy what I want.'

Would you give up your house for a man?

When she mentioned her house, that brought out another very important theme for Karen, which will probably strike bells of recognition in other women of her age. We began to talk further about her relationships with men. Now that she is in a powerful position and earning, by many standards, a hefty salary, I wanted to know if men felt threatened by her?

'I don't think I'm such a whizz-kid that they'd be threatened by my earnings. But the other side to that coin is that I've come to the conclusion I cannot commit myself 100 per cent to another human being. I have problems with people making demands on me. Of course I've had relationships, many of them really great relationships, but I've recently come to the conclusion that I'm nervous of commitment, that I'm what's known as risk-averse.

'I've begun to see a pattern emerging with the men in my life. I'll go along with the relationship for a while until it reaches a point where I'll begin to assess the situation and say to myself, "This is not my knight in shining armour. This is not the man I'd sell my house for". At that point, I know what I do: I tend to turn him from lover into a friend. About three or four men who were once very dear to me have gone that way. We become good friends and within a year they've turned round and have married someone else. They have a wife and a family, and we remain friends! It can be tough, I do miss them, but I can see that I just don't try hard to hang on to them.'

So what is the meaning of the image about selling her house?

'It all comes down to economic independence, doesn't it? Virginia Woolf's *A Room of One's Own* is now a house of your own. The thought came to me one night, when I was lying in my bathtub. I'd been seeing a man regularly for quite a long time. If things were to progress, we'd start to live together. Would I sell up my house and move in with him, I was thinking as I soaped myself? Was he good enough to give up my house for? And the answer was no.

'In my family, my father started off life as an Avon man selling cosmetics door-to-door through the Depression. Then he became a door-to-door toilet-paper salesman, and ultimately he rose through the ranks of the company to become its chairman. My mother stayed at home and was a housewife. My two brothers have both become academics. And I ended up being the business person. Maybe I wanted to emulate my father? In a sense he has been my only role-model. Maybe I'm just horribly aware of the trap of being poor. All I know is that the one person who seems capable of consistently looking after me is myself.

'On the other hand, I'd love to know why I seem to get bored very easily. Whenever I reach the point where I'm able to accomplish something too easily, I'm motivated then to move on and expose myself to a position in which I panic for the next year or so. It's as though I push a button that says "self-destruct". During those months of panic, I go around saying to myself, "I can't do this. Why did I ever think I could? I can't cope, I'm not smart enough . . . oh, shit . . . " until eventually it gets better and I can cope. Then the process starts all over again.

'All I can say is I'm delighted I did not just stay in publishing, that I pushed myself to the limit and found whole new areas of ability and capability that I'd never dreamed existed.'

Louise Mc.

What an MBA did for a primary-school art-teacher

Louise, who was born and raised in the conservative Mid-West in America, in the state of Indiana, is an enterprising young woman who has made her home in England. She talked openly about the difficult paths of her youth, her predilection for painting, and former interest in teaching art. In Louise's life, there was a slow maturing of interest in the commercial world, that eventually led to a very different awareness. At that point, she wanted more than being a teacher seemed to offer her.

Even in a crowded room, you would notice Louise without a moment's hesitation. She's tall and striking, and, when we met, she was brightly dressed in a yellow two-piece, with equally bright red nails and lipstick. Colour is Louise's predominant theme, despite the austere walls and desk of her office.

But then this efficient businesswoman is the type of person who just as easily will blend in and work with skinhead teenagers at a London youth club, or entertain inner-city adolescents whose only interest in life is drugs, with the paint brush. For Louise, becoming an organized executive has not meant death to all other facets of her life. But, she realized, to remain in the child-like unstructured world of a young woman drifting from job to job, without direction, would have meant a certain kind of death.

Like Harriet, Louise is unmarried, unattached and, at present, very aware that she is focusing all her attention on building a professional reputation and a new career. She has plenty of energy and enthusiasm. At the age of thirty, hers is a vision of the future that is more open and accommodating than Harriet's. But what, aged thirty, might appear to be an unending vista offering multiple opportunities, suddenly by forty begins to look worryingly narrow, with limited choices, and decisions taken as though by osmosis rather than through design.

What happened to the art teacher?

Many overtly ambitious young women see the roots of their non-traditional female behaviour in a strong relationship with their father. But for Louise, her mother has served as the role-model.

'My father was a lecturer in physics at the local university. We lived in a very academic environment, both in the schools and generally speaking in the town in which I grew up. Everyone more or less went on to university. Dad was a scientist, but also an artist. As a girl I went with him to art classes, and we'd spend time together out drawing. My mother had been a nurse before she stayed home to raise her three children, until we were all settled in school. Then she returned to nursing full time. She began by working in an old people's home and eventually with a friend they bought the nursing home.

'Mom is a real go-getter and she has turned out to be a very efficient businesswoman. Although she and her partner have since sold the nursing home, she is still a very active woman who attends conferences on the aged. I'm probably much more like her, in that I enjoy being busy and involved.

'I studied Fine Art and Art History at university and originally came to England during that course for a year's study-abroad project. Then I went home, switched universities and took up Art Education, intending that to be my way of returning to England as a teacher. First, however, I taught painting in an inner-city school in Indianapolis. One of the major problems faced in the school where I taught was, of course, drugs. But I had rather an easy time of it, as I was teaching ninth graders (fifteen year olds) after the lunch break, when they all would amble back into class stoned! It was certainly an interesting experience, though not necessarily good for my artistic training.

'When I did move back to England, I came as an exchange

teacher, although I was totally misplaced again by being put in a little village middle-school outside of Exeter. My second disillusionment with teaching occurred there. Although I was supposed to be the art teacher, in fact I taught everything most of the week with a couple of art classes thrown in. By then, I had been put off teaching for life. I decided to move up to London, where I joined a group of friends, and I just had a good time, working in a variety of jobs (such as a sales assistant at Harrods which must count as one of the worst jobs I've ever had!). For several months I killed time working as a receptionist with one firm, and as bookkeeper with another, both of whom went bankrupt, though I don't think due to my efforts!

'Then, in my early twenties, I began to work for an art supplies shop, beginning as a shop assistant. Within six months I was made branch manager, within a year I was managing all their London branches, and eventually I became their sales and marketing manager. By that stage, I had decided to develop my personnel and management skills. Being American, and keen on education, I realized I had been thrown into a job that no one knew how to define, and that I was floundering in the position without any theory on which to base my work. That's when I knew I wanted to go on to study for an MBA.

'My boss, however, being an East End barrow-boy who had come up the hard way, refused to give me any time off in which to study as, to his mind, I was already far too educated. The clincher came one evening when I was telling him about a part-time MBA course that was run in the evenings, so you could continue with your work. We were chatting in the pub and he shocked me when he began to confess that his real worry was I'd soon get married and leave to have babies. He also declared that if I did decide to leave to begin a family, that he would hold my job open for me to return to after any amount of time, even up to five years! I was stunned.

'Suddenly it dawned on me that I was getting nowhere and fast. He was worried about my having babies, and I was worried about my career, about my whole future. At least it threw me into action. I applied to a business school and was accepted, on the one-year full-time session rather than on the evening-only course. As I was going to give up my job, I knew that was all I could afford. I had made up my mind: I'd take a year out, study hard, and hope to improve my career prospects. I largely funded it myself through bank loans, with a little help from my parents. As I had continued working in the evenings and sometimes at weekends at a local youth club, to keep the art educational side alive, I was able to keep on that part-time work to help major payments such as my mortgage.'

And how did the young woman whose previous education had been so heavily artistic find the mathematics-based course work of the MBA? Louise laughs at the memory. 'When I was interviewed by the business school, they did warn me that they felt I was a risk to take on. "We've never had anyone with a Fine Arts background before!" they confessed. I worked hard preparing for the GMAT test, and I was scared to death of the notion of doing maths again. During the MBA course I did find statistics, accounting and finance daunting, but then when it came to marketing classes I sailed through.

'I was twenty-five years old at the time, and the other problem I discovered I had was an attention span of about five minutes. In your mid-twenties, you've grown used to the idea of life being there for you to have a good time, so to find yourself with a ton of books to read and an average of three essays a week to write for ten weeks, can be overwhelming. The first term actually was hell, but then things began to calm down. There were several other women on the course: some came from jobs with British corporations, a few hadn't done anything serious in life so far, but felt the MBA would be the key to helping them move on, and a couple were probably there to find an interesting man!'

Getting the new career started

Louise remains an involved and active person. She gives talks to other women, advises and networks. She learned through her own experience that the paths out from an MBA course may not all be lined with primroses.

'I'm really pleased I took an MBA. Before going to business school, I was in a rut and really what else could I have done? The choices open would have been to return to teaching or to try and work for the competition within the art supplies field. However, I must also admit that the short-term benefits of the MBA, for me, were debatable. Fortunately, however, the long-term prospects have been good.

'My mistake was in taking my first job too quickly. I was so desperate to prove I was employable, and good, that I worked overtime on selling myself to the interviewer. What I failed to do was really look at what was on offer to me.

'I'd come up against the problem of not having relevant business experience behind me. Although my job with the art supplier had been managerial and broad-ranging, it didn't have any recognizable and tradable prestige value. The type of job I was applying for was to become a marketing or product manager. I was feeling defeated by getting nowhere, when I saw a job advertised in the newspapers for a product manager on a range of new children's videos and recording materials. There's a level of adrenalin involved in the job-interviewing process. From an initial 150 candidates, I was shortlisted down to five. Then I was interviewed by the managing director and his wife. I was just so good at the interview, and said all the right things, that I was thrilled to be offered the position, with what looked like all the MBA trappings: a good salary and a company car.

'Well, the job was the pits! I was the most overpaid personal assistant ever. The managing director was the nastiest piece of work I've ever met. I was the only woman among a team of managers, and he was rude to us all, calling us names and he even came down to swearing at us in managers' meetings. I used to stagger out of those thinking, "What have I done? I've walked into a nightmare". Then there was his wife, who in many practical ways was my boss. There were the fights between the two of them to contend with, and the fact she disappeared to have her hair done three times a week. Then, the fact that no one, let alone me, knew what I was supposed to be doing. She expected me to tag along after her, even to the point of going on shopping sprees!

'One day we'd had a truly horrific managers' meeting, in which she betrayed me in front of everyone else, accusing me of not doing my job correctly. I was so confused when I came out that I really felt it must have been my fault. But she caught up with me and said airily, "Oh, Louise, that was nothing to do with you.

The problem began before you joined us. I hope you don't mind."
She'd used me to save her face.

'That was it, I knew it was time to quit. It came as a devastating blow for me, as I'm not a person who moves on easily and I feared it would look bad on my c.v. But there was no point in staying. Fortunately, I had been following up another lead ever since graduating. My current boss had been quietly recruiting at our business school for his newly-launched PR company. I'd kept in touch with him, hopeful for a job one day, often going along to see him for a drink in the early evenings. He had promised that as soon as there was enough work coming in he would hire me. So, I took him out for a drink and said that I was leaving my present job, looking for another, keen to move into PR, and either he took me on now or I'd go elsewhere. I had a job offer within the week.

'In those very early days of our fledgling PR business – or what we prefer today to call corporate communications – we all worked together on a flat management basis, helping each other and making the business grow. But we've mushroomed to a great degree since then and I've been promoted rapidly. I started out as my boss's executive assistant and, within three years, I'd become a senior account manager and now I have just been appointed to the board.'

Out in the business world

Louise is forthright about problems many MBA women may meet once they are out in the 'real' world. Her own problems stemmed both from a naïvety about the job market and because far too many companies have little idea of how to make the best use of their MBA employees. Louise warns that you must ask yourself even at the interview, why they are prepared to pay over the odds for someone with an MBA? What will they be expecting from you, and what will you be expecting from them? The PR business with which she is now firmly linked may not to the outsider sound like the obvious nurturing ground for MBA talents. But these companies are fast losing their old, slightly amateurish reputation, as both image and status take on a completely different outlook in an enormously competitive market.

'Even before business school, people had often suggested I should go into PR, but I had no idea what it entailed. To my mind, PR was a rather fluffy sort of business, one I associated with nice ladies parading a bunch of elephants down the High Street to promote something. My boss is very well known in the business and has been determined to put our company on a very different rung of the ladder. We call ourselves marketing and communications corporate consultants – which means we offer a mixture of straight PR and strategic consultancy. Our niche falls somewhere between straight PR and management consultancy with a marketing base. That's not really a very good niche to hold, in terms of selling and promoting ourselves. However, the mix does mean that we can make good use of MBA talents and of normal PR expertise. We need a balance of the two. The MBA personnel go in to analyse our client's company and its requirements. We need that sort of background and training for strategy input. We need the type of staff who will understand the broad business environment and its practices. PR has traditionally been a woman's field, but it just is not the same kind of animal that existed twenty years ago. Now we require good business brains and very competitive instincts.

'There is a humorous side to this change in the PR world: I have some clients who will refer to me as their "PR girl". I suppose they think of me as a secretary who made good! My boss is forever impressing on them that I have an MBA, but I expect the information falls on deaf ears. But I don't react too strongly to such comments, I just get on with my job.'

How women help each other

Louise then began describing some of the traps that MBAs in the workplace can fall into, which led to a discussion of how she recently intervened directly to help a fellow female colleague.

'The dreadful arrogant MBA reputation goes back to the Harvard Business School days, when recent MBA graduates would turn up on their first day at a job and pretend they knew everything. They'd come in, complain about the way the office was run, and expect to wipe the floor with the current staff and practices. Needless to say there was often a lot of hostility. For example, another woman MBA who came to work here fell into that trap. Formerly a lawyer, I don't think she'd ever had to learn how to get on with, or communicate with, other ordinary employees. She was arrogant, very difficult and demanding, expecting the secretaries just to jump and run to her bidding, working for her till midnight. It's taken her over a year to begin to adapt and probably in another two years she will actually be a great asset to our company.

'But there were times that the boss wanted to fire her. I stepped in, sat her down and talked calmly to her. Basically my advice was to get her act together, and to stop barking at people! I knew she could come through. She's bright and very intelligent. But you can't just go into an office and expect to change things overnight. I found myself explaining to her that she certainly had the intellectual abilities, but that she needed to work more on her personal skills.'

Single and Thirty

Louise, generously, saved the other woman's future with the company, which was one of the most refreshing stories that I'd heard in a long time, and told without a scrap of self-congratulation. The popular media love to promote an image of successful, go-getting, dynamic women who are also all 'Super Bitches'. The implied message is that you cannot get on in a male world, unless you learn to think and act like a man, while busily superimposing 'female wiles' via your make-up, clothing and a seductive smile. Louise is very different from that easy cliché.

Now we turn to the 'single and thirty' syndrome, which is certainly not as heavy as that of the 'single and forty' syndrome experienced by Harriet. At present Louise feels unconcerned about the lack of a permanent man in her life; the lack of children and the possibility this will be a permanent state of affairs, however, is another matter.

'OK,' she says with her open smile, bracing herself to talk about the tussles and triumphs with the men in her world. 'Men used to be very important to me, but, although I don't exactly know why,

I just don't feel the need to concentrate on finding a new partner. Recently I went back to see my former working colleagues from the art supply shop. They were very impressed by my smart clothes and new position, but when they said, "Who's your boyfriend?" and I told them there was no one in my life right now, they couldn't believe me. That obviously was not part of my former image. Right now, however, it is true that I am throwing everything into my career.'

Does Louise feel that the average man she meets in her working or social life would be threatened by her position, status and earning power?

'God, yes! But then I've always thought I have much loaded against me, working and living over here. For a start, I'm American, secondly, I have an MBA, and thirdly, I have a good job. What hope is there for me? American women have a reputation for being bolshy, and I am: I'm self-opinionated, independent and I have always been in decent jobs that pay good money. Whether there are more men who can cope with women at that level in America, I don't know and, interestingly enough, I haven't gone back to find out.

'Until about four years ago, I was involved with a man who is an artist and carpenter, a man I had met when I originally came to England as a student. He lived partly over here and partly in the States, so we had a coming-and-going sort of relationship which suited me fine as I always had a very active social life. Then, when I went to study for the MBA, I became very aware that I couldn't cope with him in my life. In fact the relationship was already coming to an end, but when he began talking about returning to live permanently in England, I felt petrified, fearing that with him around I'd never get through my MBA work. Not long ago, I saw him for the first time in four years, and we had absolutely nothing in common.

'But I was scarred by that relationship, and for a long time did not feel like getting involved with anyone else. What I'm beginning to ask myself now is whether a) that fear made me throw myself into my career, or b) the fact I had a new career, which I valued so much, kept me from being involved? I just don't know. So here I am now, with a new man I'm interested in, hoping something might develop. I have a lot of male friends, so I can always go out and not feel lonely. But whether I really have the time and energy to put into a new relationship is another matter.

'The man I've been seeing these past three months is in exactly the same position as myself. He too was hurt by a previous relationship and he swore that he would not become involved again and he hasn't. He works incredibly hard, travelling a lot to conferences and companies both here and abroad. In some ways we're ideally suited, because neither of us can see much of the other. There have been times when we've met for a drink at six in the evening, talked for an hour, and then both disappeared to work-related functions.

'I spend a lot of time at social functions, because in this business you have to build up contacts and network. And I do work long hours. Everyone is in the office by eight thirty and I wouldn't usually leave until around six in the evening. But there are times I get up early and work from five through to seven at home, because that's when my mind is most clear. People here are very committed to their work.

'I would like to see myself married and having children, but I just don't know how that will happen. Ideally, I suppose I'd bring up my children with the help of a nanny and keep up my working life. But could I do that in PR, which is so totally demanding? I sometimes wonder if I wouldn't go back to the youth club work and bring in my art education side again. Maybe I'll move into the design field, where I could possibly make more use of my art background and also my MBA expertise.

'There are some MBA women around who have children. But there's no way around it, women directors I see who are in their mid- to late thirties just don't have families. That was always the way for women at the top, wasn't it? Will it change – who knows? A lot will depend on what happens to women like myself in the next ten years.'

Sophie W.

Social worker turned management consultant

Sophie is a gentle soul and very funny at the same time. At first meeting, with her light brown hair almost covering her face, yet with a slightly bohemian elegance, she was neither a stereotypical businesswoman nor did she look remotely like one's image of a social worker. Sophie has style, class, grace . . . somehow you sense that an evening spent in her company would be good value.

Over a bottle of wine at her flat, with its potted flowers on the window sills and sleek cats roaming for sofa space, and occasional interruptions from a friend who was visiting for the evening, what began as a formal interview turned inevitably into a female free-for-all as three voices vied to discuss the problems, advantages, and disadvantages of being a woman in today's world.

Now in her late thirties, Sophie studied for her MBA in London when she was thirty-one years old. Her post-MBA jobs have been a hotch-potch of various fairly unsuccessful attempts to break into a different career. Sophie has strong beliefs as to what has been going on in her life. So she was prepared for the interview with notes made ahead of time.

Sophie's words ring like a gentle warning bell advising the reader not to be completely taken in by the PR gloss that comes with the MBA brochures. What is vaunted as a 'passport' to success and money, as the 'key' to the door, as the 'stepping stone' to a new and exciting future, may ultimately bring you no further forward than would an entry visa to an inhospitable country.

Being accepted to take an MBA course, Sophie feels, may well be a reflection of your abilities, determination and your own degree of willingness to take risks in life. But, what happens afterwards will then depend upon employers who, by definition, tend to be unimaginative, unwilling to take risks, and who will only see ability in terms of proven evidence.

Sophie's experience reflects that of many women's lives today. She has never followed a straight-line career path. Her jobs have pursued rather a meandering course, dependent often on other people in her life and even on coincidence. Although she feels a degree of inner self-confidence, greater than the average woman, Sophie now realizes she cannot and will not change her way of living to adapt to male standards.

Single, though formerly married, with no children, Sophie is now contemplating leaving her present job to return to free-lance, self-employed work, a lifestyle which she feels would allow her more honesty, even if less money and prestige.

Problems women MBAs may encounter

'As I now see it, there are three problems that any person, man or woman, may encounter when they look for jobs once they graduate with an MBA. If you are encumbered with one of these problems, you may find the going difficult. If you have two, the problems will be worse. But, if you're unfortunate enough to be burdened with all three, then we're talking major trouble. And I, along with a group of other women, found we fell into this latter category.

'Number One: age (or ageism). Being over thirty is a major handicap in the employment market, particularly when you consider that the MBA degree is used by many people, men and women, as a method of changing career. Job entry over thirty is often frowned upon. Indeed, many advertisements will specify that they are looking for people between twenty-five and twenty-eight years old. You can argue your worth at an interview, but your words will probably fall on deaf ears.

'Number Two: gender. I'm not saying there is any specific prejudice against women, but many business employers are looking for "male" qualities. I may sound controversial, but I am just being realistic and honest. Male qualities of style are things like talking a lot of bullshit; showing obvious self-confidence; and the ability to talk up your own experience. It's the male way, I've learned, of tackling the world. Some women can adopt that bravado style and adapt themselves to it, but others (including me) either cannot or just do not want to. For myself, I now feel my inability to act in that way is a mixture of both: I couldn't begin to act in that way, and then I wouldn't want to. There were fellow students at business school, whom I can remember as being very average, that were capable of sounding so good, and they just oozed self-confidence. Male employers can identify with that style and feel comfortable when confronted with another in their own image.

'Number Three: non-relevant previous experience. Most employers, despite the fact you have this new credential that is meant to be so meaningful, will usually only look at what you did before the MBA. If you were not in the business world, then it'll be, "Sorry, but you just don't fit."

'I became all too aware of these traps when, three or four months after leaving business school, I met up with a small group of other women who had also failed to find a job. Until that time, I had been living basically on the dole, doing the odd piece of free-lance work. After all that effort, I was furious! Yet, once we got together and shared our experience, we could see that several men whom we would have defined as "complete twits", were walking into highly paid, prestigious jobs.

'So, why were we being left out? We even went back to the school and demanded an explanation. "Why wasn't life as they'd promised it would be?" we wanted to know. No one had thought to advise us we'd have such problems with the employment market. We felt betrayed that they had not given us any special advice. Maybe, for example, we could have been advised to begin applying for jobs six months ahead of time. But, instead, the business school had continued pushing the line that the MBA would be our passport to fame and fortune. We had been so successfully psyched up over the two-year period into believing the MBA was something very special, we assumed employers would pick up that same feeling, that others in the outside world would appreciate the effort we had put in.

'The short answer is: they don't appreciate anything. The MBA is just a small element in a whole gamut of things employers might be looking for. And there are certain sorts of very conventional organizations, who were not only unlikely to take on any MBAs with the three negatives against them, they didn't even answer our letters.'

Since that initial time of unemployment, Sophie has moved on into working as a management consultant. Still there are questions in her mind about how she fits in to this world. First, however, let me retrace Sophie's steps. How did she of all people, without any business acumen, come to take the MBA degree?

On track to be a lady scientist

'When I was at school I'd always been rather good at maths. My father was an engineer and so my aptitude for maths and science was well supported. I just assumed in those days that I'd go on to do maths and science A levels, and I quite happily saw myself in the future cutting a dash in the laboratory in a white coat. I'd be the much-admired lady scientist! However, I ended up with rotten results in my maths and physics A levels, so, when applying to university, I hedged my bets and went for a joint honours course, Physics with Sociology, at Exeter. Even at university, I discovered that I was so appalling at physics that I failed those exams and only managed to get a degree because the sociology results were sufficient to pull my marks up to pass level. Finally, therefore, I had been confronted with the death of my self-image as the rather smart lady scientist, and consequently had no idea what else to do.

'At first, I was out of work so I moved back to London and began working in a community playground. Someone suggested to me that I should become a social worker and, although I have to confess I'd had such a protected middle-class upbringing I did not even know what a social worker really did, I was accepted as a trainee in the London suburb of Penge. Hence I became a social worker, by default.

'I worked for two years and then went back to university, in Surrey, for my postgraduate qualification. By this stage, I was twenty-three years old and enjoying life as a social worker. It felt as though I was doing something worthwhile and interesting. The work also exposed me to a whole side of life I'd never previously seen: forced me to come to grips with poverty and with some of the devastation that exists in many people's lives. Finally I made the great move from Penge to Catford, a distance of about two miles, but one that took me into a different London borough. There, I took on the job of senior social worker.

'Inadvertently, I had zoomed up the social work ladder. Really I'd been very lucky as I was so young, and I had been promoted very fast. But, by the time I was twenty-nine, I was then newly divorced and wondering what to do next. Further promotion as a social worker would either have meant moving into the administrative offices in the town hall, or taking a sideways move into another area probably outside London.

'With my marriage over, feeling younger than in previous years and suddenly footloose and fancy free in a way I had not experienced before, I decided it was time to do something else in my life. I'd always dreamed, for example, of living and working in Paris. And I determinedly made that my next goal. At first I answered advertisements in *The Lady* for au pairs or hotel workers. But letter after letter came back: I was far too old and far too qualified. Naturally, I became depressed wondering if I would ever be able to make this great change. But then events took over: I went on a holiday to Greece where I bumped into a couple from Paris. Two months later I received a phone call from them: they'd heard about a wonderful opportunity opening up in Paris. I should come over that weekend for an interview.

'Six week later I moved to Paris, with all my possessions packed in two suitcases, having given up my social work career and my former life. I became instead a market research analyst for IBM, which was my first-ever commercial experience. It was a terrific job, highly paid, and one that led to my developing many new friends. Plus it led to a truly great time living in Paris for eighteen months.

'But, at the end of the day, I knew it was only a temporary position and that I had to think again about what I'd be doing for the rest of my life. I needed to get back to England and into some form of "proper" career. By now, it was too late to try and return to social work, and I'd also grown used to meeting different kinds of very interesting people. That was when I read an article about a group of women MBAs at the London Business School.

They were women of about my age, around thirty years old, who seemed to have come from pretty ordinary backgrounds. They had moved from being nothing in particular to whizzo-businesswomen. Instantly, I identified with them, and the notion of doing an MBA just took root in my mind where it began growing wildly. I suppose when I set my mind to things I am very determined.'

At this point Sophie's friend joined in the discussion by suggesting that divorce can act as a major catalyst in a woman's life. Wasn't it often around the age of thirty that a marriage broke up, or children were already growing up, and that was a time when women might begin to contemplate a change?

Sophie would not agree to that as a general concept: most other thirty-year-old MBA students she met, tended to be single. They had felt the time was ripe to make a major career move based on other criteria. But as a threesome we did agree that women's lives seldom take a one-track career route. They are far more likely than men's to twist and wind their way around several tortuous bends.

'I filled out the application forms and attended an interview in Paris for a London school. Of course I'd had to take the GMAT test which for me had been an hilarious if nerve-wrecking process, as again it was taken in Paris. The test itself is American (and written in English), but all the instructions given out were in French. The other candidates sitting the exam were a bunch of extremely smooth Continentals, to be seen lounging around smoking their Gauloises in the breaks. To prepare myself for the exam, I'd practised night after night in my little Paris flat and before I went in felt that I should cope with the test. But on the day itself, I was so phased by these smooth individuals who scribbled away and who, in the break, chatted about how easy it was that I ended up feeling very depressed. I had not been able to answer all the questions and I was sure that my efforts were wasted. Secretarial course here I come, was my feeling at the time.

'However, I scored better than I'd imagined. Because they judge you on a quantitative and a verbal level, and because my results were unusual in being virtually equal in both areas, I received some bonus points for being a well-balanced individual! That in itself, I think, is quite significant too for women. Often we don't shine particularly at any one thing, but we are balanced in our attitudes and abilities. Women are often better than average at most things, without being brilliant at any one thing.'

Life at business school for the shy social worker

'The first term for me was an absolutely overwhelming experience. Some of the things they expected were the equivalent to being asked to walk a tightrope across the Thames. I'd come with little or no mathematics or work experience, and we would be set projects to complete by the next day. For example, we were tackling accountancy, marketing, and business strategy, about which I knew nothing. Yet the classes were shared with people from backgrounds like myself, and with others who were fully qualified accountants or engineers. People were using buzz words that I had not heard of, and were talking in very confident terms. I did not even know what an annual report looked like!

'One thing you do learn at business school, however, one useful piece of human psychology on which we were advised: everyone, but everyone, is very insecure when they first start an MBA course. And that leads to a lot of the bombastic behaviour I have been describing. Why are they all so insecure? Because going to business school means a huge undertaking for anyone: there's the large financial investment from giving up jobs and maybe taking out bank loans. They're taking a risk by making a clean break from previous jobs and career tracks. And this is usually in their late twenties. So, there is loss of earnings, loss of status, and an underlying fear that it might all be a dreadful mistake. That level of insecurity leads to acute anxiety which can emerge under the guise of bravado.

'During the first year, you tend to find a huge shakedown as people catch up to basic levels of ability with each other. That's when you are set more integrated topics that finally begin to call on hitherto unused skills. The quiet but persistent worker, like myself, then comes to the fore, while some of the noisy ones move over into the shadows. By their second year, most people have digested the one difficult truth: you have to work together to do well on the MBA course, rather than being in competition with your colleagues. There is no point in being secretive, hoping all the light will shine on you, because the work depends on team spirit.

Why didn't the MBA help in the job market?

Here Sophie returns to her pet topic. Coming into the employment market at the age of thirty-three, as a former social worker, she discovered that merely having the letters MBA to her name was not so very helpful. The degree itself did nothing to disguise the fact, to wary employers, that she was really a former social worker in disguise (a dastardly profession to have come from, obviously indicating a profound lack of interest in making money).

'I can see now why I was taken on the MBA course. The business school academics are looking for people with a varied and interesting background, not those who have just left university and who might see the MBA as the next step. What interests the business schools is a person who has taken risks in their life, who has done something unusual, or may be even the type who can make others laugh. They want to believe you will have a lot to offer in class. But where the business schools' registrars can afford to be imaginative, prospective employers certainly will not respond in the same way.

'In my case, for example, because in my former incarnation I had been a social worker, at business school I was seen as having good interpersonal skills. To a prospective employer I was merely seen as a non-business person. I was trying to move into marketing, for which I felt ably suited. I had spent time in Paris working in that field, and had completed a very good first-year summer project in marketing for a major company also back in Paris.

'But, at interviews, still I'd be asked the question: "But you're a social worker. What makes you think you could do this job?" I had been trained in certain interview techniques, so I'd counter: "But I'm not a social worker any more. I've just spent two years doing an MBA to show that I am determined to make this career move." To which they would retort: "You're thirty-three, with no formal experience. Why should we employ you? Normally we'd expect someone of your age to be a senior brand manager. You'd be coming in as a complete outsider. How could we justify paying you that sort of salary?"

'Another interviewer said to me: "Why do you think someone with social work experience is relevant to a management job?" My argument to that was: "In my previous career I've had to make decisions on which people's lives depended, such as whether a child should go into care or not. The decision did not involve money, but it was at least equal in weight to commercial considerations and the process leading to the decision is the same." But no one listened to me. My arguments were discounted.

'One of the other women, who was experiencing similar problems finding a job after her MBA, had previously been in a senior position with a charity based in Malaysia. That meant a position of great responsibility handling an extremely large budget. But to their eyes she had worked for a charity. Heaven help us!

'It was then I realized that if I'd joined a company at eighteen, after A levels, and worked my way steadily through the ranks, I'd probably have been far more acceptable. And that, when we come down to it, is the reality of the situation. If you're different, you're a woman, older, and just emerged on to the job-market with an MBA, forget it . . .!'

At that point in the interview the three of us, helped by the now empty bottle of wine, laughed. What are women supposed to do? I said. And Sophie admitted that she was painting rather a morbid picture. 'I've done a lot of talking and drunk a lot of wine,' she moaned. So then she began to talk instead about her current experience with a small management consultancy firm, for whom she has been working full time for nearly a year. But again the problem of identity emerged.

'For two and a half years after business school, I worked, based at home, doing free-lance consultancy work. I survived by using every contact I could possibly find and networking with all the people I'd met through business school. Most people were very supportive and I was doing reasonably well but, nine months ago, I was offered a permanent position as a consultant with one of the firms that had given me free-lance contracts. And this new position has brought me right back to my original thinking: that women continue to be judged, negatively, by male criteria; even here in this small, supposedly liberal work environment.

'Some women are basically far too honest. We tell the truth about situations and people. We have not learned to play our part in office politics; we won't take part in "the game". Whether we should join in or not I can't say, it is up to each person to answer for themselves. What I do feel now, however, is that I am being set terms and conditions that I don't want to meet. And in turn, what they are feeling (my new employers who are men around my sort of age) I am sure, is that I am a failure. Yet again I just don't seem able to fit.

'Here's an example of what has been going on. At the end of each week we have to fill out time sheets so they can keep track of what the individual consultants have been doing, and help them bill the clients. We enter into columns how much time is billable to the client, how much time was spent on what is termed research and development, and the third column is called "Other", for which we are asked to specify the type of activity.

'Well, for several months I filled out my time sheet honestly. Where I had been using time in the day for certain important but personal functions: such as being a blood donor, seeing the dentist or taking my car for a necessary repair, I filled that out under "Other". Never for a moment did it occur to me that by so doing I would create problems. Then I received a memo from one of the partners asking me to take holiday-time for such non-essential activities.

'When I mentioned this to colleagues they laughed at my naïvety. You're supposed to hide the extra-curricula time under "research and development". But my attitude was that I preferred being honest. My colleagues tell me that filling out time sheets is an art, not a science. But why do I have that uncomfortable feeling that I am being forced into lying? The client is billed for time that was genuinely not spent on their project. I just don't want to play by those rules. Similarly, I tend to come into work early before others have arrived. That time of mine when I often work hardest, goes by unnoticed. At the end of the day, I'd prefer to leave at five thirty if I've completed as much as can be done. But leaving before six thirty is seen as "sloping off" early.

'Many women face this type of problem. They are functionally and operationally sound, but they lack – often through personal choice – corporate political skills and high-profile presentation. Women's skills, which are often enormous, are likely to be under-valued. We have special skills which may pass by as quite low profile. We communicate, we empathize, we get things done, we pay attention to detail and we're honest. In corporate terms, these are all discounted. Worse, they're seen as ingenuous. And I must say, there has come a point in my life when I feel ready to say, "Stuff it!"'

Was the MBA a valuable experience?

The friend now stepped in with a good question. How, she wanted to know, would Sophie have reacted if, when she'd turned up this evening, she had arrived full of optimism to say she had decided to take an MBA. Being twenty-eight, divorced, with a history that includes running her own business, would Sophie tell her she was a fool to consider it?

'If you're taking the MBA for a career change, and you're older and female, then face up to the fact it probably won't open that many doors. However, if you go into it on the understanding that personally this will probably be a very valuable experience, then of course it is worth it. You'll learn more about yourself. You'll be putting yourself to the test, the like of which you've never dared before. You'll come away with some extremely good friends, and I suppose also good contacts.

'If you concentrate on the personal gains, then the MBA will be a very positive experience. If you remain open minded about its outcome and its ability to help in the job market, then it's fine. A lot of women come to major changes late in life, and we may have to take some risks, and try something different. I'm certainly pleased for myself I did the MBA. I proved to myself that I could do it.'

PART
3

CAREER AND MOTHERHOOD

Harriet, Karen, Louise and Sophie share one other common trait in their lives which is by no means exclusive to women MBAs. They are all single and without children. When I first embarked on my course of interviewing, one cynical woman suggested I would be unlikely to meet many women who had graduated with an MBA, who were still working and had children. However, I can report to the contrary that many of the women yet to appear in this book are indeed mothers, still working, and that they are using their MBA sharpness of mind and wit in an exceptional level of interest on the topic of career and motherhood.

Three women in this section discuss the topic. Others throughout the book will also talk about their problems and satisfaction with mixing career and motherhood. But the stories you are about to read struck me as most significant. The first such woman, Paula, is still single and without children, but she is horrified by the looming world of choices and conflicts which she will enter once she decides to move into motherhood.

Paula O.

Is it possible to work part time and remain at a senior level?

Paula O. has a senior position with one of the Health Service's major regions. For her, the MBA was not part of a career change, but a way of developing her own potential within the structured hierarchy of the Health Service. She studied part time for the MBA, over a three-year period, while maintaining her job. Sponsored by the organization, the MBA set her on track to become one of their leading lights, and she is now in a position of power from which she hopes to show the way for thousands of other women.

Paula is a refreshing fireball. You come away with the distinct impression that her sheer force of energy should be used to burn away the undergrowth that is stifling the forest (our health service), because she is acutely concerned with change in the British working practices. She can see vividly, for example, even from her own vantage point as a thirty-five-year-old senior woman contemplating when and how to fit motherhood in with her continuing career, just how backward, stultifying and downright negative the present system is. When you hear someone like Paula talking, you might be fooled into thinking the system will of course change. But there is not a scrap of naïvety in her message. What there is, in its place, is a feeling of immense power and of a remarkable intelligence.

Paula was squeezed into her cramped office in the corner of the gargantuan block that houses the administration of a major segment of our national health service. Although she had agreed to be interviewed for this book, I'd half expected her to cancel the meeting. But Paula greeted me cheerfully and we sat down to talk.

With piles of papers and documents covering every desk-top space and part of the floor in her office, there was scarcely room to rest my tape recorder.

She is thirty-five years old and went to study for her MBA when she was thirty. Now she is head of the Manpower Planning Unit for this section of the Health Service. Currently, she is single and childless, but the whole question of her place in the working environment, and of women's place in general, has filled Paula with a sense of anger at the way the system works against all women who will, one day, want to have children.

Paula was well educated and went to university to study pharmacy, specializing during her degree with a joint major in both neuro-pharmacology and pharmaceutical technology (which she described as following both the traditional male and traditional female routes). She worked at first in certain London hospitals, at the time of the re-organization of the Health Service in 1975, and later moved into the commercial sector, first as a clinical pharmacologist and then as a production manager at a manufacturing plant. Six or so years later, Paula moved into the Health Service in a more general management position, initially heading a team of forty others.

The MBA came about as a natural course of events, when she felt the time was ready to pursue a postgraduate degree. She had chosen to study for an MSc in Psychology, but was encouraged by her bosses to go for the newly-founded MBA instead, as it was felt that improved managerial skills would be an advantage to the Health Service. So Paula studied part time for three years. As a testament to her incredible energy levels, just before finishing the MBA, she started pursuing a part-time PhD in Occupational Psychology at the University of London.

Once qualified with the MBA, she was promoted to head of the Manpower Planning Unit responsible for planning for a staff of 56,000. There she runs the research unit which copes with trying to balance out the demand and supply side of the labour market for the ever-labour-hungry Health Service. Paula is extremely aware of the new labour market; in her field, she knows the skills shortage is so acute that she believes that women are definitely entering an era where they can dictate change. But as Paula knows better than anyone, there is so much entrenched

74

management thinking, within the system, that we are going to need specialist efforts to get anything on the move.

Ambition and today's working woman

'What I want out of a job is adequate pay, but I don't need a top-heavy salary. I'm much more interested in having mentally stimulating work and a good crack team working for me. No, I'd go to another job for control rather than for money. I would say I'm ambitious for the type of work I enjoy doing, but I have no great urge to be top dog. I'd quite like to be the *éminence grise* behind the top dog. For example, in my position I prepare all the advisory notes and briefings behind the actual planning decisions. In power terms, that's actually very powerful.

'The MBA for me was not a means to achieving a higher salary, but more of an entry ticket to better jobs. What the MBA does is give you confidence to try for certain positions that you may never previously have thought yourself capable of doing. The MBA basically teaches developmental and analytical skills, and it trains you in a problem-solving approach. After all the labels, what you basically come away with is an ability to analyse, clarity of thinking and clarity of writing.

'Which is where I see so many of our problems: both as women within the system and women trying to change the system. The basic level of management in organizations such as the Health Service is poor. The average manager is not degree trained; he will have a narrow, blinkered vision, probably because he joined the system in his twenties and stayed put.

'Let's state the problem women face in simple terms. Here, as maybe nowhere else, in the Health Service you have a predominantly female workforce and a blob of custard which is male middle management. Particularly in these cases, I find that men managers tend to be the type of man who married young, generally to a nurse, and she then stopped working to raise their family. The only other female role-model he has had is his mother, whose life ran along similar lines. These men look at a woman like me as oddball. So I am stuck with an Amazonian tag, and am criticized for not being "female".

'The Health Service needs more women in senior positions who are free-thinking individuals, not constrained by the "corporate culture", the culture that I define as "White man's thinking". Unfortunately, right now, they wouldn't know how to harness and make use of women's creative thinking even if they recognized it. By comparison with those male managers, even within my department, we have a group of very good, able women who are increasingly empowered. They will no longer put up with some of the dictates, for example, from the regional director.

'When I was at business school, any female who was single and around thirty used to talk about the problems women face. We gain experience, we become highly trained, then we decide to start families. And the companies do nothing to encourage or help us to stay. Look at the type of women I was just describing. By the time they start having babies they are often at Masters degree level. They go off on maternity leave and the company does nothing to take them back. Yet, the Health Service has paid for their Masters degree, paid to train them and then they let them go.

'Once they've had the baby, and got themselves settled, these women go straight back to work for the competition. They can move into the commercial pharmaceutical industry, for example, with no problem. The retail sector will give them jobs on any terms. They can choose their own hours, days of the week and methods of working, because there are such desperate shortages of well-qualified women. The labour market is actually with women these days. Yet the Health Service has not clicked on to that way of thinking yet.'

What changes can be made?

The Health Service is notoriously slow to accommodate new working practices. But Paula describes her own subtle plan of action. 'It's a question of framing staffing strategies and introducing the idea: not everything should revolve around new recruitment. Just as much energy should be spent on encouraging women to return to work and into retention schemes.

'Given that it is an all-female labour force, why do we not have crèches, or some help for child-care; part-time working, job-shares, or flexitime? At senior levels, where a lot of work is research or computer based, we could be looking at outworker systems, enabling people to spend some time working from home. But, no, there is deep mistrust from management of anything that is not nine to five. Traditional working practices within the confines of a building. It just seems to be impossible for most managers to accept that change is not necessarily a bad thing.

'It's my experience that when you are attempting to create change, you have to make it happen at many different levels. So, if you wish to put through a technical change, then you must support it with press releases, and manage it very carefully through each stage. I spend a lot of time now writing articles for house journals, giving talks to conferences, or at in-house seminars. I bring out of my bag useful case studies, role-models of women and companies who have made these changes work profitably.

'The level of intransigence I have been describing is based on fear. The managers in question fear they will lose control. What we are talking about is cultural change. All attitudes are merely socialized processes. We can't expect to shift them in one year, or even five. It will take a generation or more to create real change. I am if nothing else realistic.'

Thinking about the Health Service, I asked her why the nursing profession, the one employment group that is so obviously 99.95 per cent female, could not allow married women with families to return to work part time? Why wouldn't such an obvious group, experiencing such chronic labour shortages, be targetted for flexible work patterns?

Paula shakes her head vigorously at the shared joke on the topic. 'In this NHS region, we have some 26,000 nurses. They do a three-year training in a school of nursing and then another six months in a hospital, and then they tend to leave the service. Why? Because culturally we organize it that way. They are paid low salaries, so they are forced into looking around for a husband while still young. They marry and have their children young. And no provision or support is given to encourage them to stay in work. So we spend all this money training them, and then we let them drop out of the profession. If they do return, it's to work night-shifts, because that is the only shift where you can work a set number of hours, for higher pay.

'We treat the nurses so badly, don't forget, that few of them want to stay within the profession. Yet it's obvious we must repattern the system. Narrow ways of thinking have brought about the situation which is only comparable to British Rail in its stupidity. There, they have a 90 per cent male labour force, labour shortages, and they cannot bring themselves to employ women even to sell tickets or answer the enquiry phones!'

Are more women being encouraged to return to nursing?

'Yes, because people like me are in powerful positions enabling us to engineer such a change. As the Manpower Planning Unit, we act as agents for purchasing training places. We pay capitation rates to colleges of further education for nursing recruitment. So I can dictate what we need and force change, for example, by saying we need more mature women nurses to return to the labour force. If a woman has had her children, she is more likely to be settled and will remain in the job for a number of years. We can encourage the training colleges, therefore, to boost the quota of mature women students, by offering more money to those who take in 50 per cent mature women and 50 per cent eighteen year old students.'

How can women be kept in the Health Service?

'That's an interesting question,' says Paula, 'because the one major pitfall to avoid is that we do not start up a "part-time working-women's ghetto". These would be women taking on jobs for low pay, in low status positions, because they need to bring in money to meet the costs of the mortgage.

'Alongside the plans just outlined, I have set up career development units where we can see how best to place these women returners. High-graded but flexible jobs have to be available across

78

the board. There must be a databank for job shares. And women should be encouraged to work to the best of their potential, not lower, even though they might be working part-time hours.

'Women should all know by now that the labour market is on their side. It's time for us to go in there and ask for our own terms to be met. The lesson I would like to get out is this: you've got the skills and it's time to be assertive. Increasingly the women I see around me are becoming much more articulate and they just won't put up with the nonsense any more. All around I see women being so creative, yet organizations still have no idea of how to employ them to their advantage.

'Most of our male managers would do well with taking a spell out, working at a Marks and Spencers or a Macdonalds, and seeing what it feels like when you have to hold on to your staff to meet your customers' needs! We have several quality training programmes already underway to complement the changes proposed for the Health Service. But, with 56,000 staff in this region alone, you can imagine what an undertaking it will be to retrain them all. But the Health Service badly needs new principles behind its attitudes. We need entrepreneurial-type thinking, where managers should be in contact with society and the environment instead of being so insular. It's a question of being able to manage entrepreneurs from within, "intrapreneurship". For example in my case, I should be given deadlines and objectives, but allowed to work with a hands-off approach.'

Does Paula imagine she would probably work part time if she has children?

By this point in our conversation I was so inspired by Paula's flow of rhetoric, I had quite overlooked the fact that at the very beginning of our hot and volatile conversation, she had expressed her earnest wish to begin her own family very soon. Being thirty-five already, and wishing somehow to fit three children into her own scheme of things (albeit, she laughs, she has not yet nailed herself down in marriage to one man), she feels that ultimately once pregnant she would try to operate her job part time, working flexi-hours from both home and office.

But surely the Health Service needs women like her to stick it out and ensure that the policies and changes in which she believes so passionately are carried through? When it comes down to it, I asked, is a career not that important to someone as free-thinking and intelligent as Paula? Would she give it all up to stay home with three young children? My mind began to draw a blank trying to picture the scene at home.

Paula became pensive. 'I'm not sure that career is the right word to use here. When I set out in the hospital sector in 1974, I thought this was it: I had my career mapped out for several decades. I saw myself making certain moves which would take me up the ladder. But I no longer see it in such black and white terms. I still need to do interesting and challenging work, and I want time to do my research, plus time to read and expand my mind. It's more about collecting a life full of experiences.

'Talking to men MBAs, many of them are now feeling the same. Is there such a thing as the "career concept" any more? Will anyone, man or woman, mortgage themselves for life to one company? I know that some of the male general managers also feel that there must be more to life than that. Quality of life is increasingly being seen as of equal importance. Men MBAs have similar but different problems of societal expectations, whereas women in a strange way can be freer thinkers and can maybe afford to take more risks. And I don't mean because they might have a man to support them. Still, success and status just are not as important to women. We just are not so constrained by petty rules and by the office game. I do feel that if I begin having children now, then I've waited a long time and put in a lot of effort. I would want to make sure I had time to give to my children, too.

'Please don't think of my attempt to work part time as "a failure" or "copping out". It's more a question of hopefully moving on to something even more exciting. I continually like to create challenges for myself. I certainly don't have a problem with my energy. As it is, I work long hours here and then go to an aerobics class three times a week. I have a long-work attention span. And I would want to tackle my working-motherhood in that way. So why should I be prevented?

'You see, that's what it all comes down to. Do we women have to fit in to male perspectives and dictates? Do we have to agree to conform to the corporate ethics if we want to work alongside, or in parallel, to them? Can we not bring in some of our own attitudes and philosophies about the quality of life, and about the needs of a family to have their parents around some part of the day, not just when they wake up and before going to bed?

'But I'd make absolutely damned sure that my bosses knew how vital I am to the working of the department and that my part-time, home-based, work was going to continue being a high-status, high-profile position. Women have that opportunity now as never before. And we have to take up on that opportunity – and run with it.'

Val P.

The senior executive with an international oil company returns from maternity leave

'A job was advertised at thirty thousand pounds a year and plenty of men but no women applied. The same job was re-advertised at twenty-five thousand pounds a year and this time a few women did apply. What reasons can you give for the difference?' Val knows the answers: Women tend to be self-effacing and timid in seeking jobs; they consistently underrate their abilities and experience; and they are often put off from even applying by the mention of a high salary. Val knows that women are going to have to fight harder than ever before, if they are to hold their place in today's market.

Val has come up the hard way. She's plucky, enterprising, and a very stable and experienced executive. She holds down a prestigious and senior position in the finance department of an international oil company. And, having just turned forty, she has had to meet many challenges both professional and personal in her life. So far she has survived with equanimity and humour on her side. And Val by no means fits the image of an Amazon or trailblazer. She is tiny, very feminine, and laughs easily.

As we talk, she is sitting on her sofa holding six-month old twins in her arms, contemplating her imminent return to work.

Val's home in many ways provides a larger problem than the babies. More than an hour (on a good day when the trains are running safe and secure) outside London, the logistics of commuting and the time added on to an already long working day currently confound her. A couple of years ago, she and her husband decided to make the big break and move out of London into the commuter belt. Although the commute into London was fine for the childless couple, problems have now begun to emerge with the prospect of the twins to care for and a boss to worry about.

Their decision was made when friends, who were living in this same rural idyll, advised them of a vacant cottage coming up for sale down the lane. Within months the London flat had been sold, and the country cottage purchased. Knowing she was no spring chicken, coming to marriage and motherhood in her late thirties, Val and her husband were keen to start a family immediately.

Like Paula, Val is determined that the compromises that have to be made will not destroy her family, her job, nor her own desire to spend some time with the children. And she is in a strong position to fight for her rights. But as I said at the beginning, her story is not one of an easy ride to success. Val was a typical young woman with scarcely a clue as to where she was going, but after several chequered career moves and many false starts she has now reached an eminently responsible position.

From local government officer to an MBA in industry

'After school I ended up going to university to study Social Sciences, quite literally because I had no idea what to do. Then I pretty much played my way through university and came out with a very average degree. I began applying for a few jobs with advertising agencies, or with some of the large stores that were then offering graduate training programmes. But this was back in 1970, before the Equal Opportunities Act came into force, and I received several letters in reply telling me they did not even employ women in those positions, let alone interview them!

'At first I took a job as a travel courier for three months during that summer. But it seemed to be a dog's life and when I saw a job, advertised in the newspaper, for a research assistant at another university's library, I opted for the chance. My thinking ran that at least it would get me back to a campus way of life, which had to be more fun than travelling back and forth across Europe with disgruntled tourists. All that explains how I came to be working as an information assistant in a university careers' library.

'From that position, which was based in the Midlands, I later moved on to a job with the local county council's Consumer Protection Department. The advertisement specified "no previous experience necessary" and I remember thinking to myself that I liked shopping! Anyway I applied and was appointed to the fledgling Consumer Advisory Service. It proved to be a very interesting position and I stayed working for the local authority for five years. At that time in my mid- to late twenties I was gradually building up my own lifestyle; I had bought a house and had created a circle of friends.

'Within the local authority, I was promoted through the system until eventually I was running the town's quite large Consumer Advice Centre. However, the Government then changed and the consumer section was suddenly axed. We actually read of our impending doom in the newspapers – before word was even official – that all the advice centres were to be closed down. Realizing that competition for jobs within local government, with all those lay-offs, was going to be tough (there was certainly no chance for further career development or promotion), at the age of twenty-nine I was very concerned what the hell to do next.

'Never having been the type of person to tread water, I just knew it was time for another major move. By now I'd nurtured the plan of trying to get into industry. My family came from a mill town in the Midlands and my father had always worked in industry, so I felt prepared to make this major move. But, at the same time, I was very aware that as a woman wanting to get into industry, I was not going to be highly employable. Particularly a female sociology graduate with a background in local government!

'I had, however, become familiar with the MBA degree course during my time working for the university careers' library. And I just guessed that the one way out of my dilemma would be to play the men at their own game and do an MBA. That way I'd learn the jargon, and maybe I could make myself appear to fit into their scheme of things.

'So I made enquiries to business schools, decided on the one that offered a full-time residential one-year course, went for the interview, and was rather thrilled to be accepted. Only then did I face the problem of raising the funding! No grants were available for business school and it was going to mean borrowing the money from the bank. My family has no money and so it was all up to me. I went along to my local bank manager and came away with a loan to cover everything. First, during the summer which I planned to use as vacation time, I was to do a Cordon Bleu cookery course. Second, there was enough money to get me started on the MBA. I had decided to go for broke as I'd always wanted to do the cookery course. It was either that or take an expensive holiday!'

The MBA as a stepping stone to industry

'Friends of mine probably thought it was rather a peculiar thing to be doing: that I packed in my job, let my house, and went off for a year to be a student again. But then I've always been rather peculiar! I was still single and enjoying my freedom, so there was no problem of a husband or family to consider. In fact one friend said to me, "Val, you're the one who goes off and does the things we all talk about doing." My father was quite encouraging, but I'm sure he secretly hoped I'd find a husband there, rather than a career!

'I have to say that going to do the MBA was one of the best decisions of my life. I've certainly no regrets. Yet that is said with hindsight, because ultimately the degree did lead me to this job which has enabled me to develop so much. To begin with, though, I don't think that having the letters to my name actually made me any more employable. Despite the fact I had an excellent track record, and that I was prepared to begin at a normal graduate entry level of pay (to make sure I got in on the ground floor), I discovered that my local government background was still an enormous hindrance.

'People work from the assumption that all local government officers are useless. What they don't see is that there is a lot of talent hidden away in town hall offices that often has just been badly managed. To my mind, a lot of my experience from those days has been very useful in this new job. Just learning how to deal with the public, on a day to day basis, is a form of training the like of which you'll never get elsewhere. If you can handle the public in a Consumer Advice Centre, you can handle most situations.

'To begin with, after graduating with my MBA, I took a job with a property company as it was the first offer that came my way. I had to get a job immediately as I had all that debt to pay off. But I hated working for the company, and the job just did not suit me. It entailed a lot of running around the place, phone calls, and much talk. Now I can see that that type of work did not suit my personality. I needed something more analytical. Feeling quite depressed, and in desperation, I phoned the business school's careers' office to ask if they had any new leads. An oil company had literally just been in touch themselves asking if there were any spare MBAs around, as they needed someone in the planning department!

'It was a case of extreme good luck made even more fortuitous by the fact that, when I went along to be interviewed, my future boss happened to have a doctorate in business studies so he knew what being an MBA meant and how best to use my abilities. We discussed quite frankly my failure in the previous job. He told me that because I had overcome several challenges already in life, he felt I would be able to cope with being "thrown to the lions" in industry. He has indeed turned out to be the most sympathetic boss. It was he who appreciated that my first post-MBA job had knocked my self-confidence to pieces. And it was through him I learned an excellent lesson in sympathetic management: that you can make or break someone else's career.'

How does a woman conduct herself in a male workplace?

Val peppered her conversation with chit-chat to the babies, who were now kicking their legs in their baby-rockers, and to the nanny who disappeared to make our lunch. When she launched into the topic of women in the workplace, however, she was determined to make several points as to how women should conduct themselves.

Reflecting on that initial interview which led to her job with the oil company, she felt that women should speak up and be open about problems we all know men think about. If they're not ever mentioned, you may go home wondering why. Are they unspokenly festering like a wound that will not heal? For example, in Val's case she was aware of the powerful inborn prejudice against employing women in their late twenties; against women who are seen to be of marriageable age, who might leave very soon to have babies.

'At this particular interview, my potential boss did not raise the question of whether I might be contemplating a family, so I brought it up. Because I was single, I guessed he might be embarrassed to mention such things, but I wanted him to know where I stood. I introduced the topic myself by saying that I had no immediate plans of marrying or having a family, but that, even if I were to want a child within a few years, I would certainly return to work. I made a joke out of the comment by reminding him I had a huge debt to pay off on the loan from my MBA course!

'But I'd learned previously, when I worked in local government, about the necessity of speaking up to deter male strongholds of prejudice. Once, there was a promotion on offer; it seemed to be on offer to everyone except me. I only found out about this when the job was given to a male colleague, who had failed exams we had recently taken which I, of course, had passed. Why was he worthy of the promotion and I wasn't? I raised quite a fuss and was told that, as the job had involved relocating, which I was not prepared to do, then I had not even been considered. "You never even asked me if I'd move," I stormed back. And there lay the answer. No one had asked if I was entrenched in that town. They had just assumed so, because I had a mortgage and because I had never offered to move. So I now believe women should be the upfront ones. Just because there is silence on a certain topic, does not mean their minds aren't buzzing away, anyway.

'Most men begin with the attitude that women are expensive employees because they have to spend money to train us, and then we leave to have babies. When I hear that argument, I always retort that women leave after their maternity break because most companies do not make it easy for them to return to work. And, because of that, as I see it, industry misses out on women's commitment and loyalty. When you consider that the woman will likely have had to work for two years to earn her maternity leave, then the companies could have their loyalty on a plate if they would only make certain allowances. For example, a woman might want to extend the maternity leave or she might prefer to return on a part-time basis. By flatly refusing such options, they make the decision to return unnecessarily hard.

'Why is this such a problem? Companies should learn to look on maternity leave with fresh eyes. From a different viewpoint, they could see within it an opportunity to use that period of time as a valuable extra resource, during which they could train someone else in the position of the woman on leave. Instead of which they look at a young woman as a threat, thinking: "Oh, she'll be leaving in two years." Right now, as things stand, they are closing the door unnecessarily on women.

'On the other hand, I have to say this: that I also see many women as their own worst enemies. Too many women just don't single out opportunities for themselves to fight for. There are times when you have to force yourself to be an extrovert, to go in there and tell your bosses and colleagues that you are good at your job. If, for example, someone compliments you on a report you have completed, a woman should be prepared to acknowledge the praise and not just blush!

'I have always gone after my own jobs and promotions by keeping my ear to the ground. Another tip I give to women is where possible to bail a senior man out of a rotten situation, save face for him, and then keep very quiet! He won't forget a debt to be repaid. I really don't believe that as a woman in a male-dominated industry that you have to drink them under the table or play at being one of the boys. There is space to be a woman and to play up to their egos. There's nothing wrong as I see it with a little artful flattery. But that should not prevent you from going after the positions and promotions that you want. What I say is: don't wait for a promotion to come to you. Adopt the attitude that you can do whatever is demanded of you, and don't be too blatantly honest. Certainly never point out your faults to those above you.'

How does the oil industry view motherhood?

Val has been with her company for nine years and she has progressed rapidly. Her career began in the planning department. She then moved into economic analysis, forecasting, market and pricing research. Quite early on she made the switch to the treasury and finance departments, which was not bad going for a woman who went into her MBA degree course with no mathematical background whatsoever. How did she make this quantitative leap?

'Doing the company's cash flows and managing their finance on the money markets may sound very high-powered, but in fact it's not so very different from selling apples and pears,' laughs Val.

'Just getting into industry was the major hurdle. Managers here are not good at imaginative or creative recruitment. But it's their one great weakness, that companies are no good at spotting ability, particularly in non-conventional or mature applicants. Women tend to come to interviews with mixed c.v.s, and yet their experience is overlooked. The average manager still expects to hire straight engineers and accountants.

'Later, when I was promoted to senior business analyst, and then to assistant manager of finance, I was by then well and truly accepted as an equal of any of the men working here. That was when I became pregnant for the first time.'

That first pregnancy was a tragic experience for Val and her husband, through which the company stood by her with solid and open-armed support.

'I'd been married during my early years with the company and there I was now, at the age of thirty-seven, expecting my first baby. I was the first senior woman ever to take maternity leave and I knew that everyone I worked with was delighted for me. In the end, though, very sadly we lost the baby shortly after he was born. The disaster was a clear-cut case of hospital negligence, and the story was in all the newspapers and even on the television news at the time. I had gone well over full term without having labour induced, and then when I did go into labour the hospital did not have enough pre-natal monitors in an extremely busy period. The baby was born without my even having been attached to a monitor. As an older mother, who had experienced high blood pressure late in the pregnancy, I had actually been hoping for a high-tech delivery. But I ended up with a completely natural birth. He died after only a few hours.

'Maybe you can imagine the sort of state I was in after we lost the baby? Actually I was grateful to have a job to return to, or I could so easily have plunged into a deep depression, coping not only with his death but, at my age, with the fear that I might not be able to have another child. I'm sure there wasn't a dry eye in the company the day his death was announced.

'I was able to return to my job, at first part time, and later full time. They gave me a promotion and then six months later fortunately I became pregnant again. Presumably my advanced maternal age was the cause of our having twins, but ironically with this second pregnancy I was very healthy right through. I stayed at work as long as I could, so long as I was not risking or presenting any problems.

'Now here we are with my eight months' maternity leave nearly over. I was determined to take a reasonable length of time to be with the babies at home, as it is more than likely I will not have another child at my age. And, after our first tragedy, I really felt I owed it both to myself and to the twins to devote time to them. Just recently, I have negotiated a part-time contract for my initial return. Because I say it so calmly, please don't underestimate that achievement! This will be the first part-time contract that the company has ever written. But then, as a senior executive woman, you tend to find you're always creating the first of everything. Another woman, who was in hospital having a baby at the same time with me, has borrowed a copy of the contract to show to her employers.

'My biggest fear with having taken such a long maternity leave and then with returning to a part-time position is the concept that I'll lose touch, and the fear that slowly I'll be frozen out. Will I be ignored when it comes to future promotions? I have made efforts to prevent that happening: for example, I put my name on the company's mailing list to receive all their circulars and newsletters while at home. I want to keep up with all the internal gossip while I'm not around.

'I also felt obliged to try the part-time course of action as, living outside London, the commute would make a normal working day so very long. What I've put to my employers is this: I'll work from ten until four thirty, for three days a week to begin with, and then maybe, after I get used to the new schedule, for five days a week. A lot of my work is analytical and could be done from home. As it is, those hours would mean a regular day for my nanny. I just don't see how I could leave the house at seven every morning and not return until seven or later, and expect either myself or my nanny to work that type of day without a break. Such employment practices in themselves are cruel and unethical.

'Do I feel confident it will all work out? I just don't know. There is a sneaking suspicion I am harbouring that certain members of the company might feel I should not have my cake and eat it too. And I suspect my career has reached a watershed, that I may have to tread water for quite a while until I can go back full time and get myself on to that career path again.

'This is such an important issue for women today. Let's face it: why can't someone like me be in a senior management position and work restricted hours? Why should I have to give up all the experience and training gained over the years in my job, at this point, because I don't want to be away from my babies for twelve hours a day? My instinct tells me it's wrong to be away from children for such lengthy hours.

'Women like me are in a real catch-22 situation, and it hits very hard when you're a successful person used to being in control of your own life and working situation. This one conflict has no easy answers. But I would rather like to know how the men who work such hours deal with their wives and children? I have a feeling they don't, do they? They just leave their wives and children to suffer, or the marriages break up. But then life all around us is changing. I know many more men are now refusing to put in the 100 per cent commitment. That type of working life has always led to so many broken marriages and so much stress-related ill health.'

When I asked whether Val – just as I'd put it to Paula – wasn't letting the side down for other women by going part time, she shrugged her shoulders of the responsibility. Those babies mean an awful lot to Val. Reaching an acceptable compromise for herself and for them is all that she sees as important. She cannot take on her own shoulders the greater problems of women.

'I am an ambitious person, I agree. And one day I'd love to be financial director of a company. Or maybe I could move into part-time lecturing, or teaching. Or I could always do a PhD about how women are getting along in industry!

'I think women should be able to continue working, at senior levels, have children, and feel happy in the way they are combining both roles. But for that to happen, companies are going to have to be far more flexible with their work practices and far more open-minded. The battle cannot just come from someone like me.'

As we drove to the station for me to catch the train back to London, Val was still talking animatedly, enthusiastically contemplating a brave new future and its possibilities for women. Val mentioned a company nearby that was now offering its professional women full pay during their maternity leave. After all, they have finally seen reason: these are valued employees and so why should they be punished for becoming pregnant? The better the treatment of female employees, during and after pregnancy, the more commitment and loyalty will these companies foster in their women.

'The crunch tends to come when you've been out on maternity leave for a few months,' Val continued reflecting on her own case. 'Your cash flow has run down with all the extra costs of pregnancy and the birth, and the loss of half your earnings as a couple. Just at the same point your hormones have adapted to motherhood and you're having to face separating from the babies. Then you're thrown into the situation of having to hire a nanny for what looks like half your pay. Maybe you cannot afford to find the money at the time, at least until you would have been back at work for a month. Any normal woman just begins to debate whether it's all worth it.

'This way companies lose a lot of their women because of their entrenched attitudes. Sometimes they make it harder for women to return than simply to stay home. Where's the sense in that? Then they complain that women have babies and don't want to come back to work. It's patently not true. But something, somewhere, will have to give before the situation changes for the majority of women. Maybe the new demographic problem will finally be the trigger. I hope so.'

Sara D.

Strategic consultant

The word assertive might have been invented for Sara. I was filled with a childlike sense of terror when she grilled me over the phone. What were my motives for wishing to interview her, she asked in her deep voice? It had been suggested I would find Sara an interesting subject – she had surprised everyone she knew. It was not that she had landed a highly prestigious high-paying job at the age of thirty as a strategic consultant with a London-based firm of American management consultants; the surprise element lay in the fact she had also arrived on the first day pregnant.

What was the point of talking to her about her life and career, just because she'd gone on maternity leave soon after beginning her new job? Feeling slightly sheepish, because I felt the topic was extremely interesting, I nevertheless persuaded her to agree to the interview. Despite initial protestations ('we women can work as efficiently as men, so don't bring my child into it . . . you wouldn't ask a man those questions . . .' etc.), in truth Sara was more than happy to explore her view of the working mother discourse. And she is better placed than many to judge the inequities of the system.

Sara is very outspoken and, at first, her voice can be quite offputting, slicing through nonsense and niceness like a butter knife. But soon, when she relaxes, and some of the stiffness of what she herself likes to call 'power shoulders' begins to dissolve, then she becomes witty, perceptive and the sheer strength of her intelligence shines through. Educated at St Paul's Girls School and at an Oxbridge college (where she read history), Sara strikes you immediately as someone made for the top.

Power suits her, it fits like a glove. She does not stoop to any feminine foibles or manipulative mannerisms to make her point. Smartly dressed in a traditional suit and blouse, neatly coifed, you just would not have expected her to paint those very sensible finger nails.

Sara feels strongly that women with brains should be allowed to use them. She believes also that women with babies should not be treated as though they have no brain. She is cynical about the chances of any major revolution in social attitudes taking place, but does feel that with her exceptional educational background it is required of her that she helps show other women the way. I came away from our meeting with the distinct impression that following the early years of the struggle to combine her new career and new motherhood, she will probably be very successful: swathing a neat curve through the undergrowth for mere lesser mortals to follow.

About fellow former pupils at St Paul's, for example, she was scathing: 'They all went on to Oxbridge and then married "leading men", from which point on one never heard of them again. That was their role in life: to become the highly educated wives of *important* men.'

Why get an MBA?

'It was a very firm decision for me to go to business school. I knew that an MBA would be the necessary stepping stone for the sort of career move I wanted to make. I had a clear idea and worked it out decisively. I was twenty-eight years old at the time I started my two-year course. I had to stay in London because I was on the point of getting married. Until then I had played with the idea of attending either a big American school, or INSEAD in Paris: either of which would have been far more prestigious.

'A two-year course did feel like a very big commitment at that stage in my career, as it meant giving up my job, taking out a bank loan, and gambling that I would find a well-paid high-profile job at the end. But I had gone straight from university into a career in advertising, starting out as an account manager. At the time, it had looked to me like a fast-track career, which would use some of my native talents and creativity. I was seduced into the job by going for a number of interviews. It all looked terribly exciting.

'But eventually, despite the fact I was promoted rapidly, I found the work far too shallow. There was no challenge involved, and I felt that I was apologizing for my brain. What had grown to interest me, in its place, was the strategic work involved in helping companies improve their performance. But, from the advertising end, I knew we were coming in from the side and obviously we were excluded from any major decision-making. Which is why I came up with the idea I should move directly into strategic consulting.

'I can now see that advertising is a very traditional female career. Junior management is full of women. But once you look higher up, there's scarcely a handful of women at board level. To my mind, when an industry has that sort of paucity of women at the top, then we should be questioning the politics of the industry.

'I was quite unusual among the women on the MBA course, as I had such a strong vision of my future. I did find that too many of the women were very unassertive which surprised me, because they'd all made this incredibly tough decision to take so much time out to go back to university. For too many of them, I fear, it was more a question of copping out, a retreat from the real world rather than seeing it as a stepping stone. The MBA is still not an accepted pattern in one's career structure in this country. It may sound really awful to say this, but it is still seen as a rather lower middle-class thing to be doing; sort of like attending night school! There is none of the glamour of Harvard or INSEAD attached. But, then that might also be a reflection of the status of business in this country, and the lack of real intelligence on the part of male management.

'People in most companies in Britain today don't think in strategic ways. An MBA is not a requirement for management. Those at the top, for example in the insurance industry, may just be sitting comfortably on a cushion of accumulated money. When the cold wind of change blows, such as the new Financial Services Act, they have no idea how to respond and confront such sudden adverse market dynamics. You will find, if you look closely, an amazing lack of talent at the top in most major industries or companies. Which is all the more reason why I'm finding my present job so very exciting.'

Life on the ladder

Sara feels the consultancy firms, particularly the American companies well-accustomed to employing male and female MBAs, have a far better track record. In a position like hers you can no longer claim that it is an exclusively male domain. Although, once we turned to the question of how women (especially those with children) fit into this still predominantly male culture, Sara's attitude was no longer so benign.

'Consultancy firms, like this one, do let you use your brain. I'm still astounded by the type of work we tackle. And women have equal access to the opportunities. They consistently hire exceptionally bright people and we're very highly paid. But we work very long hours.

'The sort of work I'm involved in often takes me to America or Europe. We analyse markets. There's a lot of interviewing involved while researching the market-place. And a lot of important meetings endlessly to attend – all at board level! Here, I have been given the exact opportunities I was denied in advertising. In fact I'm still rather impressed by it all: to think that after two years of studying, I can now spend four weeks analysing someone's company, then hop on a plane and go into an executive board meeting where I'll be telling them how to run their company. Lately my husband has taken to saying, "Why is every meeting a 'big' one? Couldn't you just for once say you have to be off to a 'little' meeting?" But the truth is they are all enormous and very powerful.

'It's exciting and there's no doubt that there's a great buzz about this kind of work. But I must admit it annoys me greatly that there is absolutely no recognition from your bosses or colleagues that you may have another life outside. I'm married and we have a four-and-a-half-month-old daughter. I'm working alongside men who, to get on, are prepared to sacrifice their families. And I'm expected to follow suit. They're quite happy with the situation, and they assume I will feel the same.

'There's a whole lot of divorcees and ageing bachelors around in this industry, simply because of the demands of the lifestyle. These men are of my own age, in their early thirties, and many of them don't even have a permanent girl-friend because of the hours they work. They don't care when they go home. They have no outside pressures. There is one lovely male colleague here who confessed to me this week that he is actually relieved that his wife has gone away for a few days. For once he does not have to carry that extra level of tension: the guilt he feels about getting home so late, of letting her down on promised social occasions, yet again.

'Most of the men here seem to end up marrying either someone who just doesn't care about their absences, or a woman whom they can buy off. A lot of the partners, for example, have glamorous wives who occasionally come into the office to visit. These wives just don't know how to handle a working woman like myself! They are the ones with the big houses, cars, clothes, jewels and swanky club memberships, who spend their days playing golf, tennis or at the health spas. The price they have to pay in return is that they don't object to their husbands going abroad at the drop of a hat; that he is never home before nine or ten on an average evening.

'As for my hours? Well, I get in to work around eight and on a good day will be home by eight. But sometimes I work flat out, only going home to sleep and getting up early the next morning. I may also have to work weekends. You get used to cancelling dinner invitations at the last minute. In fact you can hardly plan social events. Then I also travel a lot. I'm very fortunate that right now my husband is working far more sensible hours. So he is the one who comes home at a normal hour to relieve the nanny. I see my daughter in the early mornings and a little before she goes to bed. And sometimes at the weekend.

'In this business we earn very high salaries, and yet when you stop to consider the sort of hours that are put in, it doesn't look so good. Although it's exciting, I would say it's a pretty bad way of living for anybody. Should anyone really work at this pitch for long? We do have families and other commitments. Yet the macho way is to pretend that you don't. And there is a lot of posturing from the partners to prove they can go the extra mile. Let's face it, clients will pay for work to be done in a reasonable time. Yet impossible deadlines are created from within. Why do we have to work weekends, to squeeze the work in to an unrealistic schedule? Why couldn't it wait another week? There are times I ask myself the questions, but you're expected to be out there gunning, with both hands in the holsters!

'Should we be asking ourselves whether men aren't toughening

97

up the rules of the game? It's as though they were saying to women, "OK, you can join us if you want, but look how nasty it is out here. We don't want to hear any soft stuff, about families needing your time. Play the game by our rules or get out." I still don't know where I stand. My daughter is little. But as she gets older, I know she will demand more of my time.

'I wonder about it all. I do believe basically women have a better sense of balance, of the quality of life. Though I cannot congratulate myself in that way, as in our marriage I'm the obsessive workaholic.

'The other major question to my mind is what happens to women at work as they become older? You just don't see too many women in their fifties and sixties around in offices. What happened to them? As I've become older, one thing I have noticed is that however bright you really are, in men's eyes you have become less of a bimbo, and therefore a less interesting person to have around.

'I fear that most people of my generation have been lulled into a false sense of security over the situation of women at work. During our early twenties, we were conned into thinking, "What's the problem? We can get jobs. We're every bit as good as the men." But once you're no longer the pretty girl with a degree, the men begin to find you difficult to handle. As time goes by, maybe you marry and you become more authoritative. Older male colleagues just don't know how to relate to you any more. So, I've begun to ask myself, are older women eased out of jobs? What will happen to our generation as we move into our forties and fifties?'

MBA, career and a baby

And then, despite those early protestations that Sara had not wanted to focus on her pregnancy and motherhood, suddenly we found ourselves skirting round the topic. And without my prompting, she launched into her own feelings and experience. There is a side of Sara that is still somewhat defensive about her particular foray into motherhood, because the style with which she handled the conception does not quite fit her image. No one knows this better than Sara and talking it through brings her anger to the surface.

'Logically, while still at business school, I felt that a consultancy position would be a good place to have children. Because good people are always in demand, I'd imagined employers would be unlikely to ease you out just because you'd become pregnant. While I was studying for the MBA, I was newly married and both my husband and I wanted to start a family immediately.

'I was twenty-eight years old, beginning on my two-year MBA course. You have to remember that this is a crucial time for most young women, when we are beginning to think very seriously about motherhood and/or marriage. It was a big item of discussion among the group of younger women at business school. For all of us the issue was the same: we had just taken two years out; we would then have to start on a new career, and aim to work at least two more years there before we could claim maternity leave. By which point we'd be well into our thirties. And who knew, maybe it would then be too late? Maybe we would discover we were infertile? The situation certainly did not seem fair.

'To everyone's surprise I jumped in! I did things the impossible and awkward way. There is still something faintly embarrassing for me about the whole discussion, which is why I was loath to talk about it. I had worked for my present company in my first summer at business school, on a three-month placement. They liked me and offered me a full-time position on graduation. At that point, in an interview, I did flag the issue of motherhood in principle before accepting their offer. Still I had another year of school to complete, so I did not feel desperate about the job offer.

'I told the interviewer (male, of course) that sooner or later my intention was to have a family. How did he feel this would affect my position as a consultant? Would it raise problems with the company? The guy handled it pretty well, though I could see he was taken aback. These are not questions usually brought up in an interview! But he referred me to some other women in the organization. Being an American firm and one with few women employees, he explained, they did not have a set maternity policy. But, all in all, I felt the prospects sounded pretty good.

'The embarrassing part was that when I arrived to begin the job I was already three months pregnant. At that point I had to remind this man of our previous conversation. I remained steadfastly unapologetic and suggested to him that I would like to take three months off as maternity leave in the New Year. He must have been floored, because the only response I received was "Fine". Actually they gave me the three months on full salary. I was under no terms eligible for maternity leave. Instead, I had gambled that if they liked me sufficiently they would go along with my plans. I just bucked the conventional logic that says you're supposed to work for two years before you are given time off as your reward before you are allowed to have a baby.

'It was nevertheless a difficult situation for me to deal with. Did I pretend that the pregnancy was accidental? Or act as though I had willingly flouted unwritten rules? To look as though my pregnancy was a mistake cast me immediately into the role of a foolish woman who is not in control of her own life. There was no way I was going to let myself be identified like that. So I just kept very quiet. I didn't believe anyone would dare ask me. And they didn't.

'I'd kept quiet about the pregnancy at business school too. Despite the fact that I was taking finals whilst three months pregnant. I'm tall and was then very slim, so nothing showed. I had also worked hard enough during the two years and figured that I'd pass reasonably well, even with the obstacles of tiredness and not feeling too well. But I couldn't risk telling anyone other than a couple of very close friends or the company who were to be my employers would surely have found out. And I wanted it to be me who would tell them, on my own terms. I started my new job immediately on graduating; that way I had four months or so of working time to offer them before I disappeared on leave.'

Pregnant on the job

Sara then told me her story about life as the newly-pregnant executive strategic consultant.

'If I wasted any time fearing that I might be sidelined on to not very good projects, I needn't have given it a thought! I was worked very hard; not the slightest allowance was made for my pregnancy. Often I was up all night writing documents only to fly to America the next morning, carrying a huge briefcase of precious reports with me, and I was six months pregnant. In a way I probably overcompensated for being pregnant. I did not talk once in the office about being pregnant or about children. There was not a single role-model for me in the company. I suppose I've been given the chance to serve as role-model for others following in my wake. But it would have been bloody nice to have someone at my level just to chat to.

'Even in the newspapers, the only working mothers in the business world you get to read about are those same two or three female entrepreneurs who are trotted out at regular intervals. But I find that counter-productive. Those women run their own companies (or say they do) and so to the public eye they're still seen as retaining a glamorous image. They are not out there having to play a man's game.

'I worked up to the day of delivery (I had a caesarian section), though as it was the Christmas period I was able to work a lot from home. My partner was away on a skiing holiday, I remember, and it was left up to me to finish a major report. The evening he returned, I phoned to explain it all to him, as he was taking it to New York the next morning. I hung up the phone and went into hospital to have my baby.

'As a mother, I can't say I find the strain too hard. My nanny is very good and I don't get up in the night for the baby, I could never manage that. But I have put on about two stone since before I was pregnant, and now I don't fit any of my work clothes! Being somewhat overweight, even though being tall I can carry it, I have noticed just does not fit the right image. The high-powered working woman is meant to be a thoroughbred. They're the thin ones. I'm sure it's back to the control issue again: overweight women are seen as having let themselves go. Women in charge stay thin.'

Entering the time warp

By now, I could hardly imagine Sara during her maternity leave. What did she do with herself? Had she been happy at home all day with the baby? Did she feel guilt at returning to this high-profile job? To be honest, Sara immediately replied, she only feels guilty about not feeling guilty. And then she began to talk freely about her time that she refers to as being 'down among the women'.

'I spent three months at home and, my goodness, I wouldn't do that again. My education and career has all been very elitist. In consultancy work, you only mix with very bright people. Being at home for three months was hell for me. Talk about an identity crisis. I kept asking myself if this was still me. I panicked that I was throwing my career away, that all the time and effort would be lost. I know I must sound dreadfully arrogant, and hope I don't come across as too much of an ogre, but my educational background led me to a natural arrogance and, besides, I feel that too many women are far too self-effacing and apologetic. We deserve to be arrogant. We should let ourselves be proud.

'There's a Fay Weldon novel, whose title has stuck in my mind, *Down Among the Women*. That's how I see my maternity leave. You move in a matter of days from the world of "dressing-for-success" and "power shoulders" to this world "down there"; literally scrubbing floors and wiping noses. You move from a cerebral world of brainpower and visible success, to a world that is bounded by physical feelings and not always nice feelings, either. I really did feel "down". And I could see how quickly you would lose that essential self-confidence. I cannot imagine how women manage to take a few years out and then return on an equal footing. After three months, my brain had turned to mush. I could not keep up with conversations. If my husband and I went out to dinner, I just was not in tune with other people. And I'm by no means a shy or retiring person.

'Or I'd be pushing the baby to the shops in her pram, and a complete stranger would stop to tell me what to do. I found it an extraordinary invasion of privacy, especially when you are used to being in charge. It was winter, and always raining, and I couldn't get the stupid pram into the shops. I look back on it all now and it was as though I'd entered a time warp. I would really like to have another baby. But I'm very aware if having one was a big step for me, then having a second will be a quantum leap.'

At that point in our interview, which had been conducted in a little conference room tucked away in the office building, a head appeared round the door. Sara was invited by a group of her colleagues to join them for lunch at a wine bar. Looking confused and perplexed, because she no doubt hated having stirred up all those unacceptable emotions again, she begged my leave, explaining that she should go, as she so seldom spent any time with her colleagues. I was quite happy to see her leave the room with that cheerful group. Either Sara is working too hard for such luxuries or she is rushing to get home before the baby goes to sleep.

I felt very confident in Sara's power, ultimately, to handle the confusion, to take the complexities on board. We need women like her − as she herself describes − to be our role-model. As to her own vision of the future? She'll always work, of that she is sure. But whether she will remain in consultancy is another question.

How could she support those working hours and deadly deadlines, with two young children? Should she even contemplate doing so? At least I told her, it was refreshing for me to meet someone so unafraid to talk of her ambitions, who believed so strongly in herself.

'My own mother was a graduate and a very bright woman,' Sara told me as we parted. 'She gave birth to me while she was still at university and then she spent sixteen years at home bringing up her children. I want to achieve whatever is possible for women today, both for my sake and hers. But, having said that, in my own terms,' Sara shrugged, 'and by the average male standards of someone with my ability and background, I don't think I've done so well considering I am nearly thirty-one. It is just still seen as extraordinary if a woman gets on at all. And, if I can't do well with my background, then no one can.'

PART
4

HIGH–FLIERS

The four women in this section have been selected by me, as being representative of women who are particularly close to the top. They are all extremely high-powered, earn high salaries, and appear quite content with their lot in life. To put it another way, these women seem to epitomize the ability to be at ease with their power, money and success.

Three of the women in the section are married, and mothers; the fourth is single and, perhaps like any single woman, given more to questioning that status, its permanence and position in her life. But then, as we have already seen with the stories of both Harriet and Louise, there is an equally strong feeling of self and of singles'-style happiness to leave us with a definite sense of balance.

Two of the stories are of American women who are living and working in London. I include them, as I did with Louise, because they are Americans who have made a deliberate choice to move across the Atlantic and settle in Britain or Europe. These women are not high-powered Americans who have simply moved in to clean up on our act. They have borrowed our nationality, its ethics and vocabulary, with all the inherent advantages and disadvantages. In turn, we can learn much from their experience of the two still very different ways of life.

In the first of these four stories, Rhoda is very much an English-woman, with all the spunk, imagination and creative energy that can come from a typical form of mild British eccentricity. Rhoda's story brings out many themes in common with several MBA women. For example, on thinking again about Rhoda, I found myself jotting down a few words that best summed up my feelings about her life: she is a woman of independence and of control whose mild eccentricity frees her in a strange way, in that it enables her not to care too much what others think or feel of her.

Rhoda K.

The high-powered MBA who leapt from a background of A levels

Rhoda came into this book as a real surprise even to me, because it emerged that we shared a past. I had been given her name along with a list of others, as follow-up contacts for women with MBAs. The initial call, as was true of so many, was taken by a secretary. But the call was returned quickly and, as I was flicking open the pages of my diary to plan a time to meet, Rhoda asked me if I had lived as a girl in a certain town. Why yes, I laughed. It turned out that both of us had been brought up in the same town and although we had not been at the same school, within the same school year we had known of each other's existence.

That new piece of information, I will admit, left me with a strange uneasiness. Maybe all women fear meeting someone their own age, after a lifetime of adult living and different experiences. Who would look the older, who would be the more successful, who the happiest? Already I had noticed a *frisson* of envy because Rhoda, according to reliable information that came from my source of names, was one of the most highly-paid women working in London. A partner, a senior executive in a firm of international consultants, on a profit-sharing scheme, it was whispered that she earns somewhere in the region of £100,000. And here was me, the lowly free-lance writer, ringing her up to be profiled in my book! Was there not something threatening about this meeting of teenage schoolgirls – some thirty years on?

How would I compare with Rhoda who, by the sound of it, was not only successfully married, but also a brilliantly successful career woman all rolled into one? Was I really about to meet The Woman Who Has It All?

One small clue had, however, already been shot out implying that Rhoda was not as straight-arrow as I had imagined. Even in this initial phone conversation Rhoda had mentioned that she remembered us both spending time, as part of a larger group of rebellious middle-class schoolgirls, in the notorious Beatles Cavern-style café in that otherwise terribly tame small town. Any girl – in those halcyon days of the early sixties, who ripped off her school beret as soon as she was out of sight of the teachers, who besported herself in black tights and white panstick make-up, who defied her parents by hanging out in this really very safe, but to us dark and dangerous, café – could not be All Bad.

Rhoda suggested I came in to visit her at the office and that we'd have lunch together over sandwiches in some quiet spot, rather than battling our way through a crowded lunch-time restaurant. Feeling nevertheless hesitant about our meeting, especially as Rhoda had such a high-powered executive title within the company, I hoped the ordeal would quickly be over.

Rhoda was ready and waiting for me as I emerged from the lift. There she stood, in her executive glory, waving her arms cheerfully, inviting me into the sumptuously and softly-furnished huge office that was Rhoda's own executive suite. Let's eat in here, she suggested and called down to the secretary for the sandwiches to be brought within.

If any woman, sitting around at home, ever dreamed of a high-powered successful high-salaried career, Rhoda's does seem to be the one that offers all the fantasy goodies. Her office itself is the realization of an interior decorator's dream, with tasteful sofas, paintings on the walls; its clean and uncluttered lines lending an atmosphere at once peaceful, calm, and very unlike the normal office environment with its usual accompaniment of tacky desks, chairs, regulation lamps and carpet tiles. Rhoda's office was more like a home.

And as we talked what I really liked about Rhoda, despite my fears of her overwhelming success is that her story like so many of the women's in this book, was not one of easy movements from A to B. Rather, it revealed a life full of misdirection and clumsy steps; the final resolution seemed to have come about because of her determination and courage. Rhoda talks with a breathless energy, an unbounding spiral of words and ideas, punctuated with easy laughter at her own foibles along the way. She also has a strong sense of narrative. More so than any other woman's story, Rhoda's flowed chronologically – as though she might be writing her own novel.

What Rhoda did

'My mother was an actress and that maybe accounts for some of my craziness! My father though was a very respectable corn merchant. Because I've gone into business, I suppose that means I take more after him, while my brother is the painter, the struggling artist. Anyway, I was sent to a prep. school and then when I passed the eleven-plus to a girls' direct-grant school just out of town. I did well in school and came out with A levels in French and English. But, although I was accepted at university I fancied going to live in France. It just didn't occur to me at the time that I should pursue my studies and spend three more years in full-time education. Maybe because of my rather comfortable background, the thought of "career" was not uppermost in my mind.

'On leaving school, I went to London to a secretarial college. Then I worked for a year in the theatre, and after that I moved to Paris where I stayed for two years. I must say I had a fantastic time in Paris. And in a sense that experience set the rest of my life on course. In many ways, I feel as though I've only made two major decisions in my life. One was to go and live in Paris and the other was to have a baby. From both those decisions all the other events in my life have flowed.

'While in Paris I went to work for an American construction and engineering firm. Remember, I was trained as a secretary and had good use of the French language. Although it was an American-based company, I was at the time the only English speaker employed there so I was involved in a lot of translation work. I didn't stay for long though, because I moved on to a really fabulous job working for a very famous French novelist (whose name I would not dare mention). I was his secretary and assistant and though it was interesting work, he was quite mad and we just didn't get along. The American company took me back, and this time I moved with them to their branch in Algeria. That was where I met my first husband.

'He was a writer, a creative man who had taken up technical writing to subsidise his attempts at novels. Dan was quite a lot older than me, but I agreed to marry him within the first three weeks, as he was moving back to California. I lived with him on the West Coast for two years. It was the late sixties and early seventies, a very good time to be living in California. I was able to work for that same engineering company, and it was there that I realized it was time to stop being a secretary. American women were far more go-getting than the average English woman of my age, and I could see that I was capable of doing more.

'Two years later, Dan and I moved back to England. This time I moved into a job in London for an American investment bank. I'd been taken on at a low level, but they had promised to give me training and career development. By now I was keen to begin moving upwards. I began working in the Middle Eastern section as part of a group of about thirteen others. We were doing financial analyses, or research and information memoranda on various companies. And I was working with some very highly-educated people. For example, one of the women colleagues, who was around my same age, was a Harvard MBA. And another colleague, a man from the Lebanon, had an MBA from Massachusetts Institute of Technology and a DBA (Doctor of Business Studies) from Harvard. And here was me, an ex-secretary, working alongside them! Curiously, I noticed that I was doing just as well as they were in the job. Maybe in some ways I was doing even better, because, by not being an MBA, I had not approached the job with strongly-held opinions on what we should be doing.

'But I think it was this exposure to the American way of doing things, that made me decide to try for an MBA myself. Although I didn't have an undergraduate degree, I contacted the various business schools and a school outside of London, offering a one-year full-time course, said they would consider me. They insisted I must do well in their test (which is akin to, but not the same as, GMAT) before I would be eligible for a place. The American woman colleague helped with my application forms, which had to be answered in essay form. She guided me in ways to make the most of what I'd been doing all those years. And I was called in for the interview.

110

'Obviously, my personality and drive were strong enough. I only had two arts A levels, and worse I had even managed to fail O level maths! One thing I discovered taking their test was that, by the age of thirty, what seemed hard at sixteen was really quite easy. Besides, working in the bank I had been exposed to numbers and had done some basic accountancy.

'The most interesting part of the test was an exercise in logic which was designed to prove you could keep your head in difficult circumstances. We were given paragraphs to read on very contentious subjects. After reading them we had to give the logical conclusion from a choice of four statements. The passages might have been downright racist or sexist, and the difficulty was to keep your calm and see what really was the logical answer. To my amazement, as I've never seen myself as a deeply logical person, I scored very highly on that part of the test with 96 per cent. It was the highest score that had ever been achieved! And they offered me a place.

'Immediately, I gave up the job with the bank and moved myself out of London for the year. I was twenty-nine years old, going on thirty, at the time. My marriage to Dan was in fact breaking up and by the end of the course inevitably it was completely over. The school itself was in a dump of a place, which was something of a comedown after all my exciting travelling around the world. And I had to face up to being the only person on the course without a degree or a professional qualification. There were twelve women out of about one hundred students.

'But it was a wonderful experience for me. The MBA course raised my confidence and made me realize I was just as good as anyone else. It opened my eyes to the fact I didn't want to work for a big bank any more, but that rather I should move directly into the business world. Before I could achieve that, obviously I had to gain some experience. So my plan was on graduation to find any job that would teach me something about selling, where I would be able to prove my worth in a quantifiable way, and from which I would probably move on after a couple of years.

'During the second term you began interviewing for jobs. I was lucky in being offered two. One was to run the business side of a language school; and the other was to join as a consultant (which, despite its fancy name, is the lowest rung on the ladder), working with the man in charge of the Middle Eastern section. It was rare for a woman to be asked to travel out to the Gulf. But the man interviewing me and I got along very well. I presume he was interested in me because I'd been working on Middle Eastern accounts at the bank. I liked the feel of the company, and the Middle Eastern connection also seemed like a golden opportunity. To my mind at the time, it looked to be the typical sort of MBA job that you do for the statutory couple of years before moving on. It paid very generously, and seemed like a nice job.

'So I decided to come here. And that was eleven years ago! Despite my original intention of staying only a couple of years, I now find myself in the position of being the longest-serving member of the company of anyone in London. I just think I've been incredibly lucky in the way things have happened.'

Could a one-year course make such a huge change to her working life?

'I didn't know anything about consulting at the time. But, looking back, I know that I could never have been offered such a job without the MBA qualification. This company hires people who have either very good business experience or a very good education. There was no way I could have even applied without a degree.

'But, if you really want to know what I think about the MBA, in my opinion it doesn't teach you very much at all. What you gain from the programme is an awful lot of help in how you see yourself.

'From a capability point of view I'm probably no better qualified, nor frankly am I better educated, than I was before business school. It's rather a superficial form of learning, simply because there is no time to do anything in depth. But, I can reason better, I write better, and I'm now definitely more analytical. I can recognize when people are bullshitting. I can recognize the buzz words, know when I'm being strung along; without having to know everything about their business. I know enough of the terminology to understand and to hold conversations. I am also confident enough to know where the gaps in my own knowledge lie, and that it's not so awful to have to ask a stupid question. That's one major lesson anyone should learn: that it is OK to ask a stupid question. It will not immediately destroy your credibility.

'The only practical information I have learned from the MBA course is on the financial side. We learned statistics, economics and finance. We did the sums. But then I found that areas like marketing and organizational behaviour by and large come down to common sense. There's not too much to learn there. No, it's really a huge confidence-booster and it also forced me to think more about myself.

'Out of the twelve women among the one hundred men on my course, we women all did rather well. It also helped us to realize that for all the men say and do, they really are no smarter than us. It gave us the clue behind the mystique of the businessman and the business world! And, for me, it led to an understanding of my own value in an economic sense. By that I mean, I am no longer afraid of asking for a high salary and in believing that I am worth a lot of money.'

I agreed with her that these are all great lessons for women to learn. But was Rhoda really such an ingenue, as the portrait she paints, at the game before business school? Somehow I felt a secretly tough person had been hiding out in her amiable and jolly self all along.

'There is one story I love to tell when I did fight for my rights, long before the MBA. I had a very amusing time when the Sex Discrimination Act first came in. This was back in my early days at the American investment bank. The Act forced us all into the position of writing a job description. That in itself was quite an eye opener. I was working, for example, alongside a male colleague and I could see quite clearly that he and I were doing the same work. But I learned I was being paid about half of his salary. My boss at the time was the nicest man and I took this glaring error along for him to see. He groaned, and said, "Don't do this to me, Rhoda." It was up to him to take the problem to Personnel. They reportedly commented, "I guess we should have thought something like this might happen." Anyway they refused to admit anything was wrong, but the next month suddenly I received an 80 per cent pay rise in my packet. I saw that as my own mini-victory!'

A high-flying career and men

Rhoda loves to disparage the amount of personal effort that has played a strong role in her life. During our conversation I found myself saying at certain major points in the story, 'But you were very brave' or 'You must have shown great courage'. In her breezy manner, Rhoda would cast the comment aside.

'Eight years ago, I was asked to move out to the Far East for this company, to set up a new office there. It was not something I relished doing as by that point I was a single woman again. I had just spent two years rebuilding my life in the aftermath of the marriage. I'd made new friends (remember I'd been married for nine years and out of the country for quite a part of that), and the idea of throwing up my new-found stability once more and going off on my own to a new country was quite appalling. Apart from anything else, I had recently bought myself a house and had just finished replanting the garden myself that spring.

'But I was then thirty-three years old and had no family ties. It did seem as though this might be the last chance for me to prove myself. Also the lure of travel, and the thought of living in that particular country, were irresistible forces.

'How did I survive? Well, I certainly enjoyed myself out there. But there is no way round the fact that for much of the time my life was very tough. I grew up fast. Starting up a new office from scratch can be very stressful, an almost twenty-four-hour-a-day commitment. After a couple of years when all was going successfully, I moved to yet another country and started up yet another office from scratch. During those years my life was hectic. But certain nagging thoughts had begun to plague me.

'In that time overseas, I had hit the age of thirty-five. And two new things began to happen to me. One, I decided I wanted to have a baby, having never before wanted a child. The decision was so strong that I knew I would have a child within the next few years, whether I was married or not. Two, I made the decision that I enjoyed running an office best. So, rather than return home immediately to the London office, I felt it best to give myself another two years in proving I could run this new office successfully.

'As it happens I fell in love in the next year. He was from London, travelling abroad a lot on business, but he was married with two young children. He also fell in love with me, but there were obviously huge problems to be worked out before we could ever be married. It still staggers me to think it took until I was nearly forty years old to fall in love.

'The last two or three years have been very difficult. Despite the fact they have been the happiest in my life, they have also been the most difficult. This is the first time in my life that I have had to live through someone else. I'm such an independent spirit that no one has ever touched me deeply enough before, so that I would share their pain. All I could do for him was stand back and be patient. I could not go through for him the hideous emotional mess of his divorce nor the agonies of separating from children whom he did not want to hurt. Things do seem to be more settled now, thank heavens. The children appear to have resolved themselves to the changed lifestyle. And, looking back, I am amazed at my own ability to cope with the crises, given that they felt so completely out of my control.

'Of course in the eyes of the ex-wife and maybe, though I don't know, in the eyes of his children, I have been cast as the arch-devil, the dreaded "Career Woman". But you know I never really saw myself as a woman who had chosen career over a man. That type of relationship just had not offered itself before in my life.'

What does her husband say about Rhoda's very successful and high-paying career, I wondered. After all, he had come from a more traditional marriage where the wife, mother of their two children, did not work.

'It's hard to say. My husband earns more than I do. Maybe it just works out between us because we are so similar. We both have careers, are strong personalities, and are pragmatic. He's possibly more of a dreamer than I am. What's important, to my mind, is why I fell in love with him, when previously I'd so determinedly clung on to my freedom. All the men in my life had been weaker personalities than me. I would never have married again had I not found a man who was as sure of himself in the world as I am.

'Having said that I used to drive him mad in our early days. I was used to a certain way of life that one adopts as a single working woman. I'd eat out in restaurants all the time, send my clothes to the dry cleaners, never think twice about spending money. It wasn't that he wanted me to be home cooking for him, but, as a married man he'd been more used to eating together at home in the evenings. He just didn't want to eat in a restaurant at the end of every busy day. So I remember one evening I made a special effort to prepare dinner and what did I do? I brought home caviar. It seemed simple and easy to prepare, and the expense was irrelevant. Now, of course, with a new baby in the house, we're home far more often than I ever used to be.'

Does her working life fit with motherhood?

Rhoda's baby daughter is just under a year old. She has a full-time, live-in nanny, and tries hard to see her daughter as much as possible, between seven and eight every morning, also in the early evenings before her bedtime, and always at weekends. The main point for Rhoda is that as a businesswoman she is now so well-established with her company that she can afford to be flexible with her time. Although she was forty-one years old for the birth, this has proved to be a very good time to have a first baby.

'When I first came back from those years overseas, I had a senior position with the company from my years of service, but don't imagine it was too easy. I had to carve out a position for myself all over again once back in the London office. My fellow partners were accommodating and welcoming, but it was nevertheless a tough assignment for me following on from running my own office for the last few years. I came back still full of energy, wanting to be more than just someone else within the office. So I had to earn my spurs all over again.

'The senior executives here are all partners. We are all still actively involved in the core business. I do business on the company's behalf and I bring in new business. After that initial phone call, it's up to someone like me to compete for the work.

'In those first few months following my return to London, I felt quite low and lacking in self-confidence. In fact I would have changed jobs, except that by that point I had become pregnant.

And I knew this was not the right time to be launching into a new career. So I decided to stay on. Instead, I worked hard and built myself a niche. I'm viewed now as Aunty Rhoda, because I have been here so long. I'm a safe person for younger members to talk to as I have no axe to grind, I'm not jockeying for position, and so I tend to be seen as an objective advice-giver by others.'

And then the conversation turned to talk about her baby.

'Did I ever think of giving up work when I had the baby? I suppose you might think that, because I could afford to. But, by the time I became pregnant, I had been working for twenty-one years, ever since I was eighteen years old. No, I never gave it a moment's consideration. Ideally, I might prefer to work a four-day week. But I can give myself flexibility here. We live just twenty minutes away from the office. And my hours don't have to be too terribly long. Quite often I conduct my interviews from home – I might invite someone over for breakfast, or for an early evening drink. People respond well to a home atmosphere as it is a much more relaxing environment in which to talk. Really, it's quite a civilized way of life. At least three days a week, my husband and I drive in to work together. He drops me off at the office in the morning and picks me up in the evenings, so we get some extra time together as well.

'He talks more than I do about the possibility of giving up work. For that I'd have to be really earning a lot! He now has his ex-wife and children to support and that counts as a substantial overhead. Even if we fancied giving it all up, and going round the world on a boat, we could not do that to her. If I didn't have to make any money at all, I suppose I would move into the art world and represent a group of painters, people like my brother who are sensitive and creative and unable to market themselves. Yes, I'd find that very satisfying.'

In Rhoda's case, pushing her way to the top does not appear to have left her with major sacrifices festooned along the way. Does she have an idea why more women have not been able to take a similar leap of faith in themselves?

'I'd say that I was lucky in going to America back in the early

117

seventies. The experience made me far more direct as a personality than I might have been otherwise. By and large women don't feel comfortable being assertive or asking for money. We fear that if we make too much of a fuss we'll be forced out of a job. But the truth is women just don't shout loud enough. A lot of the women, whom I see in the work world, don't know how to handle the organization. They tend to disappear into the ladies' loo to bitch and moan about their treatment. But that is absolutely the wrong way to go about things. I wish women could remember that no one ever does themselves a disservice by speaking their mind, assertively, without being threatening. If I have something to say to a boss or colleague, I just go in to his or her office and state my case, asking if something couldn't be done.

'Many times other women have accused me of being too direct. And yet in my counselling role here, as Aunty Rhoda, I find myself having to explain to others that same simple logic. Go into the boss and put your problem to him. Don't go in there bitching and complaining. Don't go in there just to say, "I'm not happy because of such and such." Try to go in with a picture of the problem, and your own idea of what would make the best solution.'

Phyllis F.

The American woman already at the top

We are about to enter the hallowed portals of the City. You might in fact be surprised that not one of the women so far profiled has been working in the City. Yet this financial bastion is the classic domain of the MBA graduate, male or female. Although, as I mentioned in the opening chapter, this book makes no claim to be a statistical survey of the fate of female MBA graduates, and their employment prospects, nevertheless the low turn-out of City whizz-kids, even within these pages, probably serves to emphasize that the world where money is made over the telephone and computer lines is not necessarily one that most attracts women, even at the high-powered end of the market.

Management consultancy, corporate communications, executive search, industry, running your own company, working in the public sector - such careers, generally speaking, will offer women work that is more compatible with their basic interests plus high salaries.

Phyllis, however, is very strong, determined and forceful. First, let it be said that Phyllis epitomizes the word 'formidable'. She could be to some, I am sure, a quite terrifying force. Phyllis had me quaking at the other end of the phone, when she launched into a not-so-subtle attack on my approach to her as a potential profilee. Worse, came her ego-deflating last question: 'Who are you? I'm afraid I don't know your name.'

Hastily rebuilding my resolve, I reassured myself that this was the very type of attitude I had expected to receive from all MBA contacts. Who knows better than myself how time-wasting an interview can be. Where do busy women squeeze in that extra time? Why, indeed, should they? Just because Phyllis made no outward show of being 'nice', should I be offended? Wasn't this the very stuff of much that I was writing about? 'Send me some material,' Phyllis shot out her last barbed message down the phone.

But then Phyllis, it must also be remembered, is American. Having lived there myself for many years, I was aware that a lot of Americans share a fundamental attitude towards life and other people, which we tend not to express on this side of the Atlantic. Rhoda had also spoken of a similar concept. She was often criticized for being too direct. This is what I call 'American style'. They don't want to clutter up their lives with the mess that can come from being 'too nice'. I might appreciate this concept, nevertheless, to my tender ears, the directness can come over as downright rude!

As though to prove the point amiably to me, Phyllis responded graciously and promptly to the 'material' I sent off to her. That same day she was on the phone, arranging an appointment. Searching for Phyllis's office building in the depths of the City was not easy but I was finally ushered into her office, and the lady herself popped her head round the door, asking me to wait while she sorted out an inter-personnel problem. Someone brought me a cup of coffee and I sat there reflecting on how different the environment was from that of Rhoda's, with its at-home elegant atmosphere. But then Phyllis's world in the City is very different. Here we are not talking in terms of customer service. Here we are into the dynamic world that makes up the shrewd analytical core of high-finance trading.

Photographs of Phyllis with husband and child are the only human touches to sight. A large desk, bookshelves, computer, and pile after pile of papers are the hallmarks of her daily life. From the windows there is no special view; not even much space. Yet Phyllis is on the board of this company.

Breaking into my daydreams burst Phyllis, grinning happily now the problem was solved (the problem, by the way, turned out to be one of who gets time on the valued, but shared, department word processor). Her smartly tailored suit, neat hair, and still perfect though underplayed make-up, certainly fitted the image of the executive no-nonsense woman. Phyllis has a very deep voice – a tone of voice that seems naturally to carry with it a sense of authority. With no special prompting from me, she launched easily into her thoughts on how she sees changing attitudes towards women in the business world, towards women in the City, female MBAs, and why more women out there still don't make it to the top.

Why do some women push for the top?

'For girls, especially, I believe the basis of their attitude goes back to their parents; that's how our sense of expectations is formed. My parents were both teachers and I always liked school. I did well and was respected for my talents. I think if you have a good home base and start life well in school, then you have a very powerful frame to work from. My two sisters have in a sense gone along more traditional routes: they hold responsible jobs, one as a hospital administrator and the other as a headmistress.

'My own attitude that developed out of that childhood is: if you expect things to go well, then they will do so. If you bring a child up with high expectations, giving her the feeling she will not encounter stumbling blocks, then she will likely follow your pattern and just surge ahead. At least that is how I've viewed my life. I went to university in America, following a degree in Education. While I was a student, I made a trip to Germany to take care of a university work programme. At the time, I didn't speak German, but I was interested in developing my languages, so I decided to stay on and work out there, giving myself the time to study German. After that, my next move was to Paris as the one language I really wanted to learn was, of course, French. As I had to support myself in Paris, I took a job in a French company.

'By the time I was in my mid-twenties, however, I had already reached a plateau in this chosen lifestyle. My French was not good enough to take me any higher in that type of work. And that's when I decided to go to business school. As I wanted to stay on in Paris, I applied to a French business school. The programme is a very intensive one-year course, for which you have to be trilingual. One third of the classes are in French, the remainder mainly in English, but you also need to show some competence in another European language – in my case that was German. The whole programme was quite a challenge for me as I'd been such a late-starter in learning languages. But I made the grade and did the year's MBA when I was aged twenty-seven. The only part of the process that really worried me was taking on a large bank loan to cover my expenses. I had to borrow all the money, which I repaid over a period of five years. That seemed at the time like a very major undertaking; I had no idea if I would really be able to move into a high-paying career immediately on graduating.

'However, when I finished, I was indeed hired at a good salary by an international bank. Following the MBA, I had decided to move into banking, rather than consultancy work, as I felt it would offer me the biggest challenge. At business school, I had discovered that the finance courses went well and also that I enjoyed the sort of people I was meeting in the banking world. This particular international bank had branches worldwide and I was offered a choice of where I would like to work. I chose London. I had already lived in Germany and France.

'That first job was in corporate banking. Then I moved into the treasury department, and from there into bond issues and swaps. Then I was head-hunted to this particular City position. In all my years in London, the number of women working in visible positions in banking has certainly risen exponentially. Eleven years ago, I joined a new City Women's Network and then there were altogether about thirty of us. Now, the network has mushroomed to include around two hundred, though we have widened out to accept women in management too. It is rather hard to tell how many women are actually working in the City at any one time.

'The American banks were probably largely responsible for this influx of women into banking, as they were sending over women at least ten years ago, largely, I have to admit, because women were cheaper to move than men. Those women tended to be young and single, and so they did not incur the huge costs of moving whole families. Then, of course, everyone became more used to seeing women in banking and now finally the British retail High Street banks are following suit. I do still find that type of British clearing bank is somewhat old-fashioned in their attitude.

'But, if you think about it, the numbers of women are bound to increase in the City and in management, because the MBA courses in Britain are now taking about 25 per cent women in their classes. So a fair number of women are coming through the system, being interviewed and moving into high-powered or visible jobs. And these women who come into banking tend to do very well. Noticeably, the women are not the ones who are let go during a recession or after a crash. My feeling is that because it takes so much "nowce" for a woman to take the decision to get an MBA, if she is strong enough and has enough confidence in herself to make that happen, then those same qualities of control will be carried on throughout her working life. I expect women with MBAs to do very well.'

Phyllis has strongly-opinionated views about those women who do not take themselves seriously enough in life and work. When I asked her, for example, about the differences she sees between women in this country and those in America, she at once became agitated about the numbers of women here who still apply for jobs as secretaries after pursuing an academic degree at university. That, she felt, just would not happen in America.

'The one thing about getting an MBA is that never again would you apply for a secretarial position! And if that is what it takes for women to say to themselves that they're good enough, then I feel that that in itself makes the effort worthwhile. I get very angry with women who apply to me for positions as secretaries when I find out they have a degree. In fact, the agencies tend not to send anyone now for a secretarial position who has a degree. Why not? Because I tend to ask the woman in question if she is underrating herself. That she should be using her brains, education and talent much more than she is.'

Trying to imagine the scene that would ensue when high-powered and rather high-handed Phyllis so berated the over-educated secretary, I asked her what sort of response she received in return?

'They hate hearing my comments because they have made a decision about their lives. But I suggest that it could be an unfortunate decision and especially so nowadays when everyone can type, men and women. As you saw earlier this morning, in this office we all fight over the machinery. Men have equality with women over usage of the word processors. Certain women I have interviewed have subsequently opted for managerial or administrative posts, having given up the notion of a secretarial role. And some have even returned to tell me how grateful they have been. So it is certainly time that women stopped seeing themselves as "little old me". If you have an MBA, you will stop seeing yourself that way!

'I do feel that here in Britain a word like ambition is still seen as a dirty word, particularly among women. But cultural changes are slowly taking place. This country now has more women employed than any other EEC country and the decision a woman has to make runs along these lines: do I want to be a sales lady at a well-known department store? Or, do I want to run something that gives me responsibility, more money and that is fun?

'Make no bones about it, the number of hours you will put in will be longer. You will still be trekking to work on the tube every day. So why not get paid well for a fun job? The chances of a woman working for most of her adult life are now so great, that really it is time all girls faced up to the problem of how they want to spend the rest of their lives. Why not make the most of it?

'But the idea of a woman deliberately going out to make a lot of money is still seen as very strange. Attitudes will only change when women begin to ask themselves why they continue to be prepared to be dependent on someone else. No one can predict the future. And a lot can happen most unexpectedly. So why not take precautions? Why not make sure your credit cards are in your name, even when you are married? Why not make sure you have your own credit rating and bank accounts? Then, even if today you are securely married, should anything happen to your husband or to the marriage, you will have protected yourself. Women have to learn to be proud of themselves and their abilities; to accept that that sort of preventative action will not mean that their marriage is automatically no good!'

Phyllis is married to a very high-powered and influential man. Hearing her speak I couldn't help but ask whether, even in their social circles, where the men are expected to be high-earners, it is unusual to find a wife in quite such a high-powered position?

'Not really. Over the years many women have used the same skills as I am employing to run a charity, or even the school parents' association. There's nothing magical about the skills. It's a question of calling on the same organizational abilities. I just walk in a different door. When I come in to work I pick up the phone and make things happen. There's really nothing high powered about it at all. I just get paid and some women do the same work for free!'

How do men react to a high-powered woman?

'Some men we know socially tend to ask my advice on the markets. But are the men around me threatened? I hope not! Though I will tell you the story of one of the first business trips I made up North. There was a male colleague, myself, the customer and his secretary. Over lunch the customer told me he'd brought the secretary along so I would have someone to talk to. I said nothing at the time, but he soon found out I was no secretary. It was my marketing assignment and I structured the conversation to make sure that we covered the points that would most benefit his company.'

Do women fit into the City's male-orientated world?

'It's an exciting place to be. In a small company like this one which is new and growing, you can watch it becoming better and more self-confident – rather like watching a child develop. Maybe it also takes a maverick, rather an oddball person, to move into this type of world. Remember, I left a very stable career in banking to move across here. But then our chief executive recruits by talent and not by gender. In my view, it is a good idea for women to get in on new operations like this one, where there may be more scope for responsibility and greater opportunities. Right now I'm in charge of a department of twelve people dealing with international business.

Does Phyllis dream of running her own company, or of being chairman of the board? Does she crave greater success?

'No. Wisdom has taught me what I'm good at. I do appreciate

working with people whom I respect and whose company I enjoy. Within these office walls there is the minimum of politics. We have respect for each other, and appreciate each other's integrity.

I asked Phyllis to pinpoint certain areas where the difference between men and women arose.

'The only issue for women in this sort of world that I feel is different, and therefore important, is that of clothes. It all comes back to the old story, that when you walk into a room you have three seconds in which to make an impression. So what you wear for the working day tells a lot about the impression you wish to make. Studies have shown that women who wear tailored suits in navy or grey colours project an image of authority in the work environment. I've given talks on this topic to other women because I feel it's so important. Let's face it, as a woman you can have the talent and the skill, but it just won't come across if you are not dressed correctly.'

Phyllis and working motherhood

'We have one child. I went on maternity leave at seven months and then took a further three months off when he was born. Five months away from work was a long time for someone like myself. In my opinion, I'm a far better part-time mother than I would be full time. Our child would certainly suffer if I stayed at home! I'm emotionally incapable of living in that way.

'But, equally, I believe women should not be afraid of negotiating time out of work when their children are small. Most employers today are willing to be flexible – especially if they need you.'

I wondered if Phyllis's husband has ever suggested she slow down the pace a little. That it might be better for her to work less hours in the office and to give more time to home life or the family?

She answered this with complete self-assurance. 'At the time we became engaged he in fact asked me to keep on working, so that he could change careers. Then, two and a half months after our son was born, he was begging me to return to work. Being at home all that time, I had already moved into the fishwife mode. He would walk in the door in the evening, and I'd be there resentfully saying, "Here's your dinner." He'd say, "Sorry, I'm not hungry, I had lunch with a customer." And I would fly into a rage. No, I found being at home very unnerving. Within weeks I'd turned into a hag.

'My husband is very supportive of my career. I suppose in many ways we have an unusual marriage. He takes our son to school, because he has time in the mornings whereas he is often home late in the evenings. So we treat our weekends as sacred. Running both our careers is exhilarating, but it can also be very tiring! Basically though, I would say it's a lot of fun.

'With my husband embarking on this new role in his working life, I'm often called upon to help him. Recently we have concentrated on his new project. Once I was up half the night with him, preparing a presentation, and then I had to take a train at nine the following morning for a business meeting with a customer in the North. Yes, there are times I cut it rather fine.'

Phyllis sat before me, talking animatedly about the various conflicts within her life, looking magnificent. She runs her household with the help of an au pair, who works a five-day week. There is also a cleaner.

'We actually live quite frugally. At weekends, we shop for fresh foods at the local markets. I usually ride the tube to work as we live in central London. And when I go home in the evenings, I water the flowers and look after the garden.

'I do believe the old adage of women having to be better than men. Because working women are probably running husband, family and home as well as the job. I know that any married woman who walks in the office door at eight thirty every morning will have taken twice as many decisions as a man before she even leaves the house. There is a strong management aspect to running a home that helps her cope in the office too.

'Myself, I get in to work around nine and am often here till seven, though I prefer to leave by six-thirty. Then the rest of my life I fit around my son. We try to keep weekends free for him. We always have breakfast together as a family. I have to run his life slightly by remote control, I suppose. For example, I might make him a worksheet on some maths problems and I'll check it with him in the evening. But, on the other hand, if I were watching him doing the maths, I'd probably go crazy.

'The only other factor in my life is that I do have to travel a lot on business. In the past five weeks, for example, I've been abroad for three of them. When it comes time for holidays, I won't go near an airport. So we rent a cottage somewhere in the English countryside.'

Delia H.

Handling the finance world's major accounts

Delia is by self-description North American. By that she means she was born and brought up in Canada, and worked for several years in America. Physically, therefore, she is an 'American'. But spiritually she is a European. And, like many Americans who have found themselves living here permanently, she often asks herself what motivated her to come and live and then to stay in Europe.

Rather like Louise, a similarly friendly and likeable personality with an inner tough streak of ambition that no one would dare cross, Delia finds herself as a single woman questioning particularly whether she might be married, with a family, had she chosen to stay on the North American continent where men are more accustomed to successful women? But, just as with Louise, I came away from our meeting quite convinced that she is really very happy with her chosen lot in life. Single women cannot help but ask themselves the big questions: why have I not married yet? Why did I not want children as much as other women? Would I now trade in my success and autonomy for love and a more dependent lifestyle?

Delia was another daunting woman, of whom I was initially rather nervous. The very name of the American investment bank for which she is a senior executive was sufficient to bring on the genuflecting urge. But, if she were brisk and efficient on the phone, in person Delia was charming, accommodating and another example of a busy woman who was prepared to squeeze me into her schedule. We met on a Friday in the late afternoon after work.

We had arranged to meet in her office. Asking for Delia by her surname, struggling with the Miss/Ms dichotomy, I was surprised when the man taking charge of security at reception referred to her chummily as Delia.

Despite her executive exterior, I had been given the first clue: Delia was very approachable. The woman who came to greet me was slight, average height but slim in that very American way. Neatly cropped hair, make-up still surviving after the long day, she was beautifully dressed in a deep coral pink suit and a matching designer blouse. I was quite taken aback by how attractive she looked.

Delia did not seem to be rushed. We sat ourselves down in an oak-panelled and leather-chaired conference room, where we proceeded to freeze in the icy air-conditioning.

Just like the other Americans I have interviewed for this book, Delia had no problem talking about herself. Psychologically attuned to discussing themselves, their work and their personal lives, these women from the North American continent often appear far more articulate than their British counterparts. For Delia, much of the driving force in her own life, she believes, has been the strong relationship with her father (himself an Englishman) and her position as the eldest of six children.

A family of MBAs

'My father was quite a workaholic, to whom I was very close while growing up. He was really my mentor and guide in terms of my career. Bringing me up in Canada, with a sister and four brothers – I was the eldest – my parents had the view that women should strive to do just as well as men. I have the feeling it was fuelled by the thought, not that we might never marry one day, but rather that we would always need a profession to fall back on, in case something should go wrong with the marriage. Out of the six of us, there are now four MBAs, all of whom graduated from the same university. We're all doing well, too. One other brother will probably soon be embarking on his course. My sister initially became an architect, but after her divorce when she found herself without children, wanting to make a change in her life, she also went back to school to do an MBA.'

*

Your mother must feel proud of you, I commented.

'She thinks we're all rather weird,' was Delia's rather sardonic view.

'I did well at school and went on to study languages as an undergraduate. At first, I suppose I had no real idea what I wanted to pursue as a career. But I went to Geneva for a year to study French before returning to complete my BA course in Nova Scotia. Then I contemplated taking a postgraduate degree in law, but as that meant another three-years minimum study, I took a job in the meantime running a student travel office. It turned out that I adored that job. It involved being in charge of the advertising, promotion, and planning programmes. I did very well with it and turned in a profit at the end of the year. That's when I decided maybe I should go in for business studies.

'This was back in 1974, and there weren't many women taking MBAs at the time. I was accepted at Canada's top business school, at the age of twenty-three, which made me younger than most of the other MBA students. In truth, I wouldn't have minded a background of more work experience. The school followed the Harvard method of teaching by case studies and I was really thrown in at the deep end. There I was taking accountancy classes with men who were qualified chartered accountants. I had to play massive catch-up. It was quite startling in terms of the demands placed on me.

'During that summer, I took a job with the Canadian export development office where I was able again to use my languages. I'd begun to develop an interest in the finance area, mainly because I had decided to concentrate on the areas where I was weakest – to justify in my mind the full MBA training. Already, I was quite skilled in human resources and marketing, so I just set out to conquer the next challenge.

'Quite swiftly I learned that the MBA degree opened up avenues that previously I'd had no idea were available to me. I was amazed, for example, at the number of job interviews I was called for. Maybe it was a time when women MBAs were a novelty, but I think it's fair to say that the men students in our classes probably became quite jealous of the women's success with interviewing and then with landing jobs. This was fifteen years ago and women only numbered 10 per cent of the class, which meant that out of 240 students there were only twenty-four women. And by and large the women received more job offers. For myself, although I knew I wanted to move into banking and finance, I just wasn't sure how to begin on that path. So, when the opportunity came up to move back to Switzerland, to work at a sister business school as a case-study writer, I felt that it would be a wonderful chance to go back to Europe, where I could improve my French and gain a better perspective on life.

'But I was pretty slow at sorting myself out, because even after a year in Switzerland, I didn't know what I wanted to do, or even where I should concentrate on finding a job. I adored living in Europe and that was all I knew. So I stayed on a second year and even worked in Brazil for four months. Then, once back in Switzerland at the business school, I began applying for jobs and attended up to one hundred interviews so I could begin to get to know the market again.

'Slowly, certain decisions began forming in my mind. I decided that it would be better for me to work for an American company, that I should start in head office and that I would prefer to work for an investment bank. From that point on, I was determined to get started at a really good high level. I targetted New York and was offered a job with a bank in Manhattan. So there I was packing my bags, feeling "nothing ventured, nothing gained"; that this move would be good for me as I still had the world to explore!

'It was 1979 when I joined the bank and set up my new life in Manhattan. Well, once again I had to work like a trojan, back into the game of playing catch-up. I was working alongside American-trained MBAs, and all my accountancy was on the Canadian model not the American, so I had to relearn most of those practices. I had been two years out of business school and was working side by side with these newly-graduated hot-shots. My accent lent me no sympathy value as I sounded American. It was tough.

'I stayed there for two and a half years, before I made another decision, which was to move back into the international field. It was not a totally sensible decision, as choosing to work for the bank in one of their locations abroad was seen as a sideline activity and not as part of the mainstream career path. But, I suppose that sort of choice in my life has been essential to the woman I really am. They offered me the London branch and I moved here in 1981. At that time, I was still working in corporate finance. Three years later, I wanted a change of division to make better use of my languages and to work directly with my own clients. It was time, I felt, for me to learn more about investments. By now I was more or less entrenched in London, or Europe at least. It was already too late to think about returning to America or Canada.'

Delia not only takes pride in her work, but has a deeply personal pride in her achievements and her own sense of style. Her work now involves providing advice on investments to institutions in Paris and Geneva, such as private banks and insurance companies, who have money to invest. Delia's brief is to thoroughly research and understand the markets, to offer advice on what stocks and stock markets to move into. She provides ideas on when to buy and sell, and as a salesperson, is paid on commission. The job entails a lot of travelling back and forth to European capitals and, 'An awful lot of talking on the phone. Every day I receive information from our New York research departments and I feed it through to my clients. You make friends with your clients. In many ways I'm an ambassador of the firm.

'In reality equity sales requires less of an agility with numbers than many others in the finance world. So, where the job may appear very high-powered and wrapped up within the cloak of finance, there's not much number-crunching involved. I take a more macro view. What is happening to interest rates, to gold, to the dollar? What is happening in certain countries? Are their labour relations successful, do they have sufficient profit incentives?

'The job suits me fine as I enjoy the travelling and I like using the phone. I can employ elements of my own personality such as the sense of aggression or desire to meet a challenge. Or, I can soft pedal for a while. But make no mistake, it is highly competitive. There are many brokers out there all doing the same as me. And, with the financial world in recession, we're all beginning to feel the pinch. In terms of my personal development, I would like to move more into the management-of-people side of the bank. Right now I work quite autonomously.'

But then I began to ask Delia about herself, as I was already intrigued by her story. She seemed to my mind to have shown incredible strength and perseverance in pursuing a tough, male type of career path. Was this sort of progression clear to her from the beginning?

'No! I just adored languages and wanted to travel. Mostly though, I saw myself using the languages as a tool. I didn't want to teach, nor do translation, nor interpreting. I wanted to be at the hub of things. That's about all I knew.'

But is it common to find a woman at her level within the finance world?

'Back in New York, yes. Over there the bank had a policy of hiring 50 per cent women when I joined. But working for the same bank in London? Well, there used to be three women out of fifteen people in my department. Now there are only two out of twenty-four executives. So, that brings us back again to the 10 per cent margin, just like I experienced at business school. The women who are at my sort of level also tend to be other North Americans, rather than English women. But I do believe English women are catching up. You're more likely to find them running their own businesses, operating as head-hunters, or managing departments within companies. There must be women in the financial world, but none spring to mind. And I'm a member of both the City Women's Network and the Association of Business Graduates. But then, when I look around among my male colleagues, by and large the wives of the Englishmen here do not work and only one or two of the Americans have wives currently working.'

Is the English attitude towards ambitious women slowly changing?

Delia peppers her conversation with anecdotes that bring her story to life and that also demonstrate the humour inherent in her chosen lifestyle. In 1976 when she first came to England, having just graduated with her MBA from Canada, she met some long-lost relatives. A family of bright go-ahead people, they nevertheless found it difficult to come to terms with the idea that Delia had just spent two years of her young life pursuing something called a 'Masters of Business Administration' degree.

'At a drinks' party, I noticed that they preferred to introduce me as their Canadian cousin who had just graduated with a degree in Economics. It was obviously far more palatable that way! I think that basically shows the attitude that in some ways still holds.'

So, then I came to the question that always fires a response from the single woman. Do the men she meets or works with find Delia threatening?

Remaining as cool as her coral suit would let her, Delia smiled wryly for a moment and then let herself launch into her thoughts:

'I've been told that I am; that people find me a daunting person, or threatening. I've been trying to change that perception by my own self-presentation. As I gain more confidence in the job, I feel I should be able to relax more, be more my normal, smiley self. Recently, for example, I took a whole day's communications course and there I was told that I have two distinct sides to my personality. There's the professional, controlled side and the bubbly, more myself, side. Their advice was that I should let more of the bubbly self come through in my professional capacity, and not let the controlled side dominate.

'But, as for my relations with men in general, there have been distinct problems. Quite early on in my time here I joined the Association of Business Graduates, as I hoped that would be a way to meet people, for me to help promote the concept of the MBA in England, and also to remove some of the barriers I felt developing between myself and the men in whom I might possibly be interested. By that time, I'd already realized that the barriers were partly dictated by cultural differences, but that they were also to do with my job, the way I came across, and inevitably they were to do with the disparity in income levels.

'Back then, in the early eighties, the disparity question was worse than it is now. I was earning so much more than any Englishman I met, because I was working for an American bank on an expatriate basis. Even if the man was in a very senior position with an English bank, he would have been on a considerably lower salary than myself. Things have evened out somewhat since then, but it still proves a very tricky problem.

'I can remember quite early on making a decision: if I was approached at a function by a man, who was presumably initially attracted by my appearance, and who then, on learning what I did, decided to label me "one of those high-powered lady executives", that he was probably the wrong sort of man. Obviously that type of man felt threatened by my position. However, what I now tend to do initially is to play a fairly low-key role, until I have the chance to get to know someone. I'd really prefer to be accepted as me first. Once they hear the name of the bank, and my type of position there, within the industry anyone would know what type of remunerative package that implies.

'I do tread with caution. There are men out there who still feel threatened by someone like me. They might find it easy to get on with me as a friend or as a colleague, but maybe not as a partner within a relationship. I am still earning a lot more than most men I meet, except maybe for those men working for American or Swiss banks who would be within the same bracket.

'Often I ask myself, if I'd decided to stay in America or gone back to Canada, would I be married today? If I had chosen an environment where it is more accepted to be an MBA, and particularly for a woman to have an MBA, would I have found it easier to meet my future partner? I don't know. Though I certainly recognize that I gave myself an extra hurdle in choosing to live here. I have the feeling that deep down I have always been looking for a dream man. And that, because my father was English, somehow I'd imagined that I would find everything I was looking for in an Englishman!

'Almost as soon as I arrived, however, I realized I'd given myself a massive challenge. I do find it hard to relate to the educational differences, and the class differences. It's going to take a very self-confident man, someone who can leap all the cultural barriers, who would be able to handle ME!'

Suddenly to my surprise, Delia laughed. Her bubbly self was warming up the professional exterior. Not only was she softening, she was now warming to the game of confessing all. Could the average Englishman introduce you at a party as his wife, and be able to explain your position and status? I asked her. Without a moment's hesitation, Delia said, 'No', and then began to laugh again. 'And as for the upper classes and the aristocracy, they're even worse!'

But Delia was not complaining about her choice of coming to live in this country. In fact, she was clear about the positive reasons behind her choice: even if they were intuitive reasons.

'I have to see my own choice in selecting the man's world as my place of work. One factor is that these days you tend to end up playing a man's game in this world. And, as a result of that, you often negate the female, more emotional, side of yourself. When it comes round to personal relationships, you can find yourself dealing with an area you haven't fully developed. Surprisingly, despite what I said earlier about things maybe being easier in North America, when I look back to that time of working in New York, I can see that because of the legal position regarding the hiring of women, because of concerns for equality, career-paths and opportunities, there really were no obstacles for women's advancement.

'But the counter to that was, I remember, that in order to succeed and compete in that world, myself and other women like myself had had to become *neutered*. There were so many laws against sexual harrassment, so much discussion about not making differences between men and women, that one male colleague, for example, actually admitted to me that he did not dare say he liked an outfit I was wearing for fear I'd take it personally – and the wrong way! He could possibly be accused of showing inappropriate intentions towards me.

'So when I moved to London, I found it quite refreshing and delightful to be accepted as a woman. Men make comments on my hairstyle and clothes. They'll put an arm round me and make jokes accordingly. It's nice to have it confirmed that you are different, and that you're fun to have around. Maybe career opportunities are not quite so equal and easy here, but I guess I prefer it this way.'

So how does Delia find working with these high-powered men, who can easily relate to her as a colleague, but maybe less easily as a woman?

'For one thing I won't conform to a dress code for women executives.

I certainly don't stick to grey formal suits. I've always tried to use colour and am very sensitive to the type of clothes I wear. It's important to me that I look like a woman. If, however, a particular client seems to be uncomfortable with that individual style, then I'll make the effort to dress more conservatively. Interestingly enough, the very name of this bank seems to take me past the first hurdle of the credibility gap. Clients trust me because they assume the bank would not have employed me were I not trustworthy.

'There have been occasions when insecure and rather unsophisticated men, particularly I find among the French, can create a problem. Or, an ex-broker might find me threatening and try to make my life very difficult. If it comes to that, I would suggest to my boss that he pass the client on to someone else.

'The main difference in being a woman is that I feel you have to go in to meetings very well prepared. You just know you'll be tested through and through. Maybe because I'm a woman, or maybe because I'm over-sensitive, I do feel that I have less of the skills of "bluffmanship" than a man. A man in my position might feel easy steering the conversation away from an area he doesn't fully understand, and will have the confidence to say, "I'll get back to you on that." For me, though, I need to know everything. For that reason, I probably put in longer hours than my male colleagues. There is just so much information to absorb. And it is my responsibility to be on top of it all. After all, that's what the client is paying for.

'So I tend to burn the candle at both ends. I lead a very active life both at work and socially. For example, I might be in the office before eight most mornings and stay here till nearly eight in the evening. I prefer to do all my work at the office, rather than at home, so I am prepared to be here for long hours; very often it's an eleven-hour day. Then after work, I'll go along to my health club, to a movie, or out to dinner and about one in every three weekends I work. Other times, I'll be off sailing, skiing or playing tennis. I have a good varied group of friends. Socially, I often entertain my clients. And I do feel quite comfortable taking a client to dinner, if he is single or married, or I'll take a man and his wife out. I've even gone skiing with clients. It's not really a problem. But I will confess that if I were married, or even in a firm relationship, I'd feel a lot more at ease and comfortable with the situation.'

Why is there no permanent man in Delia's life?

And then Delia brought us back to that vexing question of whether success and career have stood in her way of making a lasting relationship with a man. She has made some very strong decisions, I pointed out, leading towards her career development. Looking back at those early years in Switzerland when, as a young woman, she toyed with working at the business school. Other women, at that time of their lives, might have been induced to stay in Switzerland for the sake of a man, or would even have decided to return to their home base with an eye to settling down. But Delia targetted the career and location of her choice, and ended up working night and day for this very important bank in New York. I was very impressed by her ability to take her own life so firmly in hand, to propel herself away from typically female avenues, to be so thoroughly and totally ambitious.

'It wasn't quite so decisive as you make it sound. But I did have a strong desire to get into a field that would be a real challenge and to work my way up. Maybe being the eldest helped propel me that way. My father died eleven years ago, and I took on a lot of his fatherly, advising role from that point. I help my sister and brothers in their career decisions.

'But, I have been reasonably career-oriented and relationships have not ended up acting as an obstacle, or even as a consideration in my career changes. In my early days, I really was not ready to let relationships get in the way. I needed to be tackling new challenges and constantly found I had itchy feet. But now I've been in London for eight years which is longer than any place else. And I do feel settled here. I adore living in England and have a lot of friends. I'd rather stay put now, than move for my career again. I'd like to think a relationship could develop now in my life.

'I'm thirty-seven and still very single. I have my own flat and a social life. But the job is very demanding and I do sacrifice a lot socially by working long hours and then reading for work in the evenings. I travel a lot on business. I'm embarrassed to say that although I obviously own my own place, I have not managed to save very much and don't in fact handle my own money very well! I lost some in the recent stock market crash. But, when you have no dependents and are very busy you tend to spend a lot in order to enjoy yourself. I know I should be concentrating more on my future, on my old age. What sort of nest egg will I require?'

And then Delia made a comment that surprised me, hearing it from her efficient lips. It's just such a very common emotion felt by so many women. Why then would I not suspect Delia to feel the same?

'But you know how one always assumes at the back of your mind that you'll marry one day, and those sorts of decisions will be made as a twosome.'

Does Delia then still feel that a man will come along and sort everything out for her? And what about children, could she fit them into her life?

'On the man question, I suppose I do. Children? Well, I would have them if the right man came along and I was still capable. But I have to ask myself why my career has taken precedence for me over a more feminine/nurturing role? I think it has a lot to do with being the eldest of six — I was like a second mother to the younger ones. And still, if I need to feel that I'm not just a Career Woman, not a totally selfish person living on my own, if I need a sense of purpose, then I spend quite a proportion of my earnings helping my siblings, and their children, dealing with their education and travel problems. My own children are not something I've ever felt an overpowering urge to have. I am able to express those feelings through my siblings.'

And, at that point, Delia very graciously indicated our time was up. The professional, in-control side of her personality returned, after so much delving into the emotional female side. She had an appointment. Someone was waiting for her in the lobby. As we took the lift down together, she began to straighten up her hair and re-apply the coral lipstick. And there, true to form, was a gentleman lounging in one of the deep black leather sofas of the bank's awe-inspiring lobby. I waved Delia goodbye, and just felt there goes one contented and successful woman. Marriage and children may have eluded her – but nothing else has slipped her by.

Kaitlin N.

Engineering student turned management consultant

Kaitlin is a thirty-year-old MBA graduate who works for a major American consultancy firm in London as a senior engagement manager. Before I met her, I knew nothing more about Kaitlin than her strange surname which to my mind indicated a foreign-born husband. In reality it's a Gaelic name, belonging to her family; they changed the anglicized version back to its original form when Kaitlin was just a girl.

No one would suspect the strength and determination Kaitlin has shown to make the best use of her brain and talents. To hear her speak, you might cast her as a character in an Edna O'Brien novel. She is the type of young woman who, several years ago, one would have imagined relegated to a secretarial position; maybe venturing forth to the giddy lights of London to escape her country-girl background. But we live in progressive times, and behind that sweet and gentle façade beats a determined mind; yet still there's something of the country-girl ingenuity about her.

Kaitlin was just coming up to thirty-one years old when we met. Married for eighteen months, she has a six-month-old daughter. She arrived in London with a first degree from Dublin University in Engineering, an MSc from Cork university in Microelectronics, and an MBA from Harvard. When she told me that she now earns close to £90,000 a year, I felt like the country girl. At that stage in my interviewing for this book, I had not fully appreciated what the term 'high salary' might mean for a woman. To my mind, salaries begin to disappear off into infinity once the figures go beyond the mid-fifties, unless, of course, you happen to be a rock star, film star, top model, or run your own high-profile retail company.

Kaitlin's position was high ranking but to the outside world certainly not high profile. I had obtained her name from a borrowed list of recent women MBAs. Our appointment had not been difficult to set up, though from the initial phone call intercepted by a secretary, I had been nervous that my request would be turned down. But Kaitlin's secretary came back to me promptly. We were to meet in her office in central London early one afternoon.

The day of the interview was stiflingly hot so it was an enormous pleasure to walk through the stately doors, into the gilded and lacquered vestibule of a Gothic building that retained its original ornate ceiling, having once been a Tory gentleman's club.

Sinking back into a deep black leather armchair, I filled my time by reading one of the consultancy's pamphlets: this one happened to be a report on the state of the world's economy. Then a young woman stood before me, neatly tailored and smiling shyly; I assumed her to be the secretary sent to bring me up to the office. But the woman held out her hand and introduced herself as Kaitlin.

She was dressed quietly, in a grey-green suit, with a white cotton blouse. Her legs were bare and she wore flat leather shoes. Her auburn hair was cut simply and there was no visible sign of make-up on her face. In a sense, Kaitlin's image was the antithesis of that corporate dress-for-success image we have had hammered at us in recent years.

Our first attempts to sit together and talk in her office failed miserably as the noise of drills and high-tech machinery was far too strong for my tiny tape recorder to compete with. Kaitlin phoned around to find an empty office at the back of the building. She had ordered a pot of coffee and biscuits; the laden tray had to follow us to the other office. There, usurping the place of a mysterious man who was away on holiday, a typical male manager whose desk and walls were festooned with photographs of his glamorous wife and adorable children, we were able to talk.

And there is no doubt about it, Kaitlin wanted to talk. There is no anger in her story, no rage desperate to escape, no major hurdle she feels she has had to overcome. Yet this young woman has chosen to work incredibly hard out of a desire to achieve, to make it, to get to the top. Why? Because she grew up believing that she should use her talents and meet all the challenges presented to her along the way.

Kaitlin is clever, make no mistake about that. On top of her three degrees she is also fluent in German, French, Irish Gaelic and has some Italian. She grew up with the typical problems of being a clever female, in an environment not ready to accept such women. But she remained quietly confident of her own worth. She took herself to Harvard for her MBA. She pulled off one of the most highly-paid salaried jobs in London today. Kaitlin represents a new breed of woman. She is earnestly interested in the issues and problems of being a working mother. And at the same time, she is not going to give up her career or settle for anything less than her full worth.

Her parents may have something to do with the formation of Kaitlin's attitudes: her mother still lectures in physics at a medical school in Ireland, a job she had been doing for thirty years. Her father was an engineer. So there was a strong emphasis on science at home. Formidably, her mother also raised seven children. Among her siblings, Kaitlin has a sister who is an engineer, a brother who runs his own software company, and a sister who is a missionary. Her mother, who strongly encouraged Kaitlin's efforts to gain a place at Harvard, had herself studied for a year at Harvard Medical School.

The loneliness of the female engineering student

With that gentle brogue, there is often humour in Kaitlin's voice. 'I found primary school terrific, but that was before girls began to divide out in to those who worked and those who didn't. By secondary school, I had jumped a year and so was younger than everyone else, and at the same time, more academic. They were all interested in boyfriends and the Top Ten. I had no challenge, no competition at school. For me it was pretty much a waste of time. Probably I should have gone to a different and more academic type of school. Anyway, I don't feel I did particularly well there. I was good at exams, so I passed enough, but I just know I could have tried harder and achieved more, given some encouragement.

'I went on to university to study Electronic Engineering, where I was the only female student in a class of 180. Between school and university I went out to Austria to work as an au pair. That's why I have such good German. The family I stayed with tried their darnedest to put me off engineering, saying it was a man's world. But I was determined. However, in a sense they were proved right. The engineering school was separated from the rest of the university, and had a unique culture that revolved round the boys' determination to get drunk as quickly as possible in the evenings and at lunchtimes. I didn't have a lot in common with them. When they'd all be off at the pub, I didn't want to trail along just for the sake of it. So I made friends where possible in the arts and law faculties, though I was separated from them because I had a much heavier workload. At the time, I wished deeply that I had chosen a more sociable degree to study, something like law. I envied them all so much on the arts campus!

'After university, although I had thought about trying to move into a management type of job, I wasn't at all sure of the direction I should take. I worked for a while for the EEC, and several of my colleagues there were going on to do MBAs. So I had that definitely in mind. Already I'd decided I should do my MBA in America, and, if it were to be America, then it had to be Harvard. However, first for some strange reason that to this day escapes me, I decided to go and do a Masters research degree in Microelectronics at University College, Cork, which is an excellent research centre.

'In Ireland, engineers have a slightly higher profile than they do here; they're not only seen as digging holes or building bridges. Electronic engineering is physics with a practical bent: designing, for example, electronic circuits that go inside machines. My Masters degree concentrated on making solar cells; where you take a piece of silicon and spray gold on to it. When the sun shines on that compound, it produces electricity. It can be exciting and you do get into some very esoteric physics, predicting what will happen to the gold.

'The experience of working for the MSc was valuable. But, although the work might have been fascinating, I didn't have a good time socially there either. I was working in a laboratory with four or five others and the pressure was on me to work very hard. There were no other women. I did, however, manage to share a house with some other women who were working at the university so I had a few friends.

'After the MSc I was employed in Ireland for a small start-up company, marketing engineering products. My position involved solving technical problems and trying to find new work for the company. Again I felt stuck, and so it was obvious that the only way forward was to try for the MBA. Although I felt I should wait until I had gained more work experience, I applied as soon as I began in that job. Don't ask me why I had the courage to apply directly to Harvard. I was going to have to fund myself completely, which meant borrowing money from my mother and from the bank. But I figured that at the end of the day I'd emerge with a top degree, and that should enable me to move into a high-paying job. To my mind, the loan would be rather like paying off a mortgage – which was common at my age – I just wouldn't have the house.

'My application went in rather late. All I could hang on to was the feeling I had a reasonable chance, as I was an engineer, spoke several languages, and imagined that they wouldn't have too many female engineers applying from Ireland. I took special care with the application form, which takes quite a time to fill out. But I was lucky in knowing a former Harvard MBA who helped me on that. And then I scored highly on GMAT. So really I felt quite confident. So much so that when the letter came from Harvard in March, which said I was on the waiting list, I was already over the moon. I just felt that I'd get in. Amazingly enough, I recently found my old application form, and I can see now it was incredibly naïvely written. I did not go into how well I'd done at school or university. I simply reported that I had degrees, not that they were with Honours. Maybe they could read between the lines.'

The MBA at Harvard

I asked Kaitlin why do so many engineers go on to take MBAs, at that point unable to see the link myself. 'Because they're bright in a practical way, and they don't want to remain stuck in a technical field that is so poorly paid. They know they should move into management. In Japan, there is not the same problem, because engineers are treated like gods.'

So, why was she so determined to go to Harvard, after five years' studying in Ireland?

'In the company I'm with now, which admittedly is an American corporation, there is a clear distinction in the quality of people who come from Harvard, and those with MBAs from the other top American, British or European schools. They push you harder at Harvard. And because of that you are aware of being at a unique place; and that it's a unique experience. There's great competition among the graduate students. You're in a sort of greenhouse, where everyone is working very hard, long hours, and all are under extreme stress. So you compete even harder yourself. The atmosphere lends you an arrogance that you feel is rightly deserved.

'At Harvard, I found I was surrounded by excellence. There were guest speakers to listen to every afternoon; like David Rockefeller of Chase Manhattan Bank, and other leading figures from industry or banking. Usually it was someone of world fame and renown. Once or twice a week you'd be sitting, as it were at their feet, gazing up in awe. You were also aware that 50 per cent of the top American companies hire Harvard graduates, simply because of the networking system of former graduates.

'Strong friendships that don't wither away are formed in that type of environment. This time the situation was favourable for me socially: 30 per cent of the class was female, and most of those were also engineers like myself. Can you imagine the relief for me? Suddenly everyone else had degrees in engineering and it all seemed so normal! I was no longer the odd one out. We lived in a sort of dormitory, and that also helped us get to know each other extremely well. I was twenty-four years old, going on twenty-five at the time. And I immensely enjoyed the experience.'

What differences does Kaitlin perceive in the way American women see themselves, their careers, ambitions, and relationships with men and their British counterparts? Obviously loath to make critical comments about fellow countrywomen, Kaitlin does have this to say from her experience of living and studying in both countries:

'There are still very few women here at a similar level to me in the work world. Within this company, there are several other senior women, but they tend to be American. Far fewer women apply

147

for positions here, far fewer even apply to business schools. The statistic of 30 per cent women in my class at Harvard was high by any business school's standards. But I really believe a woman's perception of herself comes originally from home: from parents and maybe from school. In America, women may appear socially to be very man-oriented, but that's not true in the business world. All that is put aside once they get within the office walls. And they're not afraid to admit they're ambitious either. Even the American Miss World contestants will say they want to be brain surgeons. Whereas the European contenders usually talk about wanting to travel. It's a shame, but women in Britain are still encouraged to fool around in attractive-sounding jobs before getting married and giving it all up.'

And what about earning a high salary? Does she fit in with the image of women being afraid to earn a lot of money?

'Most women probably don't realize they can earn much more than they generally do,' Kaitlin says sadly. Then, thoughtfully, she adds, 'But, remember, you only get to earn a high salary like this if you work very hard. And there are sacrifices involved in that. I doubt that the majority of women are ready yet to make those sacrifices.

'Bear in mind, I undertook to spend two years at Harvard, supported by a bank loan and another from my mother – her life savings which she gladly lent me with no interest, because she was so enthusiastic. At the time, Harvard suggested it would cost me about twenty-eight thousand dollars, including tuition and living expenses. That was nearly eight years ago; I suppose it would be nearly double that amount by now. I was able to repay all that money when I began working here. But it has all been a gamble; a risk that I was prepared to take.

'Right now, earning the high salary doesn't mean a lot to me, other than that we can live in a bigger house. And that is only necessary because we are living in central London. I've often said to my husband that if we were living in Ireland, on 10 per cent of what we earn now, then arguably we'd have a better standard of living. There'd be no fears of muggings, or work, or pollution, and no problems of which type of expensive wallpaper to choose!'

The ambitious woman – her relationships with men

Then Kaitlin and I began to talk about what are crucial questions for most women. How, for example, had she met her husband, 'Donald? Surely a successful young woman of her calibre was something of a threat to men?

Kaitlin had returned from America, with the MBA under her belt, and a high-salaried career to step into. She had previously worked for her current company during her Harvard summer placement. They had offered her a position on qualification in their London office, a situation that suited Kaitlin down to the ground, as she now wanted to get back nearer home but knew she wouldn't find the right kind of position in Ireland.

'It is a major problem I do agree for ambitious women. In general, I would have to say that British men prefer their women to be less ambitious and less successful. I was twenty-seven by the time I came to London and started on my career. Quite old really to be beginning in my first job. After six months back here I was ready to assume I'd never meet anyone. And I knew that I'd never meet anyone in Ireland.

'But my husband works for the same company. He's just six months older than myself. We met and immediately started going out. He doesn't mind my being powerful. He earns more and is ahead of me in seniority anyway. I put his own ease with women like me down to his mother. She didn't work, and gave up a career to have the children, but she seems to have spent an awful lot of time in the kitchen telling her son about the world, and pushing him on. He's very receptive to bright women, in fact he's quite relaxed about the idea. And he's good about the house, more so than the average man. He does a lot of our cooking.'

The worst problem faced by Kaitlin and Donald, as she sees it, is one of time. They have a six-month-old daughter and of course a full-time live-in nanny. But there is little time, after the long hours at the office demanded by highly-paid management consultancy positions, to devote to each other. Living only twenty minutes from the office, they squeeze time by travelling in to work and home together in the car. Most of their husband-wife conversations take place on this journey, toing and froing from work. 'That's twenty minutes each way, up to forty-five minutes a day of time to talk. It's probably more than most couples find in a working day. I don't think I could survive if we didn't live so close to work, though. If I had to commute in to London, on top of those hours, that would be the end.

'Typically, we aim to be in the office between eight and eight-thirty and try to get back home for seven most evenings. But two nights a week I work late reading at home. I used to work at the weekends as well, but since our daughter was born I hate to give up that time which I so need to spend with her. Instead, I find I'm much more concentrated in my working hours. And if I do need to work at the weekend, I have to plan it ahead with Donald so he's available to spend time with her in my place.

'The only times I've encountered difficult male attitudes at work have come from the typical male consultants who work here. Their wives don't work. Those women are there to support their hard-working men, and in turn the men cannot understand how we can both put in the hours, and still survive. There are times I'm not sure myself. It comes down to the old story of being extremely organized: we have a cleaner and a very expensive nanny. And I offload as many chores as I can on to others. My husband often cooks in the evenings. Or sometimes the nanny cooks. I can't say, as I rush back home from work every day wondering what we are going to eat!'

How do the large salaries help, then? Or, to put it another way, just what does the couple earning close to £200,000 (or maybe even more as I have no idea of Donald's earning power) do with their money?

'Remember,' says Kaitlin, not rising to the bait, 'that we started out with nothing. Although my husband has been working here for longer, neither of us had previously bought property so we have a huge mortgage. At present, we have two cars, but I'm not sure if we'll keep them both. And we never seem to have much money. You get into this thing of buying nice curtains or wallpaper, as I mentioned before. It just bothers me – to be spending so much money on curtains and wallpaper!

'Still, I have to recognize that with my job, and earning power, even after all the expenses are taken out that does leave an extra thirty thousand pounds; which means we have been able to afford a very good nanny. I delegate a lot of responsibility to her. She is a well-trained and qualified young woman, not a seventeen-year-old girl who has to be checked up on all the time. I expect her to tell me about the baby, that it's time for her to visit the doctor or whatever.

'I do recognize that the financial cost of my not working would be enormous. If I were earning twenty to thirty thousand a year and, by my reckoning the running costs of a good nanny are close to ten thousand, when you take into account her room, wages, tax and insurance, then there is the cleaner – well, there wouldn't be much left over. Then maybe it's really not worth working. Except . . . I have to say I have no feeling of defensiveness about continuing working now I'm a mother . . . there's a lot more involved than just the cost of not working, isn't there?'

Working motherhood and the high-earner

Did it ever enter Kaitlin's head not to come back to work? 'No, but if we have a second child, then I might turn part time for a few years. You see, as a consultant in a position like mine, we handle two clients simultaneously, I could see myself dropping one client, and working say a three-day week.'

But would she really do that? Would Kaitlin really give up the status, the promotional prospects, would she risk entering that dangerous twilight zone – the female ghetto of part timers – being demoted from her fast-track career path? Is such a shift really on, even in the seemingly enlightened nineties?

This is where Kaitlin frowned most, and her voice became seriously engaged, now that we are talking about a subject that does seriously concern her.

'I'd like very much to work part time, but it's also a question of whether I'd find part time work ultimately satisfying.' And then she came to what I felt was the nub of our conversation. 'To feel happy about your work in a man's world, I do think you need to be working full time.

'Even in a very liberal and forward-thinking company like

this, things would become slightly different. The career path here is quite straightforward. You come in following an MBA as an associate. After three years or so, you should become an engagement manager, then a senior engagement manager; and within six or seven years you should be made a partner. If you're not getting promoted along those lines, then both you and the company know something is wrong. It becomes clear all round that it's time to move on. That sounds nastier than it is in reality: it's actually quite a gentle path and does allow you time to look around for another job. Some people work part time while trying to make a career move. There really is no sense here of people being pushed out.

'Well, I'm now a senior engagement manager, working on two major studies and managing two teams. Typically, our clients are very large multinational companies wanting to know whether they should buy another company or how much they should pay. There's a lot of financial analysis involved – all the things we learned at Harvard.

'If I were to go part time now, when I should be made a partner within a year's time, what would happen? I'd be the first woman partner here, though there are other female partners with the company in America and in Europe. There isn't really a glass ceiling as such and the company can afford to be meritocratic, but still I would not underestimate this as a potential problem. Men do worry about status in strange ways. Would my male bosses be brave and far-seeing enough to have a partner, pregnant the second time, turn part time for a few years while her children are small? Would I be able to keep up the pressure of these hours with two small children?

'I don't mind the feeling that I may have missed out something as a mother with my first child, but not with the second as well. I'm determined not to turn round in seven years and say I missed my children's growing up.

'But I'm sure there are ways of fitting children in with a busy working life that I haven't had to put into practice yet. Recently, for example, I had to meet a male colleague. He said he couldn't make a nine o'clock meeting as he had something urgent to do. I only wondered idly what it was about. But later that day I happened to see his diary lying open, and I glanced at the page. There pencilled in at nine thirty, it read 'School Play'. He hadn't mentioned to me that the 'something urgent' was for his child. That's a lesson I felt I could learn too.'

Being the daughter of a working mother who managed to fit seven children into her academic life, and the mother of a daughter who now sees her on waking, before bed and at weekends, what sort of life does she predict, or hope, for her own daughter?

Kaitlin looked slightly puzzled. It would be a difficult one for any woman to answer: 'I'd like her to be somewhere between myself and my mother. Part time maybe. My mother lectured, so her hours were nowhere near as long as mine. No, I wouldn't really see her working such long hours.'

As we parted, Kaitlin gripped my hand tightly, her face betraying the feelings that had been stirred up that afternoon. No woman has yet come up with the perfect answer. And Kaitlin has been doing extremely well.

'Don't give up now!' I called out. The words echoed down the august corridors of power, influence, decision-making and all that has been so traditionally male, for so many years. Will they let someone like Kaitlin fit her particularly female needs into that very male design?

PART
5

THE YOUNG GUNS

Maybe today's new breed of competitive, ambitious and deter-mined-on-success young women merit the title: young guns. There's something about their wonderful insouciance, their new-found self-confidence and walk-tall self-esteem, that almost begs the metaphor of gun swinging from holster.

The most obvious distinguishing factor between these three younger women (up to and around the age of thirty) and the previous section's older women mostly from thirty-seven to forty-four (although Kaitlin is an exception) is quite simply that of age. Apart from that decade of years they share much in common. For example, they have been given a great start to their careers through their MBAs; and they have proceeded to follow their dream, swiftly and diligently. In this latter section, also maybe reflecting the age gap, two of the women remain single and one is married. None of them has children.

Despite the fact that they are all high-earners, to my surprise I found them rather likeable. There was none of that hard cold Yuppie mentality I was somehow expecting to find. On the whole they demonstrated an air of kindness, thoughtfulness and depth. At the same time, that is not to say that any one of them would be likely to rush across the road to rescue you from a fate worse than death – especially if your fate clashed with a 'very important appointment'. But there are some deep feelings and emotions behind the bright, eager, ever-hopeful smiles.

These three young women also fit the general stream of MBA graduate in that, despite their relatively youthful years, they have all changed careers following qualification. Interestingly, all three had previously taken up first careers, following undergraduate degrees, within the media. All three of them had come to a point of feeling that the 'communications' industry would not offer sufficient pay, responsibility and interesting work to last them through their future years, and that a more solid career path would be found in the business world. Two of these women now work as strategic consultants, though at very different ends of the consultancy market; the third works for a City investment bank.

Sheelagh F.

She's a working girl

Sheelagh is a pretty young woman; fresh-faced, bright as a button, not at all overtly aggressive or pushy in manner and quite prepared, even eager, to talk about her new-found success in the world. At twenty-seven, she is earning around £30,000 a year, working as a senior consultant for one of the prestigious, blue-chip names that exists both here and on Wall Street. Sheelagh is another American woman who deliberately decided to make the transatlantic move and come to London to study for an MBA.

When we met there was a glow to her face that came not from any spectacular beauty, but that must have emanated instead from energy, enthusiasm, optimism and a very strong sense of pride in herself and of her personal achievements. A cynic once remarked that the people who most succeed with an MBA could possibly be classified as dumb; meaning, that they are bright, capable, pass exams, and know how to put into practice what has been preached, but they are not beset by a hyper-curious intelligence that would raise the spectre of Doubt at the feast. They are happy to be where they are, and believe totally in their own self-worth. I don't mean to be condescending to Sheelagh, but there was an element of that awe-inspiring level of simplicity about her, which may mean she will go on to even greater successes in the future.

But, first, over our lunch in a bustling City wine bar, I had to ask why this very bright young American had seen fit to grace our shores for her postgraduate degree course and her first post-MBA job?

*

The MBA's greatest value is ironically felt just before you graduate

'There are several reasons why I decided to do an MBA, but really it must go back to my relationship with my father. He was an entrepreneur who became a successful businessman and I'd always envied the way both he and my brother would sit for hours talking about the stock market. Whereas I felt dumb not even knowing how to read the stock market page in the newspapers. My brother had previously done an MBA, and he had told me about the advantages: the type of people you meet, the contacts you can make, and the salary increase when you take your job on graduating.

'I had gone to college back home as a journalism major, and on graduation had taken a job in cable television, but it was not exactly well paid, and, already in my early twenties I was becoming dissatisfied. I realized I needed to know more about finance just to get on in the world, especially as I had dreams of one day starting my own company. But more, I wanted to move into a business career and start making what I'd consider to be a decent salary.

'I don't really know why I chose to come to London, except that I'd always yearned to live in Europe. So, when I decided on doing the MBA, I applied to business schools in England. I chose one specially in London and came over for the interview. I was lucky in that my parents were prepared to support me through graduate school. Once here, then I realized it probably would be pretty hard to return to America to get a job straight away.

'It may sound stupid, but it's rather like buying a new car. As soon as you drive it out of the lot, the car starts to depreciate in value. The MBA is just like that. You're most marketable when you're still a student, in the middle of your second year. That's when the major companies are recruiting. As I was here in England while recruitment was taking place, I figured I may as well take up an opportunity with a British company or an American one based here. In about three years' time, by which point I could be selling myself more on the experience I have gained in the workplace than just the paper qualification, I would hopefully have more strength to fight for a job back home. But, having said that, I am aware that a London-based MBA does not carry the same worldwide recognition as an American one. Maybe I could sell myself as a 1992 expert by then!'

The journalism major studying for an MBA

After college, Sheelagh worked for the cable television company for three years. The job was a natural progression from her journalism degree course.

'Compared to that job and my undergraduate studies, the MBA course was a much tougher programme. The degree work in journalism had not been really difficult; not exactly taxing to my mind, simply creative. But the MBA was much more difficult, and very quantitative. I had no business experience, and no maths background. There I was sharing classes with engineers who had always been in much more challenging work and who were maths-inclined. I have to admit it was a bit of a struggle, particularly in my first year. Though by the second year, I was coming into my own because I had figured out what it takes to pass exams.

'One of the ironies of the MBA degree was that an engineer might have been able to beat me in every course and come out with better grades, but in the long run being more personable, I was more successful at interviews, and received more job offers. So, one thing you learn from such a course is that everyone has their strengths. I did have problems in returning to academic work, writing essays and producing them on time. But then there were also projects on which we worked with real clients, in real-life situations, some of which we were paid for. It gave me time to develop my skills and the make-up of the course meant that we were not only sitting in on lectures, but that we were meeting and interacting with other students and business people.

'But, there were times when I wasn't sure it had all been a good idea for me. I know the school itself had been somewhat unsure about taking me on. I was only twenty-five, which was young for the MBA course, and I did not have a quantitative background. I think in the end that I had sounded so sure of myself at the interview, so determined to get in, that when they asked what I

would do if I wasn't accepted, I retorted: "I'll reapply next year."
They felt they had to give me a place. Since graduating, I've gone
back to the school to help out with interviewing of prospective
students, and I now know what they mean. You can tell if an
applicant is not really dedicated – he or she just won't be able to
go the extra mile if they haven't got that level of determination to
win over all!'

And what about her salary as the newly-graduated MBA?

'Oh, yes, my salary change afterwards was dramatic! You expect a
certain salary level once you have an MBA and when we graduated
nearly a year ago the average starting salary was thirty thousand
pounds. All my friends are making that kind of money. I've never
actually done a cash flow to see what I gave up in terms of salary
for those two years, plus the expenses of living through the course,
compared to what I am being paid now. But the benefits to having
an MBA are more than just the immediate salary level. For one
thing it puts you immediately on the fast track, with the potential
to earn more in ten years' time. You could be on the board of
directors, or capable of starting your own high-flying company.'

Then she grinned about the concept of money. 'I'm a senior
consultant with the company. They start MBAs mid-range. And I
would say I'm ambitious. My friends are in similar positions. We
all have good cars. Sometimes it gets to me, when all your friends
can talk about is their cars, and who has what make. There are
times I wish I had some friends who were non-MBAs, just normal
ordinary people . . . I have a Golf GTI. It's a lovely car. But that's
about all I own. I haven't bought a flat yet which is foolish of me
as I'm paying a fortune out in rent at the moment.'

So what does she do with her money?

'I've been working for nearly nine months, since September. Last
time I looked in my bank account there was seven thousand there.
I remember thinking, 'What the hell am I going to do with it all?'
Of course, it's in a high-interest account, but I probably should

use my money more wisely. Being an MBA, and knowing all about finance, I'm slightly shocked by myself. But I can't really afford to tie the money up, as I do intend to buy a flat or a house. I have to spend money on clothes, of course, to look smart. But you don't see me in designer clothes mainly because the only day I can shop is Saturday, and I just don't feel like shopping then. I haven't yet had the chance to take a holiday, though soon I'll be going home to America for ten days. But even then I'm going on the cheapest ticket I could find. I am, however, toying with the idea of a really expensive trip to India later in the year – that would cost about a thousand pounds.

'Basically, I don't spend foolishly. Some of the young guys with whom I was at business school, I see them blowing their money around on travel, and eating out expensively all the time. Many of the English ones owe masses of money for doing their MBA. I must say I do think to myself at times, "Would I ever get involved with a guy so profligate with his money?" There is one graduate, for example, who says he'd like to get together with me. And I say to myself, "He has all sorts of debts, sure he'd like to get together with me. I'm prudent, and I'd get to pay off all his debts!" I just don't know if I could get involved with someone who wasn't serious about money.'

The young MBA graduate and men

Most women, I ventured to say to Sheelagh, are still tied in with the concept of appearing feminine in their relationships with men. How does she feel her success, obvious ambition, and earning level affects her relationships? Shaking back her long dark hair, Sheelagh said breezily:

'The men I'd go out with are mostly other MBAs and they know and accept I'm career-oriented. If I dated a non-MBA, I suppose he might feel threatened. If he knew how much money I'm making, I reckon he'd be shocked. But I'm not overtly aggressive and really I'm not very threatening!

'I have a busy social life because there are all the other MBA graduates from business school, many of whom are from other countries, and we all meet together. Where else would I be able to find a core group of people around my own age, all with jobs in the City? I know one person in every consulting firm, every finance company and every bank in London! We don't talk about work very much because of the secrecy issue which is very important. Anyone can guess the company names if you give away details. Also, if you were having a hard time that week at work, you wouldn't want this particular peer group to know. So we tend to talk a lot about other people and cars! We go to movies, theatres, dinner, concerts . . . the usual.

'I go on the odd date among this group. When I went back to school to do that interviewing session, one of the applicants there seemed to like me and we had a drink afterwards. Now he's a first-year student there and we're seeing each other. But I'm not looking for a serious relationship right now.'

But does she foresee problems if she were attracted to a man of her own age who was not doing so well as herself?

'That's a good question. Every now and again I do think about a former boyfriend of mine from New York. He doesn't have a professional job, and certainly no MBA. I don't know. Could I date someone now who was not an MBA, who was not on a career track? There probably would be problems because I'd be making more money and doing better. He might well feel threatened even by my group of friends, because they tend to act superior. MBAs are known for their arrogance!'

The new MBA graduate and men in the office

And what about love within the four walls of work?

'You don't ever get together with a man from the office. In that sense, sex has gone from the office environment. There is much less flirting than might once have happened. I only flirt with the young guys, in a kidding sort of way. If anything did take place, we'd all know about it. There is very little dating within the office. I've never had a man make a pass at me at work. I certainly don't have to worry about fending them off!'

*

162

So going to work in the business world is not a guaranteed place to find a husband?

'No, though it's a shame because a corporation such as ours would be a great hunting ground. There's an awful lot of men there! If I did meet someone I really fell for, I'd probably have to leave. There is no way two people can work there and be married. I do realize that limits my opportunity to meet men, as I spend an awful lot of my time at work!'

Does she spend too long at work? Does Sheelagh feel she is sacrificing her social life to the working life?

'No, thank heavens my company is not one of those corporate cultures that seems to expect you to have no family life or social life. I get in around eight-thirty most mornings and usually leave by seven. I hear horror stories about other companies where you're supposed to be there still at ten. You may not be doing that much, but you still have to be there. There's the old line of "bring an extra jacket to the office", so you can leave it on your chair and go home, while it looks as though you're still there. But there are times when we're working hard, that I do have to stay late. Last week I was here till nine or nine-thirty every night.

'But, if you're not careful, work can completely take over your life. There's always something to do, so I could stay late every evening. But I prefer to socialize after work, and keep my weekends to myself.'

As a young woman, could Sheelagh really consider giving up her life to work?

'Oh yes, I would if it were my own business. In a sense I'm thinking of this as a temporary stage in my life. I'm on a three-year work permit, and will eventually go back to America. I'm in a good position, with a prestigious secure company. But I do want more.

'You see it's not really the money I want out of my working life. It's more the type of job and the position. It's not as though my family was ever poor and that I need to make money. My father started his own company when I was seventeen. He raised money from venture capital and made a great success of it. My mother never

163

worked, she was never employed outside the house. I suppose I've always wanted to be accepted and loved by my father. Though I'm now doing best out of the four siblings and so I guess my father is proud of me.'

Does it help to be an attractive female MBA?

I suggested to Sheelagh that she had described the ease with which she landed job offers following interviews during her second year on the MBA course. She is attractive, youthful, energetic and female. Did those qualities add to the fact she was also an MBA?

I'd have to say yes. I imagine it's an asset to be an attractive woman at work, even though I've read articles that say otherwise. But then I'm not really attractive. I'm no blond bombshell. I'm just sort of average. But I can see that it was easy for me. Even compared to my brother, for example, I'm now doing very well. But it might be that I seemed to know where my niche lay, which sorts of jobs to go for. I targetted the right companies, choosing those that don't care if your MBA was with distinctions. There are some companies who hire more on personality. My brother recently quit one job, without having another to go on to. He's been out of work now for several months. Yet he's smarter than me by a long shot. I don't know why he's not getting hired. He may be coming over as too arrogant.

'Sometimes I think that women coming out of the degree programme have the advantage of "positive discrimination". If a company, like mine, wants to hire women consultants then they'll choose one of those on offer. And there simply are not that many women MBAs.

'I knew that I wanted to move into consultancy, and I had worked for this company during the summer. They offered me a job full time and so it was easy for me. I'm what's known as a "strategic consultant". We deal with an overview of companies, and advise them on how their businesses could expand and develop. Say, for example, they were involved now in soft drinks, then maybe we'd advise them to move into clothing. It entails looking at different industries, seeing how well they are doing. We analyse their portfolios to see how they could improve. This type of consulting is currently very much in vogue. In fact, I'd say that companies like mine are keeping the MBA schools going.

'On the other hand, I also have to face up to the situation that, even within a good company like this one, the future for someone like myself might not be too rosy. There are no women partners here. Right now, in the British office, there are no women at partner level, which means at times I cannot help but feel, "I'll never make it to become a partner, so what's the use of trying." Even so, I tell myself that the real reason no women are partners is that twenty years ago, when today's male partners were just starting out on their careers, there were no women coming in at MBA level.

'The situation is obviously changing and right now we have a woman who is thirty-eight years old, and who is at that point. She is next in line to be made a partner. But wait till you hear this! She was at that point, when she made one terrible mistake. She got pregnant for the first time! In fact she has just had the baby, and is off on maternity leave right now. I do hope she comes back to work. As we speak, the board is probably deciding about her. Will they make her a partner, or will they write her off? I hope it goes through for all our sakes.'

And what did Sheelagh think of women's role in the male workworld, and where they fit in once they have babies? No matter how senior the woman, she might still change her mind and decide she'd prefer to stay home with her baby.

'That's what goes wrong. Employers have been burned. They feel they lose a lot of money in training and time, if the woman does not come back. But then if their attitude was more supportive and positive, probably the women would return.

'However, this is one thing my friends and I don't talk about. We never discuss what we'll do when we have children. When I was at business school, because quite a few of the women were in their early thirties, they talked about it a lot. But I suppose among my own age group, because we just don't know anything about it, we haven't gotten involved. Myself, I can't see children out of context. To me it's all part of being in love and getting married. It's probably not worth giving myself an anxiety attack over what may or may not happen in five years' time. I'll just wait until I get there and then decide.'

The new MBA graduate and
other women at work

'I do recognize that as I become more senior at work my life could become more of a battleground, because there just are no senior women on the consulting side to bat for me. In fact, this does interest me: whether the women above me see themselves as my mentors and want to help me, or do they see me as an enemy and will do their best to keep me down?

'For the most part, the first example is true. But there are other women who I can see certainly do not go out of their way to help. There is one person here who I simply cannot get along with. She is more senior that I am, and partly I know it's that she is simply out for herself. Consequently, although I'd never deliberately hurt her I wouldn't bend over backwards to help her either. Whereas, if a woman is junior to me, I always try to see that she is working on good assignments. I'm very interested in that area of how women can help each other.

'Among the other women consultants in my company, most of them are also Americans, though some English women are now coming through. In general, I do find that British women are not so far down the line of advancement. For example, my assistant came into the company with a Cambridge degree. She is only making thirteen thousand (I'm two steps up from her and look at the difference in salary!). She has recently joined our group, at assistant consultant level, and will soon be getting a rise to sixteen thousand. Now, she's only twenty-four years old and has as well as her degree two years' working experience. She thinks this is good money. But she has just started to ask me what I think. I know she's pushing to find out what I earn. But I'd never tell her.

'What I think is: she's very bright, but she hasn't taken herself that extra step. I work directly with the clients, and I know she could not yet handle that level of responsibility. But, I have suggested she go back to study for an MBA – and right now she's looking at the application forms! I'll help her along if I can.'

At that point, Sheelagh looked at her watch and got up from the table. She was about to be late for a two o'clock meeting.

Emma S.

The history student who graduated into a major investment bank

With her bob of shining short blond hair, Emma looks like a stereotype, but I found her to be a young woman of strong and forceful views, a rare bundle of surprises.

To make our meeting, I had rushed down to the City, fought my way through the swarm of young gents and ladies in their smart suits, before I reached her steely concrete and glass high-rise office. Emma and I were going to 'grab a quick lunch'. I was learning that in the busy world of corporate finance the new-on-the-job MBA graduate can't afford to be out for too long.

To my horror Emma strode off towards an obviously upmarket wine bar, with the words, 'Are you hungry? I don't usually eat lunch. Would just a drink and some crisps do?' Feeling now dreadfully boring I trotted behind this forceful persona. 'I'll have a drink with you to start with, but I must find somewhere to buy at least a sandwich, or I'll pass out,' I confessed as I caught up. How could she go all day without lunch? I marvelled. What time did she start at work? About eight-thirty – and she tries to get out by sevenish – was the answer. Coming over very motherish, I even found myself advising her on the foolhardiness of giving up lunch. For what? I said. She is thin already. 'There's not really much time. I don't fancy a sandwich. Lunch is frankly rather a waste of time.' From Emma, I was about to hear some of the more stark realities of life in the City.

Quite determinedly, this thirty year old has a definite fix on what it is she wants from life; and when and how she would achieve that. The ensuing conversation took place at ultimate vocal level, over the din of buzzing City wine-bar chatter. Emma talked about herself – albeit at first grudgingly – and she is the type of woman who talks in short, sharp, snappy sentences – as though extra words were also seen as a waste of time.

What the MBA has done for Emma

'Why did I take the degree? Because it was a useful way of changing career direction. I'd worked as a local radio journalist after university. I'd gone up to Cambridge to read History and History of Art, and my first job was in Cambridge itself. I wasn't going anywhere very fast in radio and fancied moving to London, so I came down here and worked free-lance for a while with the major radio stations. During that time I also worked for a finance programme, there was a spot during which I looked seriously at the City. That was when I decided to apply to business school. I knew that the radio work was just not leading me in the direction in which I wanted to go. And it wasn't well-enough paid. There I was, commenting on the City; really I knew I could be doing that sort of work myself. And making more money.

'I was twenty-seven when I went to business school, which is the average age. I was a classic example of someone coming to the course from an arts background. I took a two-week maths preparation programme – because I hadn't done any maths since O level. On that induction course, we were immersed in statistics. If we could learn from the ground level to calculus in two weeks, then we knew we could cope with anything. I really enjoyed my MBA. Intellectually, it was not as difficult maybe as my History degree. It was just the volume of work that was daunting. They throw as much at you as they can. There is no time to navel-gaze and wonder whether you're doing OK. You just have to get on with it. But then it is a very different discipline. With an arts degree there's little structure. But at business school it is enormously structured. The content of the work I actually found less interesting. I love history. I could read history books happily all day long. But I wouldn't sit reading business books for fun.'

Does Emma feel her generation has grown up accepting that they'll take responsible jobs and aim straightforwardly for success? At this, Emma frowned somewhat disdainfully.

'Not really. I was at a small girls' public school and where those going on to university would have accepted they'd move into a proper career, I also knew a lot of girls, more privileged than I am, who still expected to be married to someone rich and not to work. My Cambridge friends, however, all work. As for me, I'm absolutely sure I'll never not work. I could never spend my summers in the South of France and winters in Klosters. I'd feel that I was wasting my life. I would say generally that women today do feel they should make a contribution to society. That life should not revolve around the next dinner party.'

And what about her new life in the business world? Is Emma in a rather isolated position – or did she fit in without problem?

'I had absolutely no problem in getting a job. Indeed, rather the reverse. I was embarrassed by the number of job offers I received. I went along for a lot of interviews, because I was not sure what I wanted to do. But I was offered jobs from almost every interview!

'Not many of my women friends have done an MBA. But for me it did just seem the right thing to do. One of the reasons, I think, that more women don't go on to MBA programmes is that they feel they are short of time. Your career span is quite short, if you intend to fit in children. So there's a sense of urgency, of having to get as far as you can quickly, so for many women that prevents them from moving around. But I've never seen my career as anything other than a series of short spans. I just don't plan ahead in that way.'

Surely though, compared to most women of her age, her work involves an enormous amount of responsibility, dealing with money in what has been traditionally a male domain?

'I'm in mainstream corporate finance which covers acquisitions, corporate advice, privatizations, etc. Actually now I'm in the leveraged buy-out section. The MBA has a relevance in that it helps me understand my clients' businesses. It enables me to talk to clients; before business school I'd never have been able to do that. But apart from that, I don't really use my skills. And really I don't see it as very high-powered work. Let's face it, an awful lot of women do far too little with their lives. They are under-achievers. From that respect, I am certainly handling more responsibility. But there is nothing to stop them doing more, too.

'There are other women within this company. But there are not very many. The girl I work with, sorry, the person I work with is female! Out of about 100 professionals in corporate finance, only six are women. There are two women directors in my department and that is regarded as unusual. We're definitely in the minority.

'Basically very few women even know how to read a balance sheet. And very few women want to work the sort of hours I do, with so little flexibility. Personally, I enjoy the demands made on me. But I can see why more women are not fighting to get into this world. Sometimes, I do feel that ultimately I'd prefer to be running my own show; that if I could have my own business it would be more creative. But finance is an excellent training, and there's time for that to come.'

So how is Emma with money in her personal life?

'My salary doubled after the MBA. But you have to take into account the fact I lost two years of earnings and that, during those two years, my earnings should have risen anyway. So it certainly is not a question of doubling your money overnight. Then, too, I have the debt to pay off still. Like most people of my age, there was no grant available, and I borrowed the money for the course – at 4 per cent while you are studying and on graduation it goes up to 2 per cent above base rate. It is probably the cheapest money I'll ever come across. They assume you'll pay it back by getting a good job. And I must say it does oblige you to look for a highly-paid job. The one option an MBA closes off is that of bumming around for a few years! You have to pay off your debts.

'But I never really worried about money as an undergraduate student. It just came to me that I ought to be earning more once I was working in radio, because without it I would not be able to do certain things. For example, I would not say I'm ambitious about making money. There is something rather revolting about really big money and the greed it breeds. My ambitions are more to do with a sense of achievement. But I do have expensive tastes. If I want these things, then I will have to earn them. I'm not expecting it all to come from a man. I've bought a flat, and I appreciate things like sailing, skiing, and buying paintings. I like to entertain my friends, and to go to the opera. I wouldn't say I was acquisitive, just appreciative. And I do want to be able to enjoy life.

'I haven't invested any money yet because I have no capital. Even on my high salary, I find it hard to meet my bills. The mortgage payments are huge and there is the MBA loan still being repaid. I'm sure most women would never go into such debt, because they still have a latent feeling that one day they'll meet a man who will be the breadwinner. You know, when I think about it, I never ever think to myself that I one day may be supporting someone else. I mean I've never considered earning enough to cover more than myself. I couldn't imagine trying to support a whole family. So I suppose, if in the long run I think about children, I do imagine the man will be financially supportive.'

Do men in the finance world take you seriously?

'I have been mistaken for a secretary sometimes. But generally speaking I don't think of myself as a "woman" at work. There have been times in recent deals over the government privatizations, where there have been several large meetings all with twenty-five to thirty people in the room. There they were, a lot of grey-haired men in grey suits, and me. I certainly realized then, I was the odd one out. I find that often men don't expect you to say very much, which means you have to speak to make yourself heard and visible. And then you notice they're pleasantly surprised. They just hadn't assumed you'd be a force to be reckoned with.

'Once, late on a Sunday evening, when we'd been working on a deal over the weekend, the clients came in and I had not yet been introduced. Unknowingly I got into the lift with them. They said something to me like, "Goodness, they've kept you late typing. We didn't realize there was more than one deal going on". There wasn't of course. There was only our deal. They didn't realize I was an important figure in their meetings. I didn't bother to explain. I just let them stew in their own juice when we finally all came to meet!

'Otherwise, the main people to mistake you for a secretary are other secretaries over the phone. My surname has rather a masculine ring about it. If I'm booking a table for dinner, and say just my surname, then I'll get, "OK, the table is booked for Mr S . . . " I do find that irritating.'

And how does Emma relate to other women?

I asked her if she pretended sometimes that she wasn't very ambitious, beginning to sense that maybe she was rather defensive about her position?

'Sometimes I do play it down, which I know I shouldn't, because it's not very honest. But at the sort of drinks' party, where I'd be meeting the sort of women who don't know what corporate finance is, then I don't want to sound arrogant so I tend to say only, "I work in a bank." Then they'll say, "Gosh, how frightfully high-powered." And I say, "Of course it's not. I spend most of my time photocopying." Which actually is sometimes true. Or, to make light of it, I might make a remark like, "I used to be on the photocopying machine, but now I'm getting rather good at faxing." It's partly a joke, but it's in many ways a barbed comment on the fact that we do a lot of paperwork and if there isn't a secretary around at night, then you have to do this wretched stuff yourself.

'But I can see that it is also partly self-denigration, and I do have a tendency for that. Recently, I was at an inter-personal skills course and I was criticized for doing just this; apologizing for myself. On that course, I had to stand in front of a camera, introduce myself and make a short speech. I began by saying, "I've only been in this job for a year. So I don't really know what I'm talking about. Really there is no reason for you to listen to me." Deep in my heart I know it's ridiculous – if I was going to tell them something I should have just bluffed and made them believe me. I wouldn't have to pretend I actually deal with the leveraged buy-outs. But, on the other hand, I couldn't say straight what it is I do, and not feel obliged to make light of it.'

And how does Emma relate to the men in banking?

Our conversation was now becoming more relaxed, and her 'power-shoulders' began somewhat to melt. Like any other young woman, Emma was secretly delighted to talk about her experiences as a female in this male world, and then about her own attitude towards the men.

The change in conversation was triggered by me asking whether the same young woman who had read History and History of Art, who had followed a rather normal female route by going into the media following university, did not now find the world of corporate finance, and banking in general, was . . . well, maybe rather boring?

Emma agreed, without hesitation. 'Aspects of it are mind-bogglingly boring. But then many of the people are very stimulating company. One of the privileges of this world is that the people all tend to be of a similar intellectual level. Much more so than in local radio, I can tell you! On the down side, there is less of a variety of people working here. I find that quite a lot of the true professionals in the City have never done anything else. They can be very narrow in their outlook. For example, we went to Liverpool last year to visit a client. While there, we were taken to see Toxteth. The colleagues I was with had never been to Liverpool before, probably never been up North, and they had certainly never seen anything like a race-war zone. We were welcomed on our visit by a real Scouser who said by way of greeting, "You're from London aren't you? You know what we say about you lot, rich and thick, like cream!" It was a great welcome, I could see my boss's face blanch. But in a way I was pleased to see him embarrassed because someone like him has never seen how the other half live. Sometimes I do wish they weren't so narrow.'

But does her social conscience not ever come into play? This male business world, which revolves around money making more money of itself and from itself, doesn't she ever feel slight twinges of guilt?

'No, I don't. I see no reason to feel guilty. I'm quite happy with that side of things. Money has always been the male world. And, as I said before, ideally I don't want to stay in corporate finance, but would like to run a business of my own.'

So what about the men she works with? What do they think of her? Are men threatened by her as a high-powered, successful woman?

Emma tossed back her head and for once this serious-minded young woman broke into laughter.

'I'd love to know what they think of me. I doubt that any of my male friends are so wimpish as to be overawed by the fact I'm doing a serious job and have an MBA. Yet, other men might be. But then that is really up to them, isn't it?

'The one area men, boyfriends if you like, probably find hardest to accept about me is the sort of hours I work. But then as long as the man works within the City too, he should be understanding as he would know why I have to stay at work so late. Normally, the hours aren't too bad, but when a deal is on, then life becomes hectic. As advisers to large, multinational clients, we just have to be there when we're needed. We can never admit to them that we cannot meet a deadline! A lot of money is usually involved – and enormous losses could be made if we slipped up!

'I may only go home at night to sleep and would have to cancel everything, even at the weekend. I don't mind starting early in the mornings, but I would prefer to get away in the evenings. Very often I find I am rushing straight from work to a dinner party, and I'll get there still in my suit. But then so many of my friends are in the same kind of work that we do tend to tolerate each other.

'But I won't let it happen that I stay every night till nine or ten, which some people do. Because, if that becomes a habit, you get to avoid the fact you don't have a social life. In some ways though, what I find most distressing is that you're not in control of your life. You might be hanging around waiting for the outcome of a meeting. There's nothing for you to do in the meantime, but you have to stay.

'And then, of course, I don't have only City boyfriends. With one young man I'd been seeing, I went back to his flat and stayed the night because I'd been working so late, and not getting a lot of sleep, there just wasn't time to fit in normal 'social' events. I took a cab round to his house, and the next morning we were walking towards the tube together to go back to work. I remember saying to him that it's not surprising people in corporate finance have a bad reputation for doing things extravagantly – taking cabs, having someone else cook their dinner parties, or to do the ironing, always sending things to the dry cleaners – because when you're working on a major deal you just don't have the time.

'He really got my back up because in response he said, "You think it's difficult for you, but you're bloody lucky. Just think if you had a child." And then he went on, "But of course you couldn't have a child, doing what you do, could you?"

'I was infuriated by what he said, and snapped back, "Don't give me that line on what I can or can't do. It's up to me how I live my life!" But, I suppose he had actually touched on a sore spot, and made me realize that I am in a bit of a trap. There are only so many hours in a day and I like to think that the possibilities for my life are endless, and that I can do anything I want. But basically he was right. I wouldn't be able to fit in having a child with this kind of work, probably I would not even be able to fit in a marriage. But right now, I don't know if I'm missing anything. I go swimming and play tennis, and I go out for dinner, or occasionally I give dinner parties. To do that, I'd shop one day, cook the next and give the dinner party on the third night!

'I'm just not a domestic type of person. I do cook, but I don't really see why I should. Often I prefer to get a take-away. Really, there's no need to take life too hard. Domestic things get in the way and if I want to spend the evening with someone, I'd prefer to bring in take-away so we can really spend the time talking.

'My sister is already further down the line than me. She's far more successful – as a head-hunter. My mother never worked, but both my parents brought us up on the assumption we'd have professional careers and work most of our lives – not just for a few years until we married. I do think the whole business about children, for women like myself, is a very difficult one. I don't know anyone who has solved it really successfully. My sister, for example, is married, has a two-year old and is now pregnant again. She has continued working, with the help of a highly-expensive nanny. But there's no way around it, she has to handle an extremely difficult balancing act every day. The whole thing is emotionally fraught. She's well paid, but then her outgoings are very high, too. Good nannies are very expensive.'

I wondered if Emma would like to think of herself marrying a man who worked similarly long hours?

'Oh, I think I'd be quite tolerant of the hours. But then I wouldn't really want a marriage where we'd meet up at six and spend every evening together. I still would see myself as being independent. I don't think that to be successful marriage has to follow the old-fashioned conventional style. I really would not want to give up everything I do, to be with one person all the time. I'd expect him to have lots of interests too.

'I'm not saying the man would be second string, because I really believe in passion. Marriage shouldn't be domestic, mediocre and boring. You shouldn't be irritable with each other. I just wouldn't want a marriage along the model so many have.

'I look around the office and see how the married men spend their time. There's not much sexual flirting going on at work, everyone is far too ambitious for that. But the married men work terribly long hours and don't regard it as a problem. As far as I can see, they don't want to go home. There's just no incentive to go home, which I find desperately depressing. There are obviously no arrangements with their wives to do things at night, and, if all that's going to happen is they go back to watch the television news and have dinner on a tray in front of the box, then it's no wonder they don't go home. But it really is sad. I just wouldn't want a marriage like that.'

What does Emma dream about?

'I'd like to travel more. One day I'd love to take six months off and go around the world. I might have to do that between jobs, or maybe my generation will do our dropping out when we're older and have grown tired of success and money!

'In a way I think the decision not to marry or have children would really free someone like me tremendously. I'm not saying I have made that decision yet, but if one day I did realize it would not really be for me, then I'd be free to do other things with my life. I'd feel less tied to a particular place, for example, and I wouldn't worry about selling my flat. I could be more carefree. Yet, another part of me still likes the idea of a good marriage – for the companionship – and I do enjoy children. So I just don't know. I haven't started to worry about it seriously yet!'

Kelly P.

Young, married, and an MBA

Kelly is one of those females who conveys an air of her own vulnerability and 'niceness' at the same time as being sharp, bright and very articulate. Twice I had had to call off our arranged time for the interview, because of the tube and train strikes that were crippling the south-east at the time, but even in those introductory phone conversations, her voice did not ring with any MBA super-confident style. There was no secretary to fend off the unwanted; no hint of 'let me see if I can squeeze you in to my busy timetable'.

Kelly was about to turn thirty-one. Married, she and her husband have been an 'item' since she first went to university at the age of eighteen. In this year of working, since graduating with her MBA, she has become a newly-fledged consultant in corporate identity – a management consultant working with one of the leading design companies.

Not only did Kelly impress me with her fresh-faced straight-forward, no-bullshit attitude, but her offices were in themselves a delight. So very different from the steely, efficient grey and chrome of the City. Here was a fairly rambling warren of floors, offices and even a tasteful works' restaurant on the premises.

We had lunch together in one of the private rooms, reserved for their clients to the side of the restaurant. Our conversation ran way beyond its allotted lunchtime, because Kelly is a thinker and an ideas person. As she relaxed and unwound, thoughts just came pouring out.

Many of the first impressions I had of Kelly are commonly experienced by colleagues and clients, and she talked freely of the problems a young, attractive, and not outwardly aggressive woman can have in the business world. Her comments are peppered with humour and some very neat turns-of-phrase. Fair-haired and classically pretty, Kelly had come to greet me in a knee-length, navy-blue softly-draped dress. There was no jacket, no pretence at overt sophistication.

When I asked her about the 'young/attractive' quality, and how that persona is treated by the type of male corporate client she would have to deal with, this was Kelly's response:

'I have a twenty-minute credibility gap with most new clients, or with any man who is my senior. In that period of conversation I have to drop enough data to show that I understand, that I'm super-alert; and make sure that I ask extremely intelligent questions to help them get over the initial hurdle. In that twenty minutes, I know that they're absorbing the fact I'm female, young, and that they're sizing up the way I'm dressed. I know that I promote an air of naïvety around myself that is greater than the reality.

'Also, because I dress down and will not go around in severe suits, I have to overcome their prejudice. But I know I can do the work in the end, and really do not see why I should wear fancy dress to impress that upon them! We are, after all, a design firm and of course I stick within our own limits of the dress code. But we are supposed to present an image which is slightly different from that of the City as we are expected to be more creative. Still, the consultants do tend to dress fairly conservatively. It's the designers who can go around with spiky hair and torn jeans!

'I wouldn't say I'm ever taken as the secretary, though that may be because I never go places except by appointment. However, if ever I'm out with the boss, I notice that answers are always directed at him as though I were the 'notetaker'. But I don't stamp my feet about things like that. They'll learn. When it comes down to the job proper, we work together with clients over a period of months, then there is time to develop a good working relationship. Provided you feel you can do the job, then you may as well be yourself.'

The design company is noted for employing an individualistic bunch of staff, because Kelly then commented, 'In fact I'm quite rare here as a Thames Valley White Anglo-Saxon Protestant. I stand out from the crowd, being so very normal!'

*

Kelly's surprise at finding herself in her well-paid and responsible position (though she refuses to see it as high-powered) goes back to early days and her own very typical route through school, university and early jobs. Never did she see herself as anyone very special; certainly not anyone likely to move ahead and achieve. So, let's go back to the beginning. Where did the road to the MBA begin in her Thames Valley White Anglo-Saxon Protestant life?

The girl not destined to make it

'I went to a private girls' convent school, the type of place that cared more about raising well-behaved young ladies than any academic achievements. Going to university was not part of the culture, so I just never really thought about it. Sometimes there wasn't even a Sixth Form in that school. My parents weren't graduates, my father was an entrepreneur and my mother stayed at home. But somehow I got the idea in my head of going to Oxford, and I decided to apply to read Psychology. I did it all myself, arranging to do the extra Oxbridge term for the entrance examination on my own – with the support of the local girls' high school. It might all now sound as though I was very ambitious, but really it was just something I fancied doing. I was astounded to get an interview. They are far more flexible than people imagine and were probably interested in me because I was doing it on my own.

'I was offered a place and so went up to Oxford to study Psychology. My parents were rather thrilled and so were happy to support me. However, I was very nervous and I didn't have a great sense of self-worth. I was convinced that they had made a clerical error, I shouldn't be there and that fairly soon my false position would be rumbled. I had a great time there as a student, even if not in the traditional sense as I met my husband-to-be in the very first week and settled down with him. I came out with a good second-class degree and was only rather miffed that David, who had announced he was trying for a first-class degree, got one. I kicked myself then that I'd never even thought to try.

'After university, David wanted to stay on to do a doctorate in English. I had no career plans, had not done the milkround, and had the feeling maybe I should go back home into the family business, which is in boats. So I took a one-year diploma course as a personal assistant, which in fact was a glorified secretarial course. There, I did decide to go for the silver medal (the top five) and achieved one, which was eventually quite useful in my business life.

'The course benefited me in that it offered a bottom-up view of the business world. Everyone else there was going on to be a high-powered secretary. And at the time I thought that was the route I wanted to go; that it would be interesting to be the totally trusted and reliable side-kick of a captain of industry! I imagined I'd see what goes on at the top, without having to bear any of the responsibility. It's a very feminine way of handling situations, isn't it? But it had not occurred to me then that I could go up the main route myself. I had never thought of power for myself.

'Eventually, following that course, I did go back to my father's business, but I was bored out of my mind. Everyone there had known me since I was a child, and I knew I would always be a pale shadow of my father. I was missing David, and so I went back up to Oxford to live with him. During that time, I decorated our house and applied for secretarial jobs. An agency offered me a position as a secretary in the publicity department of a publisher's. And this was where the big change in my ambitions came about.

'I discovered that I enjoyed working in publishing and that my innate talents were recognized, as I was plucked from the secretarial ranks and promoted, once a year, until I ended up as a senior editor. Publishing is well known as an industry where women can advance from the secretarial level. It is a common route of entry for university-degreed women to move into secretarial work and progress up the ladder. So in some ways my choice of employer had not been too bizarre.

'By the latter two promotions, however, I nearly bottled out. I had become nervous of taking on a more responsible part, because the decision-making was quite financially loaded. I'd try to say I had changed my mind, but I was coaxed along and persuaded to take the promotions. Nevertheless, there was a growing level of frustration in me, partly at the fact I was so poorly paid for such a high level of responsibility (publishing is notoriously low paid) and also at my own level of ignorance. I was making some big deals, but there was no intellectual theory to back it up, and I just felt that I was floundering.

'By then, you see, I was a commissioning editor – for an academic publisher – and I had financial targets to meet, to be aware of costs and print runs. But also, I felt strongly that I was an interface between the board and shareholders on one hand, and the creative authors on the other. In the end, I was just finding it exhausting. There I was, acting the role of shock-absorber and taking all of the emotional flak. Maybe I was too protective of the authors, but I really didn't feel I could carry on.

'I do think, now, looking back that it is also a very female predicament to plateau out in an industry like publishing. It is based on a harem structure, with a few men at the very top and a lot of very good women scurrying around beneath them. At that time there were no female directors, though I know that situation is changing now. But it left me with a lot of uncomfortable feelings.

'Just how do women fit in the male work world? The signals women give out are not necessarily the ones managers are looking for. They are expecting us to be aggressive and acting hungry. But they overlook the fact we might be very good for the company without behaving as though we have an overdose of testosterone!'

Making the change from publishing to the MBA

'A friend of mine was doing an MBA at the time. I could see the change happening to him. He just seemed to be acquiring a sense of purpose. Remember I was burned out and working for very little reward. I just did not want to carry on for ever with more of the same. Of course, I had begun to contemplate the usual female alternatives. I thought about having a baby, but David and I were not married then and our relationship was not going through a very good stage. Then together we came up with a plan, of which we came within inches, to buy a run-down Victorian rectory, which we would have done up and run as a hotel. The life of trimming the roses – and bringing up loads of children on no money – was very nearly mine! Meanwhile, however, David's career was not exactly flourishing. He had failed to finish his PhD and had been sidetracked by the theatre. He joined a rival publisher in Oxford also as an editor, and so we were working in direct competition with each other.

'The rectory fell through and I decided to apply to do an MBA in London. I didn't fancy moving right away and studying abroad, because of David, but I knew that London attracted a lot of recruiters. I didn't really expect to be offered a place as I had no strong idea of what I would do at the end of the course. I just didn't want to stay in my trap of being underpaid and over-stimulated. On the application form, I remember writing down that my plan was for a portfolio life in about five years' time. I saw myself in some sort of consultancy work (which would be both flexible and highly paid), that I might also be involved with the family business, and working for environmental groups. Somehow, I thought that would be laughed at; that I should be saying I wanted to end up running Jaguar! But in a way it is all working out, because not only am I now a consultant, but I am also on the board of Greenpeace.

'I did well on the GMAT scores and I was lucky in that my father, horrified at the thought of me going into such debt, put me on a low salary with his firm which, with the help of my grant, actually kept me through the course on better money than I had been in publishing. I was twenty-eight when I began the MBA, and I celebrated my thirtieth birthday while taking finals.

'The MBA was ultimately everything I'd ever hoped for and more! I'd come from a career where I was used to managing a few people, where I'd also been in charge of my own domain and able to delegate to others. It came as a shock to find myself back again with no status, having to do everything for myself. I was just one student out of more than 100. Everyone else seemed to be very dynamic and super-intellectual, and also very international. It was as though they were all able to converse in a myriad of different languages. They seemed like super-people and I felt very ordinary.

'In our group work, the dynamic was quite fascinating. There would always be only one or two women out of the group of eight. And in the early weeks I found that if I spoke, it was as though no one had said a word. No one listened to me, conversations did not change direction on the basis of my suggestions. I couldn't believe it! I had after all experienced a couple of years of being listened to. The other woman in our group was a shy Chinese girl and so, for three or four weeks, it felt like being a ghost. But then the results came back from our first essays and overall the girls had done very well, against the typical male accountant. And suddenly I was being courted to write up our group reports. It was not only good for me to witness the change, but also very healthy for those men to have women around. Many of them are reformed characters now.

'But I loved being a student again. I lived in a tiny flat, which my mother had bought close to the business school. I was able to work very hard during the weekdays, with no distractions. And at weekends I could go to Oxford to be with David. So I had the best of both worlds. I felt that I was learning a lot, which gave me confidence, and a degree of security. The work on an MBA course is not only intellectual, as you're being tested all the time as an entire person. This is where I was able to score; my people-skills mattered as much as an ability to add up.

'Just being sensitive to people meant I was more likely to receive a pat on the head from the strategy lecturer, than being able to crunch numbers. I felt very good about that, as it validated all those "soft" qualities that women have. On the whole, the other women on the course also came from arts' backgrounds, rather than from accountancy or engineering, and we did just as well as the men. Ultimately, business is not just a hard, numbers oriented game.

'During the recruitment session in the summer of my first year, I applied to the big consultancy firms – one of those offering the real glittering prizes. I did well in those rounds of interviews which was terrific for my morale. I took a summer placement in a financial consultancy firm to test myself further by working in the City. I was given a project to complete on the airline industry, and I was rather pleased with myself. I completed the report and they actually moved upon the basis of my suggestions.

'But, during that summer, I also became more conscious of the fact I was missing being with David and that I was looking for ways to give him more time. So, when it came to the final round of interviews I selected jobs in human resources or in corporate identity, which would reflect the softer sides of MBA work. Fearing having to make an outright decision myself, I rather hoped I'd only be offered one job out of the bunch. Well, in the end I had several offers and had to weigh up which one I would most regret if I turned it down. It seems ridiculous to me, now that I'm here and love the work, that I might have seriously contemplated working anywhere else.'

Working in the 'soft' sector of corporate identity

When asked directly about the company and why she feels she landed this much prized job, Kelly shrugged her shoulders and confessed she was still not too sure why they offered her the position.

'The interview didn't really go well, not compared with some of the others. It seemed to be very friendly, but more like a normal conversation. Some of the high paying strategic consultancy firms will give you a business problem to solve on the spot. I enjoyed those because I'd got the knack of thinking on my feet. But here, the whole approach was softer and I did not feel that I had done very well, or that I'd even been sure of what to say. I did find out afterwards that they had not been sure I was tough enough for the job. My last interview was with a very horrible, rude director who was testing me to see how I would react under pressure. He was seeing whether I could handle being constantly disagreed with. He also feared that I was not showing enough ambition. Once offered the job, I joined them immediately, conscious that I needed to clock up two years of working before I could dare to get pregnant!

'By the time I joined them, however, I had had a most unexpected boost to my self-confidence. It came as a big turning-point for me, because I came away from business school with a distinction. I most certainly had not expected that. As finals approach, you are getting marks, but you have no idea how you are doing compared with everyone else. I felt that I might be reasonably high, but not in the Top Five! I regarded it as such a wonderful prize that I've been cheered by it ever since. I even had a dream the other night that it was taken away from me.

'Being a consultant I have discovered is rather similar to being an MBA student. We work on case studies and come to decisions about companies. In the first stage, the work is involved with picking up data, analysing the situation and then making recommendations. But, the next stage is just as important when you are helping the client accept your decisions. It's all very well coming up with the right answers, but you then have to persuade the client of their value, and help them make use of the information.

'Corporate identity can have rather a vague sound to it; to many MBA students it's too much of a "touchy-feely" concept. But I love it, because it's to do with the central notion of the corporation. What is its identity that makes it unique? How does it look, what are its values, how does it behave? Does its behaviour reflect its beliefs? It's like psychoanalysis, except that it is for corporations rather than individuals.

'Often a large part of our work is involved in looking at the culture of the organization and how it may bring about possible changes. How does it compare with its competitors? We have to take a very holistic approach. We need to understand it fully, and we must be aware of the signals it is giving out. For example, does the company pay lip-service to caring for its employees and yet, when we go in, we find that the staff toilets are dirty? We watch everything and take sneaky photographs of things like styrofoam cups left lying about and unkempt toilets. There's a sort of Egon Ronay side to the work!

'Fascinatingly, the company bosses may feel they are coming to us for a face-lift, when what they are going to get is a mind-lift. They see us as a design group and may ask for a new logo and brochures. But we offer a service that goes much deeper. Sometimes, it might entail holding up a mirror to them, so that we can emphasize a point. As we are a design group, we can offer a two-fold service: we, the consultants, are the thinking machine. We have client contact and assess whether their aspirations make sound business sense. We may test that out over several months. Then the designers go in and provide changes in the visual sense. We work as a team, maybe four to ten people on any one project.'

I asked Kelly what it was like to walk in on a new job as a new MBA recruit? How did she convince people that she could do the job?

'You come in with your new MBA badge and clean shoes, that first day, to work among twelve other consultants. Quite a few of them have MBAs, but others have come from the consultancy background and you do get the feeling that they think you're going to be much too "ivory tower". So, in the first few months, you have to prove that you have some credibility. But basically you're going to learn the job by experience. You're sent out in teams and you learn as you go along. I found that for the first three months, I was always on best behaviour. Then, within six months, I'd gained a lot of self-confidence. There's almost a 50-50 ratio of women working here, so that is no problem in itself.'

What about children?

I questioned Kelly about children. Where did they fit in to the picture? Would she wait the two-year statutory period? And would that be accepted happily by her new employers?

'I want to start a family, but it is a terrible problem to know how and when. As I said, I feel I have to work the two years first. Even at my interview, although no one brought up the topic, I raised it myself and asked what the arrangements were for maternity leave. I was told upfront that maternity leave would be very inconvenient, and that a pregnancy would be frowned upon for at least three to four years. I even saw my notes from the interview; they'd underlined "Wants to have children"! But I have a hunch they'll come round to it. The company is not too male-orientated and, as an experienced consultant is a very rare commodity, they'd be loath to let me go. Besides it would be such a waste.

'But, even at business school, I used to moan to the registrars about the fact it was a two-year course. It is a massive price for a woman to pay to take two years out – just before she's thirty – to study, especially knowing she'll have to work for at least two more years before starting a family. That would make me thirty-two. And I resented it bitterly at the time. While I was on my MBA course, David and I got married and he has moved since to London to be with me. He had to follow me, as I was the one with the good job. Even so, it was unsettling for both of us to trade down from a large house in Oxford to a tiny flat here.

'But David seems very well-adjusted to my success. He says he's happy for me, and has always egged me on to try for the next stage. Recently I asked him if he felt threatened by my success, he just laughed and said, "not remotely". But then he has been having problems with his own career. Being a man and with his PhD work, he started higher than me when we were both

187

in publishing. Now there is a big gap. He has applied to do an MBA, but has not yet been offered a place on any programme. Suddenly, there seems to be an enormous rush for places, and the fact he failed to get the PhD seems to be going against him.

'So far he has not been able to take the MBA route to find an easy way out of his trap. He says he would like to work in television. But, since moving down to London, he has been effectively unemployed. The past four months he has spent doing up our flat, as we bought it cheap to renovate in the hope of proving a good investment. David says he is prepared to play the opposite role if we start a family. The trouble is we're both competing to child-mind!

'Besides I do have a problem with that idea. I don't really want to be the breadwinner. And, for similar reasons that husbands want their wives to work, I just fear it would be more interesting for him to work than to stay at home. It could drive a wedge between us particularly if he was only doing it to be nice, rather than because it was something he very much wanted to do. For example, it might just be that he's been finding the recent interviews demoralizing, that he's already losing the edge of his self-confidence.

'But, in truth, I am beginning to panic about babies. I don't want to wake up one day and find I've left it too late, that I'm too old. If I did get pregnant soon, I would definitely try to come back full time. But ideally I'd prefer to work a three-day week, and maybe only focus on one project at a time.'

And what if she had stayed in publishing, I asked, wondering if in the long run that might have been an easier environment in which to begin a family, as it is notoriously a women-oriented industry?

'I escaped death by getting out of that. I'm absolutely thrilled things have worked out as they are. I'm much more purposeful now about what I want to do, and how I could work in the future. For example, as I mentioned I'm on the board of an environmental charity. That, to me, is the real value of an MBA, almost more than earning a lot of money. I have something to offer other people.

'I feel that I'm incredibly lucky being part of the generation of women who are having an easier time, more so than the pioneers did in previous generations, many of whom became completely screwed up by their efforts. Some turned into quasi-men, others succeeded, but they could not combine family with a career. But among my group of female friends, quite a few have had babies and none, as yet, have given up their jobs completely.

'Mind you, all of them have babies under a year old. Very often the question seems to be "What will happen when I have a second baby?" That's the current group angst, "Can we do all this and have two children?" That bothers me too, because I'd dearly love to have at least two children.

'I'm pacing myself better now, trying to get a feel for how I could adjust my life to accommodate a child. I'm not lying in bed worrying that I've not become a superstar. I'm much more aware that during the next six months I need to earn some Brownie points here, which will see me through my projected maternity leave.

'What worries me is that the hormones do seem to affect women that way and I see it all around me. Whatever you think beforehand, the baby ultimately becomes all-important. But although it seems an entrancing idea, that you fall in love with your baby and give up everything else, I also see that as a problem: one day you'll wake up and come out of that dream world to find your confidence has gone, you've no job, no money, and cannot get back on the career ladder. I just hope things will change to help women with these decisions.'

After our interview, I scribbled a note to myself: Kelly is certainly a potential future leader among women. What happens to someone like her, over the next few years, in her choices about having a child and whether she will manage to stay in work and enjoy her motherhood, will be a route-marker for other women of her generation and those coming along behind.

PART

6

WORKING WITH MEN

Maybe you're thinking by now, that all these women are too good to be true. Everything has been far too easy for them in forging their way forward. Offices and companies you have worked for, or have even contemplated working for, may have shown their blatant anti-female colours, tingeing your attitudes with a strong touch of rust. The women in this section of the book, struggling to take their place in the male world, have by no stretch of the imagination found the battle impossible. But they are all honest about admitting that they found it tougher than they'd imagined.

There is wisdom to be culled from their views and comments, and much to be learned from their experiences already gained. These women, for a variety of different reasons, are either more honest than some of their predecessors, have a stronger sense of reality (or cynicism) or, in some cases, they may just have been plain unlucky. Whatever the reason, I feel their stories are perhaps even more worthy of our attention than some of those who have had it easy. These women have come up through the school of hard knocks. For someone like Marion, who leads off this section, her experience has led to greater strength in adversity, to an almost irresistible desire to keep up the fight and win, and to a wonderful sense of humour.

Marion F.

From shorthand typist to the boardroom

Going to meet Marion involved an hour's drive out of London; she had been particularly welcoming and helpful in making the arrangement to get together on a Sunday. Though I had not relished these interviews encroaching into my own private time, which of necessity is spent with my children, I could understand that working in industry way out of London, she did not have much free time during the week. Besides, Marion travels a lot on business and our interview had to be now or never.

But I could not have spent a nicer Sunday afternoon. Marion is fun. She lives alone, in a most unusual house on the edge of a forest. She has come up the hard way and exudes a sense of deserving the peace, quiet and luxury of her chosen home. Besides, she keeps the house crowded with guests and her own diary crammed full of events. There are also four cats to keep her company and a huge garden which, she looks at it despairingly, is just not her 'thing' to keep under control. Money and status through her job have brought a richness to Marion's life that she would never ever have imagined.

At thirty-seven, Marion is now a product manager, responsible for around £100 million worth of sales for one of the nation's largest industrial manufacturers. Her sales trips have taken her primarily to Eastern Europe and Japan. Bold and intrepid, as she related her stories the image flashed through my mind of those Edwardian lady travellers who took on the world – and couldn't care less what anyone had to say about it.

As we wanted to talk in relaxed surroundings, we walked through the village lanes to the nearby pub that serves excellent lunches.

Marion is all too aware of her single career-woman status, conscious that it makes her an oddball, a misfit, both at home and at work. There are men around in her life, but no one has yet appeared to tempt her to give up the peace and serenity that come from having a home of her own. She has no family responsibilities, no ties that as she well knows can bind too hard.

Marion doesn't have much to do with village life. She works long hours and has also built up a small but successful business setting up music dates in a local hall. There certainly is no room for her at the Young Wives or the Women's Institute.

The servile secretarial life

'My background is rather unusual, particularly for someone with an MBA. I was born in a small industrial town, where we lived behind our little corner shop. I went to the local grammar school, but was not expected to do anything special there nor with my life. So, despite the fact I got seven O levels, I left school at sixteen. Only four of us actually left then, and one of those was pregnant. But then no one encouraged me to stay on. I just wasn't seen like that.

'So I went off to learn shorthand and typing and started working as a secretary – a shorthand typist would be a more accurate description. I was working among a lot of Oxbridge graduates, and slowly I began to realize that although I didn't have the right vocabulary, or accent, I was just as bright as they were. That pushed me to begin taking A levels, through a correspondence course.

'Still I had to carry on with the job. But, by now, just being servile and taking no responsibility was making me feel hopeless. I was becoming exasperated. So I started looking for TOPS courses – until I realized they weren't for people like me who really wanted to get on. They were aimed more at teaching secretaries to become PAs.

'But once I had my two A levels which I'd achieved in six months, I was given a place to take a Business Studies degree course at the City of London Polytechnic. When I began the degree course, I was twenty-three years old and I had already been living away from home for seven years; I was working in London and had a bedsit, so, with a mature student's grant, I just continued living there. My parents certainly could not have supported me, and nor would they have done. To their mind, I was mad giving up a wonderful job as a secretary.

'But I had already worked out that I should concentrate on moving into a management job. The four-year, very practical, undergraduate degree course was intended to help me make that transition. It was one of the female lecturers who encouraged me to go on further; who suggested that I should go to business school to take an MBA. Until she mentioned it, I hadn't been aware such places existed. By then I was twenty-seven years old, and that's getting pretty old in the life of a woman, so it was a difficult decision to apply to business school for two more years of studying. On the one hand, I was fed up with being a student. But on the other hand, I knew that if I went to interviews even with my degree, they would only see a sixteen-year-old school leaver, a mature student with secretarial work experience. That still did not fit the sort of role I wanted. I might indeed have ended up again as a glorified secretary. I hadn't worked like mad, simply to finish up where I'd started from.

'I tried a couple of job interviews, and already was warned that my expectations were far higher than that of the average employer. One interview I went along to was for a job with a brewery. They told me they had never employed a woman before. So I told them they should try. These companies just weren't ready for someone like me. So, when I was offered a place on an MBA course in London, and as grants were still available for mature students, off I went. After four years living as an undergraduate, living on next-to-nothing, the new grant made me feel quite wealthy.'

Marion and I then talked about how she fitted in with the business-school crowd. Although twenty-seven is quite a normal age to be studying full time for an MBA, graduates tend to come with prestigious first degrees, maybe from reasonably high-flying jobs, and with an in-built level of self-confidence, even of arrogance. Had Marion felt herself a misfit among that crowd?

The MBA: key to the door

'I got on well with everybody and even ran the magazine for the first year. But I continued living in my own place, and so I also had a social life outside the graduate-school walls which made me something of an outsider.

'One of the first things was to train myself away from the servile, secretarial attitude; so I never made the tea, or acted as the wife or mother to other students. The secretary answers the phone, types her boss's work, and generally plays the part of his wife in the office. I'm obviously a born organizer, and so it can be all too easy for me to slip back into that role. However, my organizing side still emerged because I found myself busying them all into teams to get the course work done. I was not going to be wasting my time, so I had to make sure they all pulled their weight! Academically I did not find the MBA work as challenging as my first business-studies degree course. But what an MBA gives you is something else: it's an attitude that comes from being forced to compete with others, against time pressures. It gives you the confidence to know you can handle anything in the business world.

'I don't know what you'd call it in my case: sheer determination, or an inner drive to get on, but I never stepped back again. I just knew on graduation that I could get a really good and interesting job. So when it came to our last year and we were applying for jobs, I let nothing stand in my way. I aimed for industry because I knew that the finance world, or going into consultancy, weren't for me. I wanted a job that would mean doing something "hands on"; something essentially practical, where I could be responsible for making things happen. All the interviews I had were very positive about me. So in the end I was able to choose this company.

'Bear in mind that no other woman on the course with me even applied to industry for a job. They felt unqualified or that they wouldn't be accepted. There I was applying for jobs that specified they wanted an engineer with languages. I knew I didn't fit the bill, but still I'd be offered the job. Men will apply for positions for which they know they're not qualified, whereas women tend to be too easily down on themselves. I chose this company, because I came away with the feeling that they liked me and were prepared to design a job to fit me.

'While at graduate school, we took some psychological tests to find out what type of career would best suit our personality type. The psychologist kept pushing questions at me about my mother's and father's influence. I don't know why he kept pushing the point, because there was nothing for me to say. Finally, he gave up the unequal battle and decided I had an enormous need for achievement, and that's what drives me on. I know that some friends have described me as brave. But I don't see myself that way. It's more that I have had no choice. But, on the other hand, if I'd have been given everything on a plate, maybe I wouldn't have ended up with that same level of drive. You need that type of grit and determination in this kind of work. Otherwise you might give up at the first hurdle.'

Landing the job

Marion's face comes to life most vividly when talking about her job. Although she refuses to live and die for her work, she does admit that her career is the single most important part of her life, consuming most of her mental and emotional energies. Until recently, when she was travelling extensively around the world on business, the job did in fact take over. There was no chance of a social life, no room even to meet a man, let alone time to squeeze in a relationship. Right now, she has curtailed the travelling and is finding relaxation through her fledgling music business – which also provides her with a far wider range of friends and contacts in her social life.

But the job, which pays on a modest post-MBA scale, is one which fits Marion to perfection. There is more to life in her terms than an astronomical salary. Responsibility, autonomy, achievement, status, peer-respect and power; these are all qualities that are important to her.

'On paper, I had nothing particularly relevant to this company or to the job I was appointed to. But I do get on with people, and that seemed to come across at the interview. The director who recruited me, I've since learned, has a reputation for using his instincts when hiring. In many ways, it was a brave decision for them to take me on. I had no knowledge of the business, no scientific background, and no languages . . . all necessary ingredients. For the second interview, I was invited to come to their head office outside London. A female chauffeur picked me up from the station and I was brought to an ancient building with its huge sweeping staircase, and a view of cows. The director in question told me I had to meet the rest of the board. "Do well," he told me. "I want you to come here." And I was offered the job immediately.

'Within weeks of joining, I was sent out to Eastern Europe to negotiate contracts, develop the market, and manage the men out there. It entailed quite a leap of faith. I could imagine them sitting around saying to each other, "Shall we let this crazy woman loose on Eastern Europe?" But I wanted a job where I would be dropped in at the deep end, and indeed I was being left to swim and fend for myself. It was far better than being stuck away in a back room, acting as an analyst or writing learned documents. After six weeks with the company, I was making a solo trip to East Germany and in three months I was the first westerner to enter Poland after martial law had been imposed.'

The all-male work environment

Were there problems for Marion working in such an all-male environment? She was thoughtful for a time, and then said truthfully, 'There were problems at first, partly because of my MBA, also because I was younger than most of the men, and lastly because I'm female. There was always that suspicion, I felt, at the back of their minds that I was only taken on because someone liked the look of me. At the time, there were no other women at my level and that was in 1981. On the technical side, there was a woman qualified with a PhD who had been with the company a long time. But she was a scientist, not a manager.

'There was also a certain amount of bad feeling in the department I first joined, as I had come in on the same level as men who had been working there for ten years. The company had been in the process of "losing" people due to a re-structuring, and then I turned up recruited from the outside. I'm sure in some ways I've received less help, being a woman, than if I'd been a man arriving new to the department.

'Little things would reveal their innermost feelings. If I went with my colleagues to the pub, for example, and ordered a half-pint of lager. They'd be sure to come back with a pint. They were obviously saying, "If you're one of us, then you have to drink like us." It might appear stupid, but I understood what was going on.

'But, after a while, things began to settle down as I started bringing back contracts under difficult circumstances: such as from Poland during martial law. I was the first person to go out there representing a western company and I made that trip alone. Then, the fellas started coming in to my office and saying, "How did you do that?" I'd begun to be accepted on their terms. But it took time.

'Even though I've often been dealing with men who have been entrenched in this male-dominated industry for centuries, once travelling away from home I've always found them charming. I think they're entertained by the fact that I have come out to visit them. On another trip to Poland, for example, I went to visit a factory. The man who works for our company out there is in his mid- to late fifties. I was very concerned he might resent me. But he came to meet me at the airport with a bouquet of flowers. At the hotel, there was only one room with a bathroom which they gave to me. My boss, who had brought me along, and this man had to share the other room. Nevertheless, I felt it beholden on me to muck in and drink vodka with them until the early hours of the morning . . . as I see it you have to show willing.

'My next big foreign trip was to Japan. Again my bosses weren't too keen on letting me handle that situation at first. I had to undergo an internal interview to be given the position. During the interview I remember asking what the Japanese businessmen's attitude was towards women. "They despise them," was the retort. "Well," came my riposte. "They need educating, then." My interviewer didn't sound too enthusiastic about my chances of survival out there.

'Eventually I made the trip and I went alone, which was not good form for the first time as I should have been introduced to our clients and agents. I had a Japanese translator, who expressed his terror for me. However, I attended my first meeting, entering the room barefoot as is the custom, and sixteen businessmen had turned out to see me. Again it was fine once the ice was broken. They were delighted to meet this tall, crazy woman from England.

'My bosses had pretended to be nonchalant about the trip. But the minute I was back the director phoned me, obviously nervous as hell. So once again I felt the company had really given me every opportunity possible. Certainly they have taken risks for me. And in turn, I've broken down a few barriers for women in the international trade arena. It's easier now for other businesswomen to go out to some of these countries.'

What about personal relations with male colleagues and men in general?

By now Marion and I had enjoyed a couple of drinks and, as in most interviews, there had been plenty of talk about our individual lives, feelings and ideas. Once those barriers are down, few women can resist talking over the more deeply-felt personal issues of their lives.

Marion paints a picture of a fun-loving, convivial woman at work; someone who likes her bosses, enjoys being appreciated by them, but also someone who, at the end of the day, would never dream of spending her social time with any of these colleagues.

'I think the male executives at work tend to find me entertaining. The first time I went into one of their board meetings, I had on a bright red suit. But not only that, my blouse, shoes, nail varnish and lipstick were all red. I saw myself in the mirror in the ladies room and thought, "Marion, what have you done?" I get the impression they quite enjoy having me around. I certainly brighten things up. I don't always dress so colourfully, but I don't worry about conforming either, unless I'm travelling or meeting clients. Provided you look smart, a woman can get away with anything, in my opinion.

'On a personal level, however, business men just aren't my type. When I'm travelling of course there are always the wolves on the prowl, and they're usually the British men. But, as a general rule, surrounded by those conventional men in grey suits, I find I can keep my eye on the work pretty easily,' she laughs at her revelations to herself as well as to me.

'The music world introduces me to men whom I tend to find more attractive. They're down to earth, far more sexy, and humorous. But then I don't fit their type. I'm often chatted up at the concerts I arrange. But once asked what I do, and I tell the truth, I can watch them immediately withdraw. So, I have to ask myself, does it matter? The sort of man who'd want a "little woman" wouldn't interest me, either.

'But still I think some day I'll meet someone. I've been a late-starter in everything else, so why not love and/or marriage? I might want children, too, if I met the right man. By this stage in my career, I think I could fit a child in quite comfortably. I'm certain I'd keep on with my job. Just imagine it, if I wanted to take maternity leave. That would give my bosses a nice shock to the system. It would be good for them. They've never had a woman manager go on maternity leave before.'

Later that afternoon, as we were walking back to Marion's house, we were chatting more on the issue of the 'single-woman nearing forty and-the-lack-of-available-men' crisis. Marion began describing how often she feels resentful of the fact she is independent and self-supporting; and that men who are her equals just don't seem to marry such women.

'Once, I went along to a company Christmas party held in a private home. I brought along a tame man as my partner, but I was wearing another of my very bright outfits: short dress, tights, shoes, lipstick, nail varnish, you name it. Well, when I walked in you could have cut the silence with a knife. They all went quiet! These men I knew so well, and their "little" wives were standing around in groups; men with men, women with women. I felt like Jezebel . . . or Joan Collins! The wives glared at me – I certainly am the odd one out.

'But I used to notice the same kind of event at business school. I'd get along very well with the men in school; they were interesting and intelligent. But when they invited me to dinner or to parties unfailingly they'd introduce me to a wife or partner who was a nice quiet little woman. If even the business-school men choose to marry women like that, what chance do I have of finding a partner?'

But, even as the words left her lips, Marion was quick with the rejoinder, 'I'm happy with the life I have, right now. Don't get me wrong. I'm not desperate to share my life with anyone. I love my home, I have a great career, and an interesting life with the music business. All in all, it's a good lifestyle. The man would have to be bloody good to make me give any of it up.'

What's next?

'I've been with this company about eight years. And in my present position as product manager, operating almost independently, with complete responsibility for a line that sells around one hundred million pounds worth of goods a year, for two years now. I probably could have made more money by moving around. But in terms of "total lifestyle" I know that I'm better off this way.

'I've invested a lot of time in my career at quite a late stage in life, and I'm aware of that. Now I'm concentrating more on finding a balance, on making sure I have quality of life. More and more people, men and women, are striving for that balance these days. I have already said to my bosses that I'm no longer prepared to work overseas. Though I will still take on some travelling, of course.

'All my women friends, outside the company, tend to be in education or nursing. They're taking responsibility in their jobs, but it doesn't go any further than that. They have partners, so they're not solely responsible financially. Whereas I am, and I mean to carry on making money. Looking back, when I finished at business school, I was broke. I had been a student for six years, and on top of that, I had taken out a student loan not all of which had been spent. When I had the offer of a job here, and had to move out of London, I was put in the position of buying my first home at twenty-nine, using what remained of the student loan as the deposit on my mortgage. Apart from that, I had absolutely nothing. Not even any furniture. I lived out of cardboard boxes; though I did have a washing machine, the working woman's closest friend.

'It took years before I began to feel well off. And it's only really now that I am beginning to feel comfortable. I hold down a good position in middle management, and have every hope of going further. My mother would probably be shocked to hear me talk. "Why do you want to do all this?" I can just hear her saying. "What's wrong with what you're doing now?" I'm sure my parents are proud of me, but they certainly cannot begin to understand why I push myself so hard.

'On the other hand, my mother never once has suggested I might be happier if I were married. She's seen too much misery for women in her life to believe that. My own sister has been married, divorced and remarried. Now she lives cramped in a small flat with this new man and her children; her life has always been a struggle, and there has never been any money around. That is certainly no ideal way of life.'

Marion shrugs, 'I don't envy her one bit. In fact I do as much as I can to help her children, to show them there can be more to life. I'm single and happy, what do I really have to worry about?'

Liz B.

The unwelcoming male-dominated industry

Liz is a bright, cheery, friendly woman, happily married and well-educated through the acceptable route of a first degree in Economics. Surely someone like Liz would find moving into the male business world easy? Her credentials are as good as any man's. But Liz unfortunately took on what she describes as a 'prehistoric' male industry as her target: where bright young women MBAs are not only frowned upon, at times it seems they are well and truly trampled upon. 'Just my luck to choose a dinosaur,' she jokes.

Liz and I met during the afternoon, in one of those dull, conventional, corporate conference rooms with their formica furniture and instantly forgettable decor. The company itself was feeling far from dull and forgettable, in the throes of a fierce take-over wrangle. So, Liz confessed, she had plenty of time on her hands. No one knew what the future held in store. And, at that moment, it was pretty obvious Liz could hardly summon up the energy or enthusiasm to care.

Following her undergraduate degree, she started life working for a major American manufacturing company, in their finance department. She'd noticed in herself an interest in personnel or marketing, and that most of the high-fliers in the company had come in with MBAs. Her boyfriend (now husband) was studying at the time for an MBA in London, and he highly recommended that she should follow this path. Imagining that you had to be really brilliant to get on an MBA course, Liz applied for a one-year programme outside London. And she was surprised to be accepted.

Although she still grudgingly admits that getting an MBA gives a woman credibility, Liz was feeling quite bitter about her post-qualification experience with this British-owned industry. She readily admitted that they have proved to be very backward over attitudes towards their women employees, which makes her something of a pioneer. 'But I didn't want to be a pioneer.'

Taking time out to pursue an MBA

'I didn't think I'd get on to a course, because I imagined you had to be really clever. But in the end I have learned that is just not true. I found it difficult to reach the decision to give up my job for that year. I had to support myself, which is why I chose the one-year course. I had a flat and a mortgage, so I rented it out when I moved away from London and went into shared digs with three other women graduate students.

'I can't say I found the course very enjoyable. Everyone was so intense. Several people hadn't studied for ten years or more and they just worked solidly. There was me, keen to have a social life and everyone was stuck in their rooms working. Basically it teaches you to work to strict time pressures. Yet I knew I could do that. I began to feel I should be working harder, but already after six months, we were looking outwards towards getting jobs. I do think the older people on the course found it quite tough going. There was one guy who was forty-five, with a wife and children at home. It was a lot for him to accommodate. And many of the people there had given up highly-paid jobs. For me, I was only twenty-five which is quite young for an MBA student – and to give up a year of my life wasn't the end of the world.

'There were only twelve women out of 120 people on the course. It amazed me really that the percentage of women was so low. Just like after university, I didn't have a problem finding a job – because I applied to industry. When I was at university, there were only twenty women out of 100 students doing economics degrees, and even at the application stage, no other female, apart from myself, bothered to apply to the manufacturing industries. The other women economics students were going into teaching, or similar typically female careers.'

*

So, I asked her how women fit into the manufacturing industries, sensing the answer. Very badly, according to Liz, especially if the industry in question is of the old-fashioned variety.

'I was really naïve when I came here for the interview. I was looking for a certain sort of job, not at the type of industry. I hadn't noticed the attitude that prevails towards women. Maybe I should have looked to see how many women were in senior positions, for example. They just do not have a policy here of promoting women. I would never work for a company like this again. I'd rather aim for an American company or a more service-based organization. If the company is forced to be competitive, it has to be more dynamic and less set in its ways. Here, I'd say they're simply looking for a certain type of man!

'There are no other women here at my level (or above). The only other women are a couple of grades below me, and the rest are secretaries. That immediately presents me with the problem of how I access the male networks, if you see what I mean. I don't go into the loos with them, or out on the golf course, so I miss out on a lot of basic information. The only gossip network available to me is at the secretary's level.

'And then that, of course, encourages the attitude that if a group of women is talking, they are gossiping. When a group of men is talking, it will be about work. It does wear you down, and has made me feel that maybe I would rather be in a typical female type of job.'

I asked her to describe her job specifically.

'Basically I'm the highest graded non-accountant here. I work in the Treasury, which to my mind is really like bookkeeping only on a higher level. Our main area of work is in terms of funding the company's borrowing requirements. We act as advisors to the various businesses and for that I have to deal with all the major banks. Although I had not planned to go back in to working for finance departments, when interviewing for post-MBA jobs I discovered that despite my willingness to switch career-tracks, employers were only interested in my past experience. So in a sense, the irony of my degree was in being channelled back into what I had previously come from.

'I've been with this job for three years. I'm thirty-three years old and am earning thirty-two thousand pounds, which is good money, but I know it should be higher. In my time here, I've managed to consolidate my base and I would like to progress further, but I notice buffers against that development all around me. This is why certain people, and particularly women, can find it so hard to move on. My boss has a unique point of view on all this. He once told me everyone has a reason that will hold them back (they might be fat, or bald, or talk too much), mine just happens to be that I'm female. He says that there's nothing I can do about it, so I shouldn't waste my time worrying. I'll just have to persevere and try to overcome the obstacles.

'Similarly, I once asked him about my salary level. He said that he always pays women five thousand pounds less than men who are their equals, because women leave (to have babies I presume he meant). Then there is also the question of my job title. I'm called group banking manager, when I should by now have the title assistant treasurer. A man at my level has the title. But my boss admitted to me the other day that others (men) in the department won't let me be so graded and he dare not confront them. Ultimately, all this is going to have an adverse effect on my career, as I've been to see a couple of head-hunters recently who commented on the title. My boss's reaction was that I could use the correct wording on my c.v. and he'll cover up for me! But the head-hunter also felt that my salary should be higher by my level. In my book, I'm "Up Against the Corporate Brick Wall".

'I'm just waiting to see what happens with the take-over. I can't stay here. But I don't want to walk out until I know if we're going to be made redundant. Or maybe someone better will move in and take charge.'

Working with men within a prehistoric corporation

'There aren't actually any men MBAs working here, as far as I can see. Mostly, they're accountants, which provides another obstacle in my way as the company line seems to be to promote qualified accountants.

'Some of their old-fashioned attitudes have to be seen to be believed. For example, to have a certain sized office you have to be a certain grade. By mistake, I ended up with one of these offices, though I wasn't at grade level. Some of the other men, who were slightly higher in rank than me, complained that I was being favoured by this office. In the end I actually got an office half its size! I don't know if it's the fact I'm younger than them, or that I'm a woman, but it obviously drives them mad. The most antagonistic men, I find, are those in their fifties. They can be incredibly hostile, I suppose because they feel most threatened.

'It's not even that I'm particularly aggressive. I just do my work and act civil. But I do refuse to pretend I'm an empty-headed secretary, and that's what makes them uncomfortable. As I see it, one of the problems these men have is that their wives all stay at home, doing nothing much. They tend to talk to me in the same way they would address their wives; as though I'm about five miles behind them in terms of being able to pick up new information. To their minds, I probably am aggressive. That's a word always used against a woman if she is not acting the "silly secretary", isn't it?

'I tried socializing with them and being pleasant, when I first joined the company. I asked a few of my colleagues home for dinner. I wondered why their faces looked horror-struck! Maybe it's just not done around here. Certainly no one's invited us back again. That's the type they are – utterly dull and boring.

'But I do find that women are often their own worst enemies. I remember when I was at school, I was about seventeen, and there was a debate, "Are women equal to men?" Out of the class full of thirty-four boys and girls, I was the only one along with the teacher to vote yes. I was appalled! Can you believe it? Maybe that's the result of mixed education. A lot of the other girls were very intelligent, but they had no inclination to push themselves. It seems to me such a waste of their talent.

'Even now, I often find it hard to meet women friends who are like me. I play netball in the evenings. I know they think I'm strange. I have a company car and they cannot understand how I could have a car when I'm not a sales rep. Their sights are set so low. Mostly they're teachers, or they're women at home with children. I really wish more women would do more with their lives. It certainly brings me down to earth, when I'm worrying about a problem at work – which probably means I'm worrying about millions of pounds – and they're talking about the price of chops.'

*

Does this set-up make Liz feel like giving up working? Or just moving to another company?

'It's difficult to assess at the moment because this experience has dragged me down so far. I used to be ambitious, so I hope it's just the effect of this environment. Some of the people here seem to me to be of a very low standard. And I know I've a lot more to give. But I can't stand waiting around being bored.

'In some ways I'd quite like to work part time. I really don't want to be at work all the hours God sends us. My husband is a management consultant, and although I work quite normal hours, we don't have that much time together. I've looked around at more "female"-type jobs. But they just don't pay, do they? I glanced at some teaching advertisements, for example, and I genuinely thought they'd got the numbers the wrong way round. I couldn't work for that kind of money. Temporary secretaries get paid more!

'I am at a crossroads. I recognize that. My husband thinks I'd be better to stay in work of some kind. I'm not desperate to have children, and in fact we may not ever get round to having a family.'

Is her husband ever threatened by the MBA woman?

'Oh, no. One of the major reasons I went out with him was just that: he was never threatened by me. A lot of men I've known have gone for less intelligent women, but he's not into all that male thing. That's why I'm still married to him. He's often said that, given the opportunity, he'd love to stay at home. Ideally we'd probably both like part-time jobs. He cooks. If I'm not hungry, I don't even bother cooking in the evenings. And often it's him who does the shopping. He wouldn't dream of asking me to iron his shirts!'

What about maternity leave?

'On past experience, I'd say there's no way they'd give me back my job. You should see some of the things that happen. If I hadn't witnessed it all myself, I'd have said this was a woman being paranoid. But I've lived through these things. Our financial controller, for example, became pregnant. We're not talking about a secretary, but a woman at senior level. They pushed her out. They basically made it so difficult for her to return that in the end she took voluntary redundancy. It was appalling to watch. They kept on at her saying, "We can't keep your position open, so why not take redundancy?" She was going to fight them, and at one point she was prepared to take legal action. But things got so bad, her boss had to intervene because he feared she might have a miscarriage under the strain.

'And then, in the end, once she'd had the baby, this woman ended up acting completely to form. She took the redundancy and stayed at home. I could have died! She had totally let the side down, ruined it for other women. But I know deep down it was because they made it so difficult for her. Once she'd had the baby, she probably felt unable to keep up the battle. The men just kept on acting as though they couldn't understand why she wouldn't take the redundancy. They certainly know what game they're playing. Someone in personnel recently said to me about this woman, "Oh, she's so happy at home with the baby." But I heard from another source that she hadn't really wanted to make that decision. She just got worn down.

'You read about all the extra women now in the work-force, but I can tell you I don't see them. We used to have more women in the Treasury department — at high grades and on high salaries — than any other within the company. Now they've all gone. I remember when one woman followed her boyfriend out to Hong Kong, giving up her job. One senior man commented with an ingratiating smile, "She's following her heart".'

Hilary M.

*Trying to find a niche
in the market-place*

Similarly to Liz's experience in the previous section, Hilary came
to her MBA ably qualified, with an undergraduate degree in Maths
and several years of suitable work experience in advertising. But,
as with Liz and Sophie, Hilary has also found herself somewhat
stuck: locked in that no-win situation which just may, she feels, be
the product of quite radical, often subtle, anti-female thinking.

Not that Hilary would strike you in any way as an earnest
feminist or campaigner for female rights. A charming and palely
attractive young woman of thirty-one, newly engaged, living with
her fiancé in a beautifully decorated flat, she exudes an air of
poise and self-confidence. But when Hilary talks, she does so far
more honestly and more directly than you might have been led to
expect from her exterior persona.

Maybe it is simply that Hilary, as with the Young Guns in the
previous section, is a product of her generation. She is comfortable
being forthright and down-to-earth; quite capable of calling a spade
a garden shovel.

This was well illustrated when I asked Hilary if getting the
MBA had instantly improved her career prospects and earning
capacity?

'What makes success in our world? Earning one hundred and fifty
thousand pounds a year? It really makes me mad when people talk
that way. An MBA doesn't have to mean necessarily a good job at
double your salary. It might simply mean a growing experience;
something that could lead you into more interesting areas. Who

knows what will happen in life? I'd hate to think of being so circumscribed.

'The whole business of getting an MBA is imbued with mythology. If you're honest, you know your life hasn't really changed overnight. It's just that you've had every chance to spend two years working on projects, analysing companies without interruption and for the most part, with interesting people. There's no doubt I feel more confident about tackling things. But an MBA doesn't make you instantly brilliant. If you're good at your own PR, then I think you can build on the mythology and give yourself a certain degree of mystique. But you have to watch out, because it can mean one hell of a bluff to keep it going!

'I'm not sure even now why I went to business school, I mean I'd never heard of such places. I'd gone from university into advertising and had reached the stage where I felt that I needed to learn some more. The people who were really succeeding in advertising seemed to relate to their clients' businesses. I had friends who were taking MBAs and I just thought what the hell and applied. I put myself through all the usual hoops to get in – and then I had to find ways of financing myself there.

'I had just turned twenty-five when I started. I was turned down for a grant and had no help from my parents, so I managed to pull together a small scholarship and funded the rest on special business graduate loans.'

How sexism rears its ugly head

'You'll find the women talk about this peculiar fact of life at business school. There are loans for business graduates arranged by the banks. But, whereas the men are offered these loans without problem, the women have had lots of trouble. I came from Sheffield and my bank was still up there. I went to see one of the manager's assistants and mentioned this special loan and he said, "What's that?" He'd drawn a blank. I told him, "It's a wonderful thing. You lend me money, unsecured. I don't pay much of it back until I've graduated and then it's at a low rate for a couple of years." His comment was, "Why would we do that?!"

'Anyway, I filled in the forms and surprisingly it was turned down for approval. I was only twenty-four then, but I was in a reasonably well-paying profession. The bank had the gall to ring my mother to ask her to guarantee the loan. I'm sure if a man had applied that wouldn't have happened. They actually said to me, "It's all very fine in theory, but what if you don't get a high-paying job afterwards? What if you leave to have babies?" Looking back, I think I should have sued them. Their attitude was appalling. Finally, they agreed to lend me some of the money, but not all. The financing was a real millstone round my neck. Yet, what makes me even more mad is that they'll give an undergraduate student an overdraft without batting an eyelid.'

Hilary now works for a European mortgage company that has moved into the lucrative British market. It's a start-up company and a position that she landed by following a newspaper advertisement. But it is not her first post-MBA job.

Finding the job that fits your style

'At the end of the MBA course, I hadn't a clue what I wanted to do. I knew I shouldn't move back into advertising as I'd already wanted to make a change. But I suppose I have chopped and changed rather a lot. In my first job, I landed a plum MBA position and was rather highly paid. But I've since lost that advantage by moving around. At the end of the day, I would say I'd probably be happier running my own business. So many women seem to have this dream. There are a couple of women friends who would like to go into business with me.

'I really think women are not as good as men at the game of office politics, which can make life difficult unless you're totally committed to your job. At first, though, I decided I wanted to go into banking. And investment banking looked to be right for me. I applied for a number of positions and was offered one by an American bank in London; in international corporate finance. I knew nothing about corporate finance, mind you, other than what I had learned in theory. But you have to have an MBA for the job. In fact I'd say you have to have an MBA to breathe there.

'But I learned about the American way of doing things during my

MBA programme, because I had gone to Chicago to do an exchange term. Compared to my experience in London, the American schools are very competitive. The style of teaching at Chicago was not case-study based, so it was very academic – and frankly the teaching was very dull. Most of the other students were young, and, although I was then only twenty-six, I felt almost geriatric among them!

'The real problem in America, and I'd hate to see it going that way here, is that you virtually have to have an MBA to get a high-powered job. So they all try to get it out of the way, after their undergraduate years, while their parents are still paying. Although you are supposed to have had some work experience first, I found they were often nineteen or twenty years old – and that made for a very dull environment. In London, the graduate students were more broad-based and it certainly made for a more interesting educational experience. The other large problem was they tend to work very hard. Employers over there will ask to see their grades, and salaries are marked down accordingly. Yet, despite the differences, I seemed to do rather well, without all that effort.

'So, when I joined the American bank I could see the picture clearly. Nearly everyone had an MBA and, consequently, the fact you have the degree is almost meaningless. I might also have had no previous work experience, as far as they were concerned, because they treated me like a complete moron. It was rather like being a new student again. In fact there's some truth to that, because, for all that the letters MBA sound good, you have only emerged with a basic overall picture following two years of theoretical work. It is like starting all over.

'There I was on the photocopying machine or doing other menial tasks, with no acknowledgement of any breadth of knowledge; working for a salary that had more than doubled from its previous level. In the end I had to leave because they wanted me to move to their New York office, and I just didn't want to go at the time. So I took another job with a merchant bank. Then I had a brief spell with a corporate communications firm, but that was a very unpleasant experience. They seemed to be very excited by the idea of hiring me, but then did nothing to help me discover my place within their organization. We ended up on very bad terms. I even omit that experience from my c.v.!'

*

Then Hilary described a scene which spelt out some of the aggravation women can experience in the very male world of City finance. Summing up that type of attitude, Hilary also describes being told, maybe tongue-in-cheek, but with an element of seriousness behind the joke: "You can't even think of being a banker if your teeth are crooked." When asked why, the reply went: "Because it shows you don't come from the right family background" (i.e. the right, or moneyed, background would have given you access to dentists who'd straighten your teeth).

'For a time I moved back into the City, working for another bank, in the loans syndication department. I enjoyed that, until I was moved to the Trading Floor. That was a truly awful experience. I hated it! The place is vile. You're working without daylight, trapped at your desk for terribly long hours; the atmosphere is hot, sweaty and smoky. Why would anyone want to work in such an environment? Forget how much money you can make.

'I'd not really thought at that time of having problems through being a woman in this world. But I was working in a team with two chaps who were slightly younger than myself. They did not have MBAs and they resented my presence terribly. They went out of their way to make life difficult for me, withholding information and just being unpleasant. I'd hate to say that it was because I'm not the four-inch heel, four-inch mini-skirt type. But it just could be. One of them was quite extraordinary. He said to me, "Hilary, one thing I've never understood about you, why aren't you married?" He went on, "You can't be a whole person unless you're married." I remember thinking, "Hell, where do you start with someone like this?" I wouldn't dream of questioning him about his personal life. Basically, I suppose he disapproved of my being there.

'So eventually I left and for a while worked on my own, or worked with a fellow graduate from business school on free-lance consultancy projects. We put to use the material we had learned and marketed ourselves. For a month, I also took some time off and went to Africa. This was meant to be part of another business project, but I also knew it was an opportunity to travel that might never recur.'

Now, in her new job with a mortgage company, Hilary is working in a multi-functional role as a manager, also involved in selling and marketing.

'It's good at long last to be putting to use my MBA skills. I was interested in being in on the ground floor of a start-up company, because you learn so much more that way.'

Would you hire an MBA, I asked her, bearing in mind she talked of setting up her own business?

'Oh, yes. I find it easy to work with other MBAs. I know it means they will view the big picture. I trust their way of thinking.'

But does she feel that MBAs are accepted well enough in this country?

Hilary laughed. 'When I was in advertising and would tell people I had a degree in Maths, they would always say something like, "Oh, I failed maths O level six times," as though they were in the right and therefore I must be in the wrong. Then, when I went to business school and would say, I was doing an MBA, people would say, "I nearly went too, but I decided it was a waste of my time." How very nice, you then think to yourself. But maybe people are threatened, I don't know what the answer is. Among my old friends, quite a few did tell me they thought it was rather an odd thing to be doing – going to business school. But then most of my friends are either professionals, who are earning well, or they're artists who live on nothing. At one stage, I would say I must have been earning more than any man I might have gone out with, but not now.

'My mother never worked. She was rather concerned that I was giving up a good job and going into all that debt. My stepfather was quite positive about it all, though. I have two younger sisters who both work in the City. My fiancé? Well, he has an MBA too. But he went on his course a year after me, and it had nothing to do with me. We hadn't met then. He's in consultancy now, but he's just become a local councillor and may well decide to go into politics. In which case, I suppose I'll have to get a good job to support him!

'We'll get married some time – don't ask me when – he's far too busy right now. I suppose we'll have children one day, but I don't see how either of us would have the time or the space for a family. He can hardly fit me into his diary as it is! He works hard in his job and then is out most evenings on Council work. Still, it makes him quite an interesting person. When he's awake! If I were the type who'd expect a man around every evening, then he would have been a very bad choice. But I'm terribly independent – which is one reason why I worry about children. I can't imagine being dependent. I'll always have to work at something.'

Janet A.

Time to strike out on your own?

Janet's work life is based from home. There's an office in the upstairs back room. But we met in her pleasant flower-filled living-room, an experience which made us both feel somewhat guilty as though we were ladies of yesteryear, able to spend their time at leisure. But married, and thinking seriously about having children, setting up her own business is all wrapped up for Janet in attempts to blend her work life and family life together to become part of a whole. Indeed, her feelings mirror those of so many women.

Janet's new business is that of a property developer. Now in her mid-thirties, her previous career has followed quite a typically female chequered path. She started out as an undergraduate with a degree in Psychology; moved from there to a job in publishing, on the production side; and on from that to take the MBA at a northern business school. She emerged with her MBA eight years ago and began a new career in banking. Over the years she worked for two American banks based in London. And then she decided enough was enough. Janet was not, in her soul, a banker. Corporate working practices were just too inflexible. And what about all those other dreams of hers?

Janet is a warm personality, who I would imagine is also a very gregarious person. At first meeting she does not let it be known that a tough and determined heart beats firmly within.

'I'd been brought up in Hong Kong and only came back to England when I was eighteen to go to university. My first job was in publishing in charge of the production of the book jackets. And then I moved into the marketing department. But I felt very lost in that company, never progressing far. It was full of young graduates, all jostling for positions! So I went to business school. Though when I first started on the programme, I remember thinking, "What the hell am I going back to university for?", I discovered that I absolutely adored that time. There were only sixty on the course and, of them, just six or seven of us were women. But it was a really great group of people. We worked as a team a lot, on case studies. And I went to New York in my second year on an exchange programme.

'When I left university the first time around, I hadn't taken finding a career seriously. But now, at business school, I fitted much more into the system and took job hunting very seriously. I decided to aim for banking and really blitzed the banks in London. I received a number of offers, but in the end chose a North American bank as I felt they would know better how to treat a woman, and certainly a woman MBA. But, there my optimistic thoughts ended!'

Does a woman MBA fit into banking?

To be blunt, says Janet, it didn't really work out at all.

'I joined at the same time as another guy from my class, plus a couple of others from a London business school. The London MBAs were started on higher salaries, we knew that. But then I found out I was on a lower salary than the guy. And he was younger than me. At least the salary levels were laid down by our grades, so I was able to put my rate of pay right. But I must say it made me feel very suspicious of them. Would I always have to be on my toes? Basically, the answer to that was yes. I never trusted them again.

'Even as an MBA, you go in as a trainee to learn banking from the ground level, though I was aiming towards becoming a marketing manager. You do have to learn the job right through. But I began to feel very chagrined because I never quite lost that tag of "trainee". It's as though you're always being treated as that "nice little girl". Banks are full of women, but at very low levels. You can see the change by working there: at the bottom levels, it is all women. As you go up the ranks, there are more men. And at the top it's all men. Women work in the "processing" stage, basically they're the equivalent to a computer.

'My biggest problem, however, was with senior men or men at my own level who were not MBAs. Particularly so with the English men working there, who tended not even to have a university degree. They'd worked their way up for twenty years and resented all of us MBAs, and most especially me for being a woman. Nothing was ever downright unpleasant, but there was always the feeling of not being taken seriously. They'd crack jokes and I was supposed to laugh along. It got quite boring.

'In the end, I left because shortly after I was married – and of course they all knew that was happening – I was offered a job in their Chicago office. They expected me to move out there the following week. I was absolutely dumbstruck. The position was not even within my area. I refused the move and then that refusal was used against me, when I complained about not being further advanced, that I had "turned down this wonderful job". But I knew they would never expect a man with a family to move out in a week. In the end, I resigned and I soon found a job with another American bank which, in terms of equality, treated me much better. There were more women in senior positions and a lot of MBAs working there. It was just a different culture.

'Finally, with this new bank I was able to shed the overhanging image of "trainee". I had been able to start afresh and project a different image. I'd given that quite a lot of thought and had deliberately changed the way I dressed. This time I was determined to go in at a certain level, with a certain image. I had always worn suits to work, but now I felt that I was constraining my personality with the conventional little grey suits. I decided to dress more how I felt; that I'd wear fuschia pink or bright green if I wanted to. To that end, I moved more upmarket, buying designer styles, rather than four buttons and a little collar. I felt that now I had enough self-confidence to dress as me.

'I stayed there for eighteen months, but although I quite enjoyed my new role, my heart was just not in it. I could play the game, but deep down I wanted to start up on my own. Now that I was married, it seemed to be more of a question: "How am I going to spend the rest of my life?" I felt that I needed to be more in control of my time. So that was when I decided to move into property development and, as redundancies were being made at the bank, I worked on them to make me redundant when they didn't really want to. There was a fine line between getting the redundancy and resigning. But in the end they let me go – and I was able to use that money to invest in my own business.'

The one big grudge Janet still bears towards the banking community, and its attitudes towards women, are the questions she was unfailingly asked at interviews about her intentions *vis-à-vis* marriage and children.

'I always answered that I would continue with my career were I to begin a family. My attitude on that one is quite simply: you should lie through your teeth. You have to take a party line and stick to it. Why should you tell them anything? Until it really becomes an issue, don't put your cards on the table. You can react and become uptight, or you can push it out of the way without making a big issue of it. But, whatever, it is they who are putting you in a difficult situation. What used to aggravate me so much was that they were asking me to make a value judgement for what I might do, about certain events, in five years' time. They wouldn't ask a man at an interview, "Are you intending to leave this job in two years' time to move on to a better one?" Yet whatever the reasons men or women have for leaving, the facts remain the same.

'To be honest, while I was working for banks I did feel I would continue even if I had a child. How I would really have reacted I don't know. One of the reasons that I have set up on my own is with a view to starting a family. I had gone beyond wanting to work within the corporate structure. It seemed such a waste of people's time and energy, having to be there from nine to five (and more). I'd watch people just idling time away talking to each other. And it seemed to me such a bad way to run a business. There was no flexibility in hours, and it was obvious there'd be no flexibility if I did have a child. I'd seen a lot of women who had children staggering into work, looking like death, trying to handle it all.

'Even so, once I'd left and set up on my own I did feel guilty, as though I'd let the side down. I really felt that I was letting down women's struggle for advancement within large corporations.'

Setting up on her own
as a property developer

Why did she choose property developing of all businesses? Why not something more traditionally feminine? Was this a way of putting her MBA to full use?

'My father was an architect and I've always been interested in property. It was something my husband and I felt we would enjoy working on together, though he's not come into the business with me yet. That would be too dangerous. He works as a consultant. Of course, we have picked what has proven to be a difficult time in the property market.

'When we embarked on the business, property was booming. Then it quickly slid into a recession. It is an incredibly capital-intensive area, which takes all your nerve to withstand the strain of waiting! I used the redundancy money as my basic income on which I lived for the first year. I had to borrow a lot of money to get the business going. We bought a house to renovate, with the intention of selling it off as flats. But our money was tied up for a very long time before we began to get an injection of profit. For example, the first house was finished in the September, and we did not sell the first flat until the March and another in April. That meant we went eight months of paying out interest without making a sale. It was pretty scary.

'But I was able to take that as a salutary lesson on how best to proceed. You must make sure you have enough money to see you through at least eight months of not selling.

'Am I using my MBA fully? Absolutely, in the sense that I don't think I ever really made use of it as a banker. It is difficult to describe just what an MBA does do for you. Psychologically, it builds you up in self-esteem and hence self-presentation. You come out from the course with an overview – from which you're supposed to rocket into a top job. But it's not really like that. You tend to go, as I did, to a big corporation as a little cog; usually within a very narrow area, so there is no way you can use the MBA skills. At least when you're running your own business, you have to look at every aspect of the work. And I really craved more ground-level involvement.

'As a banker, I felt very much on the outside of someone else's business. Bankers don't produce anything. And as a cog in the machine you have no input. If businesses want money, they'll come to you for a loan. I've always had a drive in me which is not very typically female: to show myself that I can do something. I used to think that if most women didn't get MBAs, then I wanted one!'

How do the men she mixes with treat the MBA woman?

'If you're talking about the builders, just the fact I'm a woman is bad enough! Working with non-professional men is another whole ball game. I'll certainly grow up in a business sense, if I can learn to handle them! Some of them hate having me around, they think I'm wasting their time. I don't know if they all realize yet that it's my business. They probably assume I'm the boss's wife sticking her nose in.'

Did she find it easier turning to the banks for loans on her new business, coming to them as a former banker herself?

'I don't know if it's an advantage or not,' she laughed. 'Maybe I anticipate too much and I probably give them far more information than they actually need to know. But I've had no personal problems regarding men and my MBA. Though that could be because my husband is very self-confident and certainly doesn't seem to find me threatening! Mind you, I'm not a very threatening person. My choice of man had to be someone who could cope with me as I am. I'd already had time to establish my personality and character by then. At one stage, I was earning more than him and I think he was relieved when he got a rise and moved on ahead of me again. But it wasn't a big problem.

'Looking back, if I recall, I did feel rather odd after business school, before I met my husband, when I would have to tell men I met at parties what I did. Very few could cope with the information. It did seem to work as a direct turn off!'

The next two stories share certain elements in common with their predecessors in this section. But they also stand quite alone. Alison and Bridget are both older in years (we're not talking really old here, merely about women who merit the term 'wise'). Both would say of themselves that they came up the hard way through the School of Hard Knocks.

Neither Alison nor Bridget sailed through school and first degrees with an inbuilt air of her self-worth. Neither found her path to the MBA degree opening easily. But they are both survivors and delightful survivors at that. Both women studied (in fact Bridget is at present in the middle of her MBA programme) part time, while continuing to work and support herself.

Alison has finally set up in business on her own as a management consultant to the hotel and catering industry. Bridget most likely will stay on with the same company that now employs her. Both talked about problems they have faced with the men in their lives. Men with whom they live and who have not always treated these women's attempts at self-betterment with the type of support and loving admiration any woman might hope to receive.

Why is it I feel both Alison and Bridget have something special to say? Two women who have not yet scrambled out from the scrum with an armful of glittering prizes? Why is it, I wondered while writing, that I chose to finish the book with their stories – in my own way emphasizing their comparative lack of success? I think it is because their message is humble, honest and most likely universal.

The message reads that, even without the glimmering lights of a life right at the top, there is much to be said for persevering, for trying our best, and just getting on with life.

Alison C.

You don't have to hang too much on those letters: MBA

I was introduced to Alison through a roundabout route. Describing my on-going book project to one of those women who seems to succeed in business life without really trying; self-educated, a prime doer, I was hurt to see her mystified look at my notion of talking to women MBAs. Why would anyone be interested in them? came the question. But she knew Alison, who had put herself through the MBA course. Alison's got a new baby, she confided. She's set up in business from home. 'I think she's doing OK.' Already I sensed a certain tension in Alison's tale.

Her home-based office is in the suburbs of one of our large southern cities and, being a hopeless map-reader I found myself going round and round the roundabouts, *en route*. Alison had begun to worry at my late arrival, because she had set aside time to talk in her far-too-busy day, and feared that the baby would soon be coming home from the child-minder's, thereby neatly finishing off our chance to talk.

Alison's early story mirrors that of many women. She began as a schoolgirl with a low self-image and with no one offering her sound career advice (or if they were she refused to listen). Her main feeling was that she was bored and wanted some fun. Later years have been influenced by a variety of different jobs, yen to travel, and by the different men in her life.

*

The schoolgirl who couldn't wait to get out

'I suppose my education was pretty standard: an all-girls' school, the child of professional parents. I got my O and A levels, but had no desire or intention of going on to university. My mother was quite Women's Lib for her time and really pushed for me to go to university, but I refused. I just felt I was not academic enough and I seemed to lack the confidence. At our school, either you had three or four A levels and were going on to Oxbridge, or you left at sixteen. I was somewhere in the middle. Most of the girls I knew were leaving to go to secretarial college. But I'd taken my A levels at seventeen and I wanted out, to go somewhere with not too much hard work. I wanted to be free and have some fun!

'But I was also very practical and as well as Chemistry and Biology, I'd taken Domestic Science. Somehow I've always been interested in catering. Another of my great influences was my grandfather, who was an entrepreneur. He would bring me from the North down to London on business trips and I was fascinated. But I wouldn't have had a clue how one got into business or management. I really felt my only way forward was to go into catering.

'So I went to the poly, where I could begin at seventeen and where they offered a vocational catering course. It was an HND course which embarrassed my mother no end. But I was doing it with a view to one day running my own catering business or acting as a consultant.

'Following my time at the poly, I went off travelling to Australia, America and Canada for a few years, working in different places. Ostensibly I was studying fast food and catering abroad. While I was in Australia, it dawned on me I would need some more education so when I came back I had that in mind. I began working for some catering facilities, helping them with recruitment and training staff. They suggested I should apply to the Hotel and Catering Training Board, and indeed it was through them that I was sponsored to study for the diploma in management studies. Eventually I was promoted to a training development organizer, studying graduate recruitment and selection.

'So, by default, I had begun to do well in my career. I was married for the first time by then, and life was looking up. As part of my research studies, I returned to the poly where I had been a

226

student, and they asked me to apply for the position as assistant lecturer in management studies, related to hotel and catering. And there began a new branch of my career! I became a lecturer. I was just over thirty by then, but soon realized I wasn't very happy as a junior lecturer. I'd been used to working very hard and I was bored by the rather easy hours and long holidays. I just wasn't being stretched.

'Once again I'd reached that point of thinking I needed more formal education. Still, I didn't have a pure degree, and certainly not a Masters or a PhD. I was getting very frustrated. I began to look around at the business schools and was accepted on a pilot course for a three-year part-time MBA programme that was just starting up. It was a cheap way of doing the course, but caused quite a bit of concern at the poly among my fellow lecturers who were basically annoyed at having to cover for me on my day release. The timetable had to be planned around me and, after all, it wasn't doing them any benefit – only me.

'But I really enjoyed doing the course, and by now I knew I wanted out of lecturing, to get back into industry. The MBA would be my ticket out. It was a very tough time, though. There I was in my early thirties, taking on all this extra work, and my marriage was breaking up around me. We'd been having a lot of problems, but the pressures of studying made it worse. In many ways I think it's the wives, husbands and children of the MBA students who really deserve the praise. There's such a lot of reading to do. I've never been able to sit down and read a novel since doing the course. You become very task-oriented and learn to skip read. If anything it trains your mind to over-target your time. You probably become a very unpleasant person!

'There were only about three other women on the course. They mostly had brought themselves along and were great. One had applied because her husband had wanted to do the MBA and he had recently died. In a way she was doing it for him. The men were all sponsored by their companies or organizations. They tended to be in their forties, middle management types, and I know they found it even harder maybe than I did. I know that a lot of the men found coping with essay writing very hard. They were not used to passing exams based on essay writing – which someone like me found easy. But we developed a lot of comradeship from sticking it out together and many of us still stay in touch.

'I felt good that I finished the course and achieved the qualification. It was all done through my own merit and drive and it gave me back a sense of control . . . that I could do it. Looking back though, I think my mother might have been right. I should have done a proper degree after school. Maybe I would have moved on further by now, and at an earlier age. Graduates today don't realize how lucky they are. They can move straight into a well-paying, high-flying career straight from university. If you're a woman between thirty and forty now, however, you'll probably have worked harder to get where you are.'

Was finding a job hard after the MBA?

'I'd already decided I would go into my own consultancy work. But that decision might have been influenced by the fact that employers look at my c.v. and see me as someone who is unreliable or maybe flippant. I've moved around a lot. I've done too many different things. What they don't see is that it is my drive and ambition that has pushed me on. I might have preferred to do a full-time MBA, but there was no way I could afford to take two years out to be a student at that stage of my life.

'But anyway with my marriage over, I fancied getting out of London and away from England for a time. I'd gone to the Mediterranean to give a talk to women in management in the hotel industry. While there I'd had a look around and made some contacts. So I decided to target work there. It was time for me to get a bit of sunshine! And, secretly, I had met my future husband there and wanted to know if anything might come of things between us. I stayed there a year and a half, working hard and having a lovely time. One of my clients, however, was linked to a big hotel chain back here and eventually I was asked to come back and work for them. I was newly married, and my husband had been working in the police force out there. He was quite happy about the idea of coming to England and getting himself educated, too.

'So, back we came, and I ended up earning not very good money, but bearing a fancy title with the large hotel chain; working on their strategic management development. That involved a lot of exciting work because, as an outsider, I was able to take a good caustic view. None of their staff had any management qualifications, so I was the most advanced.

'Things might have continued well, but then I became pregnant! And I just found that the workload, often including weekends, was going to be too much. I made the decision to leave and to set up in business on my own. My husband is not working, as currently he's studying for his management diploma on day release. I'm bearing the full responsibility for running our home, the child-minder and our personal lives. It's quite a load, I can tell you. There are times I feel guilty, knowing what it was like when I was studying because I just cannot give him the support he probably needs. But I can't. There's nothing left to give. I can't really be stretched any further.'

Work and motherhood

At that point Alison's husband brought the baby back from the child-minder's. Seeing we were still hot into our discussion, he offered to take their little boy out for a walk, to the shops, to keep him away from the house and his mother for another half-hour. Her obvious stress at the situation made me feel strangely guilty because on this occasion, as my own children were away for a week on holiday, I felt like a single woman with no cares or responsibilities on my mind. I put that feeling across to Alison.

'Yes, I find it unbelievably tough. I just don't have any time for me. Sometimes I compare myself with other women consultants who have husbands who support them. They can work a three-day week, because they have nothing else to do. My little boy goes to the child-minder's from eight until six-thirty, which I know are very long hours, but I need that time for my work. It's stressful for him and for me. But I'm away a lot and my husband has to be free to go to his classes.

'The child-minder costs me six hundred pounds a month – that's seven thousand a year I have to consider making before we can begin to live. I'd love to have a nanny, but as she would have to live out such people are hard to find in this rather affluent area – so that would cost me even more. If I applied for a job, no employer would be thinking I'd have to earn all that simply to be able to get to work. They assume you'll have a partner to support you.

'The type of work I do, much of my time is spent on the client's worksite. Sometimes I'm literally living out of a suitcase, just like a sales rep. And I don't have an understanding wife at home. When I get back, my husband's had enough and he tends to go out. I'm earning well, but I have to pay for anything I can to be done: a weekly cleaner, a painter, a decorator. Anything that will buy me time. Otherwise I'd go totally insane!

'Recently, a friend asked me to meet her – she said let's go out together. And I explained that it would have to be in the lunchhour. She couldn't understand why I wouldn't meet in the evening. I had to say it was because of the baby. "Why not have your husband look after him?" she said. Do you know, it had never even entered my head to ask him. He does so much when I'm away, has to spend his evenings here at home with the baby, that I wouldn't dream of asking him that favour when I am at home.

'This year, since going into business on my own, I've made three times as much money as ever before. And what have I learned? At the end of the day, it's not a question of how much money you make. It's a question of feeling good about yourself, that you're leading your life how you would like to.'

I asked Alison then whether she resented having to support her husband while he is studying. Some extra income might conceivably help them pay for a nanny? Alison shrugged, looking rather tired and depressed about things.

'We have our arguments. But he's a Mediterranean and he expects his wife to do certain things for him. He'll come in from his day out and I'll get the food ready, while he watches television or reads the paper. I'm the one who organizes the house, cares for the baby, arranges the childcare, and I make the money too. I bought this house and arranged to have it redecorated. To be honest, I feel like a single parent. But that's the way it is.

'It's all very well for men to talk about how nice it would be to have a wife who earned a lot. But when they're back home, facing the reality, I think many a man would probably find it difficult to cope with – particularly if he were a traditionalist used to being looked after by a wife.'

Alison, the businesswoman

Alison began talking about her work life in the time we had left. Suddenly her mood perked up. The rather unpleasant emotions raked up by discussing her complicated marriage, and complex motherhood arrangements, were pushed out of the way. Now she could talk about something in which she reflected a lot of self-confidence. Now Alison cheered up, became funny and relaxed. I'm sure a lot more women than like to admit it are actually far happier when dealing with work issues than they are dealing with family or domestic problems. But then, is there any reason why they should not be?

'Yes, I'm doing rather well running my own consultancy business – for the hotel trade, but also within the fields of medicine and pharmaceuticals, financial services and telecommunications. At long last; it's as though the worm has turned. My experience is now being seen as a valuable commodity. Not just my paper qualifications, but my real experience. My father's advice was to make myself into a "marketable commodity" and now I realize, instead of being seen as flippant, I am in fact very highly skilled.

'The MBA is hardly ever mentioned, not even as letters after my name. I might just make an indirect mention of it to a client. In the catering industry, the qualification is hardly recognized any way. So it certainly has made no difference to the type of earnings I receive. Maybe its long-term influence has really been in how I view myself.

'The one thing I know I have to offer is that I speak the same language my clients speak. I may now have an academic background, but I don't confuse them with jargon. Maybe, too, at long last the fact I'm a woman is now working to advantage. They don't see me as a threat. Very often the large management consultancy firms have hired young guys, the Yuppies, with virtually no work experience. The men I have to deal with bristle just to see these young whizz-kids turning up in their BMWs. And the work they failed at is passed on to me! So I'm not out to change that system by any means.

'Going in as a free-lance consultant, or outsider, my unique difference is the training and experience I have previously had within the industry. So, for example, I never offer just straight management courses. I'd rather integrate courses with training and then stay around to see the results. I am very able to help people sort out the wood from the trees.

'I'll organize everything for them: arrange venues, co-ordinate meetings, and feedback information to the clients. I'll analyse the data, set up workshops to discuss the analysis and really make them face up to the feedback. Then together we develop a personal action plan so that, along with their staff, they are working as an efficient team. I make it my business to be around, to absorb everything that is going on.

'Very often, I find that other consultancies will use their senior account managers to go in for the initial discussions and then they pass the job down to someone else. Whereas, if I see a client, they know they will be working with me. Even if I bring in others along the way, they will always have me as their main point of contact. I know this is why some companies frankly prefer to work with free-lancers.

'In order for me to survive, I have to deliver quality. I have gained good experience from the service industry. You work long hours, are not always paid too well, and you have to deliver quality . . . or the customer will move on. I know I am better than other consultants, because I'm so often called in to pick up the pieces of someone else's mess!'

So then we came to the vexed question for self-employed women, or those running businesses. Does Alison feel she is charging enough? Suddenly Alison's face brightens.

'No! I'm sure I undersell myself. I know other consultants might charge almost three times as much per day as I do. Now why aren't I so expensive? I don't think I feel inadequate, but I am aware that I have not been through the high-flying graduate schemes with their glossy c.v.s. And I'm just not capable to talking myself up in that way. When I go in to see a company, I know I'm delivering goods that are far better than they'll receive elsewhere.'

*

Does Alison, I pushed the point, have the feeling that if she asks for more they'll then see her as greedy, or that she will have outpriced herself? It is, after all, typically female to think that if you are average or medium priced then you will be acceptable. But, if you ask any more they'll shake their heads?

'The core, to my mind, is my need for them to like me. Whereas a guy in my business might go in for the hard sell, I build up a friendship, a lasting relationship, with my clients. That way I do benefit by receiving a lot of repeat business. Or I'm brought in to rescue them from other consultants. In the end, I don't find that money is the only reward.'

So is she working on putting her rates up? Without a moment's hesitation, she flashed back:

'Yes! I'm trying very hard. My aim now is to earn enough money so I can afford a nanny for three days a week, to do quality work, but to get by without feeling I have to be working every minute of the day. I would actually like to spend some more time with my little boy. I just have to summon up the courage to change my prices!'

Bridget B.

The businesswoman who decided to go back to school

I've saved Bridget until last because she is something of a treat. She is like the wise woman of the group. Now turned forty-five, married young with a son who is already twenty-three years old, Bridget has never stopped working. Not only does Bridget work, but she has also struggled her way up the ladder, almost solely on her own drive and determination. No privileged background, no high-flying career track have helped her along; merely pure guts and will-power to fuel her steamroller activities. And now, when other women might take their success for granted, Bridget is embarking on an MBA, studying part time in the evenings while continuing to hold down her well-paid and influential job. And she still has time for her friends; acts as 'mother' to some of the younger ones on the course; and continues her heavy involvement with one of the women's professional networks.

To my surprise, Bridget lives just around the corner from me. So I was able to take a stroll early one evening to meet her at her flat. Looking back, I hadn't taken into account how generous it was of her to spare me the time. She had just finished studying for her first-year exams, as well as working full time, and she squeezed me in too! Bridget is one of those people who make a truth out of the oft-quoted axiom, 'If you want something done, ask a busy person.'

Her flat was impeccably furnished and spotlessly clean, one of those places where you instinctively feel like taking off your shoes in case you might soil the carpet. But the living-room also bore the relaxed symbols of daily domestic life: an ironing board was still up and one of the chairs was strewn with heavy text books from her academic duties.

The very first obvious question was why Bridget bothered to get an MBA, when her experience must have taught her pretty much all there is to know about business life. When it comes down to it, once you have the odd grey hair to your head, does it really matter that you pile up the letters after your name?

Having no previous university degree behind her, suddenly education in its own right had become important. Bridget had grown to believe in the significance of the MBA.

'I do think it has become beneficial now to gain the degree. It teaches you a way of thinking, directs you along certain lines. It will never train you to be an entrepreneur, rather the opposite. But it will teach you a logical approach to a business-based problem which is quite usable in the workplace.'

But that is Bridget at her serious best, in her business-like mode. Let's switch tracks to discover the real person who is far more interesting. Being tiny, slender, and rather neat by nature, Bridget was able to curl up in the chair; after a while, she relaxed and began to talk as herself – woman to woman – about her life and experiences.

The chequered career

'I had a lot of ill health as a child, which meant I did not do very well at school. I couldn't take A levels and so university was out. I started my working life in a bank at about sixteen or seventeen, but I didn't like that very much even though I progressed rapidly. Then I left and went through a series of jobs, ending up in administration and credit management. At that point, I became interested in computers and took some exams.

'But I was married at twenty, and had my baby at the age of twenty-two. In those days, the climate wasn't right for women to keep on working, so I stayed home for a few years with my little boy, except that then I got divorced and, with a young child to support,

I went back to work. I began my new working life as a PA to an accountant and moved on to take over their office management. I was doing all right, earning quite well, when I moved into a more senior position with an engineering company. With them, my job was more involved in the computers, and basically I was working as a systems analyst.

'Then I moved on to a fashion company, running their group administration. For five years, I ran that company very successfully. By now I had a secretary and people working for me. I was even offered a board appointment on one of their loss-making companies, which I was able to turn around to be profitable in under a year. But I was beginning to feel fed up. I was working weekends, running the whole show: including doing their marketing and advertising; and it was all becoming a terrible strain. I still didn't even have an A level to my name. So, I decided to take a nine-month break to give my future career a good thinking through.

'However, eventually I found another job with the company for whom I am still working. Originally I went to work for them for six months. It's an international group that operates divisions in real-estate and shipping; a real multi-million dollar operation. But still I'm not qualified, though my position is now as group auditor for Europe. I'm obviously not really an auditor but rather a trouble-shooter, and an in-house management consultant.

'Still feeling the lack of anything by which I could prove my intelligence, coupled with getting older, I began sending off to universities for brochures. I can't say I'm awed by people with degrees or paper qualifications, because I'm not the type to be awed by anything, but I noticed that my initial reaction towards them was different to my reaction to other people. Maybe because this company has American connections, it encourages its employees to pursue education even if you're older.

'I had heard about the MBA degree, so I approached one of the business schools. At first, it did seem as though I just wouldn't fit in, without having any A levels. They expect you to take that GMAT test which I just may not have been ready to do. But then I discovered the part-time MBA evening course at a local polytechnic. It's not as prestigious a programme as some of the big name business schools, but at my age I felt that didn't matter. The thought of waiting until I was ready to take the GMAT was offputting, as I didn't know how long my motivation would hold out. I might have found something else to fill my time.

'The polytechnic advisors felt that my years of business experience would be just as great a contribution. And they thought I must be intelligent to have achieved all that I have done in life. This is a three-year course, and I also felt that that would give me time to get up to standard on some of the courses. And in fact, even without an undergraduate degree, I've found that I fit in as many of the other students have arts degrees and we're basically all starting from the same point. I've just finished my first-year exams, and I think I've done all right on most of the papers.'

What does the MBA course mean to Bridget?

'My primary motivation is not to get an MBA just because it will be so useful to me in my career, but more as a personal achievement for me. I needed to do it, to prove something to myself. Although, now I've embarked on the course, I think it will actually be more useful than I'd imagined. I am old for the course, but not the oldest by any means! I'm forty-five now which means I'll be forty-seven when I finish. The average age on our course in about thirty-three. There's a group of twenty-six to thirty-five year olds, who form the bulk of the class, a couple in their late thirties, and one man who is probably about forty-eight.

'There are a couple of other women around my age. One is a lecturer at the poly, who is very bright academically, but who has no business experience. The other is also a teacher. There are quite a few teachers on the course; they want to move out of the classroom into the management of education. I find they can learn the academic material, but they're not very practical about what goes on in the real world.

'But I mix well with the young ones. The group I sit with is mostly of men and women in their late twenties, early thirties, and they treat me as an equal. I find it opens my mind, and I can see better now how young people think. We study a lot together, visit each other's homes, eat spaghetti and drink cheap red wine together. It's a great leveller. The older men in our class have more trouble than the older women at mixing in. But I, for example, was elected their first-year student representative, which made me very proud.'

Does age really have an effect on your ability to study?

'There are times I suspect it does. Tests were conducted to see how intelligence works. Young people were found to use one particular type of intelligence which is geared to their metabolism, because they need to be learning new material. Older people, by comparison, tend to rely on proven fact, experience and they relate new information to knowledge previously acquired. Basically, at my age, you cannot do things at such speed. And you know you just cannot do everything. I used to be able to go out dancing, drink till three in the morning and go to work the next day. I wouldn't try that now.

'Also, I've noticed that I just don't have the ability to go on accumulating new information which they can do. It's as though you've got a lot stuffed in up there already, and there's no more room! It's certainly not an open cupboard into which you can shove more material. Against that, there is probably a higher degree of motivation when you're older. You're less likely to get side-tracked.'

How does the part-time degree work?

'My company has sponsored me to do the course, which means they pay the fees and the books, and know not to expect too much of me. They're not insisting that I pass, for example. The sponsorship is of benefit to them because I'm unlikely to leave them while in the middle of the course, am I? The studying is done at night school, two evenings a week from six-thirty to nine-thirty. We cover three subjects each time, in a series of lectures.

'On those evenings, I leave work around four-thirty, dash back home to change into my jeans. Then one day a week, I have off for study leave. On that day, I might go to the library, or have some extra maths coaching, but there is also more studying time to be found then and in the evenings too. I have to confess that like most of my fellow students, I only truly got into the regime the month before the exams. Before that, I tended to be writing up the essays the evening before classes.

'Quite often on my study-leave day, I catch up with housework. As I see it, I have a certain amount of time available to me in life. And there's a finite number of things to be done. When I fit them in is up to me. I have a full-time job. I also run a home. And I'm working for a degree.

'My son, who is now in banking himself, lives at home. Both he and Jim, my partner (I don't know why we never got married, we just didn't), expect certain things to be done by me, just because I've always done them, which is an added burden.'

Previously in our conversation, Bridget had used the term 'time management', such a popular word among women – who know there is so much to juggle with in the day – so now we talked about how she really works out her time and all those various commitments.

'In my first two terms, I found one of the biggest problems was that after the evening lectures, I was still in overdrive and I just couldn't sleep easily. Then, of course, I had problems working hard the next day at the office. By the third term, however, I was beginning to plan ahead, to make better use of my time. Now I read in the lunchtimes, I take in a book and find that by devoting forty minutes a day to reading I can get through quite a lot. Weekends I leave for project work.

'A typical week for me would be doing some preparatory reading in the lunchtime; finishing off course work the night before lectures; then two evenings a week at night school. Friday night I give myself off, and weekends I'll use to catch up on other work. There's also a great deal of stress and worry involved, that I'm not doing as much as I should be. Basically, the course intrudes on your everyday life. There's no time over just to have a bath and wash your hair!

'I tend to find that I come home from work, make dinner and then have to find three hours in the evening in which to do some work. When your stress levels are high, and you're having to crank yourself to work for a couple of hours around nine, then by midnight you can begin to feel good, and the whole pattern is restarting. You've just got back into your work, so now you won't sleep and it'll be hard to function the next day. So far I've been able to keep up my end at work. I do realize that I'm in a very well-paid position. So of course I worry about risking what I have now, for what I might have one day after the course.

'The big question you have to work out is this: where are your priorities workwise, domestically, emotionally and your need to fulfil yourself?

'I find I'm self-evaluating all the time. Will the MBA mean so much to me at the end of the course? I know it will have meant a lot in terms of personal achievement. But will it bring me a better job or more money? By forty-seven I might be thinking, "Well, I've had high-powered jobs before and I know that they demand incredible levels of commitment and do I want that again?" One of my girlfriends is now working as MD of a huge concern and she is very well paid. But the work load and the demands are stressing her considerably.

'I'm at an age when I would really consider what it is I want to do. The MBA should help, but arguably I could have achieved that or more by staying where I was and just negotiating better terms! Going for the educational qualification will in fact slow me down for three years. Will I ultimately give more impetus to my future career by having done the MBA or not? It's very difficult to know. It'll depend on how motivated and how fit I am when I reach the end. Come and see me in two years' time and we'll see how I do!'

Which side of your life tends to lose out?

'Your social life. You can't squash too much into life. My pint pot was pretty full to begin with. Some things have to give. I have a lot of female friends and I've had to give up seeing them. Jim got pretty fed up this summer, because we keep a yacht down on the south coast, and I just couldn't find the time to go there with him. Dinner parties are a thing of the past.

'Interestingly enough, college becomes a clear substitute for your social life. College itself is a form of escapism. I go along wearing jeans, carrying my books under my arm. It makes me feel young again. I've become so used to being treated as an executive at work, it's nice to be treated just like one of the girls.

'Because we work together in teams, you get used to being supportive of each other. I get loads of phone calls at home from fellow students. We'll chat and talk about our problems, and say to each other, "If I ever see another book I'll scream!" Socially, therefore, it distances you from your other friends. I've had trouble talking to people who are not studying, because everything else seems boring and irrelevant to me now. You try to have a conversation with friends and they'll say, "How's night school?" But if I try and tell them, they're not interested. That glazed look comes over their eyes, which basically means it was only a polite enquiry, and "please don't bother"! Whereas with your peer group, you all want to talk about the experience. In short, it takes over!'

Did her close friends think she was mad?

'No, not really. Some have told me they wouldn't want to do all the work, or that they couldn't. But others have been fascinated and one friend will go on to do some kind of business degree. Those of us involved do tend to be persuasive. We know it's good for you. It wakes you up, makes the brain move faster. And you learn that the more you do, the more is possible.'

So is Bridget really enjoying the course, or in her secret heart does she feel the strain is not worth it?

'Hand on heart, I'd say it's a mixture of both. Even if I don't pursue it to the end, I can honestly say it will have been a worthwhile experience. Already it has filled a huge gap for me: given me exposure to studying at this university level. So at least I know what people mean when they talk of university life!'

'But of course it's a strain. It's bound to be, isn't it? As you get older your fear of failure becomes greater, because you have more to protect, like your reputation. What I've found difficult to come to terms with is this: as you progress up the work ladder you become used to thinking you're rather clever. And you certainly don't appreciate having it demonstrated that you're not half as bright as you thought you were! You're surrounded by people well your junior who are picking things up twice as fast as you are. So there's a lot to come to terms with in yourself. You're forced into a realization of your strengths and weaknesses. At least you're unlikely to be so dismissive of others in the future.'

The MBA and the men in her life

Bridget is pretty, and as I've mentioned previously, tiny, petite, almost bird-like. Simply because of her size and looks, she would impress men as a likeable and charming woman, someone they would like to have around. But she is also a formidable force, with a strong sense of herself and of her personal achievements. Has this mixture of qualities produced problems in her life?

To some degree, she admits it has because she is a mix of the traditional, old-fashioned type of woman, and of the new version hot off today's presses.

'My business success hasn't put Jim off, because he's used to working with women in high-powered positions. In itself, that can be mildly irritating when I feel like being cherished and looked after. But there have been some problems over my studying. I remember him once saying, "Don't you think you're getting a mite obsessive about all this?" And that was because I had been featuring college work as the prime importance in my life. Particularly close to exam time, I was probably unbearable to live with. The exams are so important to me, but they're almost meaningless to anyone else. Other people will say to me, "Congrats", or "Tough luck" if they were hard, or, just as irritating, "I'm sure you've passed," when all I can think is I'm sure I screwed up on Question Three!

'But when Jim said that I did realize I'd been giving him a hard time. I don't know if families always understand what they're getting into. They might say, "Jolly good, go ahead." But when it comes to it they'll interrupt your studying to say, "Where's the cheese?" And you're thinking, "Sod it, I don't care where the bloody cheese is!" I think it came home to me that I was probably neglecting Jim somewhat when I saw him ironing a shirt – it was the first time I'd seen him doing that in sixteen years. I'm sure it was very good for him!

'I don't think he's really minded, though he did get pushed out of shape when I wouldn't come on the boat with him. He's glad this first year is over. When a man is doing an MBA, his wife is much more likely just to accept his long working hours. The other women and I talk about these things at college. We admit that for us the picture is totally different. The guys on the course still have everything done for them; all their meals cooked and laundry arranged. I got very cross recently about the shopping. Jim and my son are used to having everything provided for them, and they dared to moan because the fridge was empty. For someone like me, the domestic routine – organizing the cleaning (we have a cleaning lady), the shopping and ironing – all lands back in my court. A man does still expect loyalty from you, doesn't he? He wants you to be around for him!

'I just think men are used to being selfish and that most women don't know how to be selfish. The number of things I do that I don't really want to . . . for both of them. And I'm no shrinking violet either. But I made the decision with this course, that whenever things came up and there was a conflict of choices, that I must do the work. I think both of them have been quite surprised at my attitude. I mean I have been called selfish, which I must admit amused me. I was amazed to see that when you stop giving in every five minutes to their demands, you get called selfish. It just means to me that the man in question is not getting his way at that point in time.

'But, if you've always run the home, it can be a problem to stop. I don't like seeing the house untidy. I've had to stop myself rushing round clearing up the mess, when I should be reading a book. Yet it's hard. And then I find it very irritating when they turn round and say to me, "My God, this place is a mess!" Who's made the mess?

'It's a problem particularly of my generation, more so than the younger generations. They seem to have different relationships with their men. Jim and I are a very traditional couple. He does the wallpapering and I do the cooking, washing, ironing and shopping.

'At college, we women all talk together about the difficulties the MBA course is creating in our lives. We tend to chat together over a drink in the canteen. We don't go down to the students' bar, or we'd never get back to the next lecture! MBA students are quite controlled. But although many men also have a problem fitting it into their lives, women quite clearly have the much greater problem. We have other burdens to carry too, like periods. Three of us had quite nasty periods during exam week. And no allowances are made for that. It just makes life tougher and harder.

'But, if you've got the determination to do it, and most of us on the course have, then you'll overcome. That's why I say it's so important to remember that you're doing it really for your personal sense of achievement. Just think of all the stories you'll have to tell your grandchildren.'

EPILOGUE

Epilogue

Demographics, it is widely mooted, will be the single strongest factor bringing women more firmly into the workforce across the board. With a shortfall in the number of workers available, particularly in the skilled, managerial levels, companies as we have already begun to see will begin making alterations to their working practices to adapt to women's presence. More, there is a strong body of opinion that women are not only going to be encouraged to seek places 'at the top', but that they will be very welcome. Women bring to management, to senior executive positions, a different set of values, of work ethics and a wider understanding of the balance that should be maintained between work, family life, leisure time, and one's inner sense of well-being.

In a recent conversation with Laurence Handy, director of studies at Ashridge Management College (which offers what has sometimes been called the Rolls-Royce of MBA programmes, because it is so high-priced and high-prestige), he emphasized the college's interest in attracting more women to the programme. Because of the type of course offered at Ashridge, a kind of part-time, full-time course which is usually sponsored by the candidate's company, it tends to attract the more mature students (in their thirties or forties). Consequently many of the men as well as the women arrive at the college with a background well-entrenched in family life.

'We ask the men as well as the women about their family commitments and whether they have discussed with their partners and children the implications of doing the MBA programme. We feel today that men should also be addressing these issues. With a fair proportion of women on the courses, who naturally tend to talk about concerns regarding their children, I've seen it is helpful for some male managers to be exposed to this type of attitude. They learn so much about relationships, about a new style of caring, and about how important these issues really are to the working woman's life. The more domineering man may be surprised to see that there are other ways of working. They end up full of admiration for some of our women candidates.

'What often happens in our culture is that men who see themselves as high-potential turn into workaholics, devoting themselves 100 per cent to their career. The very word leadership carries a pronounced masculine connotation, and leadership styles tend to be male in concept. But I do believe men and companies are starting to change somewhat, partly because the women in their lives are beginning to demand that they change, and also because they are being influenced by women working with them at an equally senior level.'

So we should take an optimistic stand, that women will in fact be able to change in the next few years some of the ways men have grown used to working. Shall we assume that during the next decade, and beyond, while women take up increasingly influential roles in the workplace, that issues such as the extreme length of working days, the ability to mix work from home with office-based work, the need for time out to take care of children when they are ill or need our presence at school, will all become accepted as the norm – and not something to be frowned upon as symptoms of the fact women don't fit? Shall we assume that certain of the more old-fashioned industries, such as the one described by Liz, will indeed die out like the dinosaur – to their own benefit as well as ours.

I would hate to think for women's sakes, as well as for their children's, that there really is no room in top management either for women who have children, or for those who refuse to commit themselves to twelve-or-fourteen-hour days. We are beginning already to feel the effects on society of a culture in which there are no home-based women to pick up the pieces. Caring for children is just one issue, but there are also the huge numbers of elderly parents who will be in need of support and care, the growing numbers of disadvantaged or mentally ill – all of whom used to be the domain of the middle-class married women, who did not need to work for an income and instead devoted their lives to charitable concerns. If we envisage a future where men and women are both locked into office regimens from eight to eight (and more) every day, then who will be around to help with all the other aspects of our lives?

Cynics have suggested to me in the course of writing this book that women MBAs might be doing well right now, but what will have happened five or ten years down the line? Will they still be keeping up with the struggle? Won't they drop out because of the pressures of family, or to start their own businesses? Any research so far completed into this topic has come from America where women MBA graduates have been emerging for a longer time than in Europe. One sample from Harvard Business School, women who graduated in 1975, discovered that ten years later, 40 per cent of the women were by then ambivalent or frankly not interested in positions of increasing responsibility either in corporations or in businesses of their own. However, back in 1975, there was a very different type of business atmosphere, and the few women MBAs then around were such a new phenomenon they might have been as pressurized by the loneliness of their solitary positions as by any other aspect.

Among the women I have interviewed, I felt a strong determination to continue along their path to success, but only if the job would continue to support them, allow them to change and adapt their working lives around changing home lives, and so long as it continued to be intellectually stimulating and challenging.

The business world does seem to have reached a point of no return in terms of change. Now both men and women feel there are many more opportunities available and that attitudes are shifting. Increasingly people are saying that they want more out of life. They want interesting, challenging work, but they also want time to themselves. Marriage is no longer a hard and fast institution, which, once entered into, is guaranteed to be a mainstay for life. More and more women, and these can also be women in top jobs, are single parents, with all the extra family commitments that that entails.

The likely pattern for the future will be moments when working women and men reach natural break points in their careers, when they will stop and consider what they are doing and what they should be aiming for.

That is the sort of world we should be working towards: one

where men and women feel freer to explore their own levels of excellence within work and at home. Perhaps our goal should be for greater flexibility, non-rigid stereotypes, mobility within and out of work, together with a shared sense of caring and responsibility towards the family from both men and women. This can now be achieved – we're on our way to the top!

APPENDIX

Useful Addresses

Ashridge Management College
Birkhamstead
Herts 4PN 1NS
Telephone: 044 284 3491
MBA – f/t

University of Aston
Management Centre
Nelson Building
Aston Triangle, Birmingham B4 7ET
Telephone: 021 359 3011
MBA – f/t & p/t

University of Bath
School of Management
Claverton Down
Bath BA2 7AY
Telephone: 0225 826826
MBA – f/t & p/t

University of Bradford
Management Centre, Emm Lane,
Bradford, West Yorkshire BD9
Telephone: 0274 542299
MBA – f/t & p/t

City University Business School
Frobisher Crescent
Barbican Centre
London EC2Y 8HB
Telephone: 01 920 0111
MBA – f/t & p/t

Cranfield School of Management
Cranfield Institute of Technology
Cranfield, Bedford MK43 0AL
Telephone: 0234 751122
MBA – f/t & p/t

Durham University
Business School
Mill Hill Lane,
Durham DH1 3LB
Telephone: 091 374 2000
MBA – f/t & p/t

European School of
Management Studies
108 Boulevard Malesherbes,
Paris 75017
Telephone: 47 54 65 00
Grande Ecole degree in
Management Studies

University of Edinburgh
Department of Business Studies
William Robertson Building
50 George Square,
Edinburgh EH8 9JY
Telephone: 031 667 1011
MBA – f/t

University of Glasgow
Glasgow Business School
57 Southpark Avenue
Glasgow G12 8QQ
Telephone: 041 339 8855
MBA – p/t

Henley Management College
Greenlands, Henley on Thames
Oxfordshire RG9 3AL
Telephone: 0491 571454
MBA – Modular, f/t & p/t

University of Heriot Watt
School of Business and Finance
Studies
35 Grassmarket
Edinburgh EH1 2HT
Telephone: 031 225 6465
MBA – f/t & p/t

University of Hull
Dept of Management Systems
& Sciences
Hull HU6 7XR
Telephone: 0482 466236
MA – Management Systems

Imperial College
School of Management
52/53 Princes Gate
London SW7 2PG
Telephone: 01 589 5111
MBA – f/t & p/t

Kingston Business School
Kingston Polytechnic
Kingston Hill
Kingston upon Thames
Surrey KT2
Telephone: 01 549 1141
MBA – f/t & p/t

University of Lancaster
Dept of Marketing
School of Management
and Organizational Sciences
Gillow House
Lancaster LA1 4YX
Telephone: 0524 65201
MA – Accounting & Finance,
Business Analysis, Marketing,
Organisational Psychology,
Systems in Management,
Management Learning

Leicester Polytechnic
School of Management
P O Box 143
Leicester LE1 9BH
Telephone: 0533 551551
MBA – p/t

London Graduate School of Business
Sussex Place, Regents Park
London NW1 4SA
Telephone: 01 262 5050
MBA – f/t & p/t

London Management Centre
Polytechnic of Central London
Marylebone Road
London NW1 SL5
Telephone: 01 486 5811
MBA – p/t

University of Loughborough
Loughborough LE11 3TU
Telephone: 0509 263171
MBA – p/t

Manchester Business School
University of Manchester
Booth Street West
Manchester M15 6PB
Telephone: 061 275 6333
MBA – f/t & p/t

Middlesex Business School
(Middlesex Polytechnic)
Bus Ed Unit, High Street
London W5 5DB
The Burroughs
London NW4 4BT
Telephone: 01 202 6545
MBA – f/t & p/t

University of Newcastle
upon Tyne
Dept of Industrial Management
Newcastle upon Tyne NE1 5QU
Telephone: 091 232 8511
MBA – f/t & p/t

University of Sheffield
School of Management and Economic
Studies
Crookesmoor Building
Conduit Road
Sheffield S10 1FL
Telephone: 0742 768555
MBA – f/t

Sheffield Business School
(Sheffield Polytechnic)
Pond Street, Sheffield S1 1WB
Telephone: 0742 720911
MBA – f/t

University of Strathclyde
Strathclyde Business School
Sir William Duncan Bldg
130 Rottenrow,
Glasgow G4 OGE
Telephone: 041 552 7141
MBA – f/t & p/t

U.M.I.S.T.
University of Manchester Institute
of Science and Technology
School of Management
PO Box 88
Manchester M60 1QD
Telephone: 061 236 3311

Cardiff Business School
University of Wales Institute
of Science & Technology
Aberconway Building
Colum Drive
Cardiff CF1 3EU
Telephone: 0222 371200
MBA – f/t & p/t

University of Warwick
School of Industrial and
Business Studies
Coventry CV4
Telephone: 0203 523922
MBA – f/t & p/t

f/t = full-time
p/t = part-time

The Association of MBAs, 15 Duncan Terrace, London N1 8BZ (01 837 3375) offers an advice and information service for those interested in applying for an MBA course, and a networking organization for MBA graduates. They can be contacted regarding loans available to MBA students. Their *Guide to Business Schools*, ed. Paliwoda and Harrison – gives information on all the schools listed below. Contact AMBA for details.

City Women's Network, 925 Uxbridge Road, Hillingdon Heath, Middlesex UB10 ONJ (01 569 2351) is a network for women who work in the City or in similar senior professional capacities.

Women in Management, 64 Marryat Road, Wimbledon, London SW19 5BN (01 946 1238) is a support, networking and resource organization for women nationwide working in management.